# Feudal Society in Medieval France

University of Pennsylvania Press
MIDDLE AGES SERIES
Edited by
Edward Peters
Henry Charles Lea Professor
of Medieval History
University of Pennsylvania

A listing of the available books
in the series appears at the
back of this volume

# *Feudal Society in Medieval France*

## Documents from the County of Champagne

Translated and edited by
Theodore Evergates

University of Pennsylvania Press

Philadelphia

Library of Congress Cataloging-in-Publication Data

Feudal society in Medieval France: documents from the County of Champagne / translated
  and edited by Theodore Evergates.
      p.   cm. — (Middle Ages series)
    Includes bibliographical references and index.
    ISBN 0-8122-3225-9. — ISBN 0-8122-1441-2 (pbk.)
      1. Champagne-Ardennes (France)—History—Sources.   2.   Feudalism—France—
  Champagne-Ardennes—History—Sources.   I. Evergates, Theodore.   II. Series.
  DC611.C457F48   1993
  944'.3—dc20                                                    93-19240
                                                                    CIP

# Contents

# *Illustrations*

# *Preface*

Anthologies of medieval texts, ranging widely in time and place, accord scant attention to the practices of feudal society in the High Middle Ages. Beyond the frequently reprinted descriptions of fealty by Fulcher of Chartres (ca. 1020) and of homage by Galbert of Bruges (1127)—both highly simplistic representations—few nonliterary texts are available to the English reader. This collection attempts to redress that omission. In drawing from the abundant sources available within a single French province, it seeks to present a coherent picture of a complex and evolving society at the very time when fundamental social, economic, and administrative institutions were being formed.

In the translations, I have tried to facilitate comprehension by modern general readers. Several texts already available in translation have been modified slightly to that end; the rest are translated here for the first time. A few technical terms are retained in parentheses, while explanatory comments are given in brackets. All dates are converted to modern style (in Champagne the new year was reckoned from Easter). Personal names are rendered in English except where the French forms seem familiar (for example, Henry the Liberal, but Jean of Joinville).

I thank R. C. Famiglietti for a critical reading and many suggestions that materially improved this collection.

# *Acknowledgments*

The unpublished documents presented here are located in the manuscript collections of the Archives Nationales (Paris), the Bibliothèque Nationale (Paris), and the Archives Départementales of the Aube (Troyes), Haute-Marne (Chaumont), and Marne (Châlons-sur-Marne), whose directors have authorized the translations. The Reverend Joseph J. Gross has graciously allowed the publication of his translation of the Rule of the Trinitarians (Doc. 93). And the following publishers have kindly granted permission to reprint or to make translations of documents they have published:

Archives Départementales de l'Aube: Docs. 1, 74, 86, 103
Burns & Oates Ltd: Docs. 83, 85
Champion-Slatkine: Docs. 20, 98
Cistercian Publications: Doc. 79
Columbia University Press: Doc. 78
Comité des Travaux Historiques et Scientifiques: Doc. 47
Penguin Books Ltd: Doc. 90
Presses du CNRS: Docs. 18, 52, 57A-B, 73
University of Nebraska Press: Doc. 32

# Introduction

## Feudal Society

In France the term "feudal" has served two quite distinct historiographical traditions. The more recent descends from the eighteenth century when it was employed, notably by Montesquieu, to characterize a type of society. That broad conception of "feudal" has been recast and popularized in our own time by Marc Bloch's *Feudal Society* (1939–1940), the most influential synthesis of medieval social history in this century.[1] Bloch used the term to encompass the fundamental traits of post-Carolingian society, which he conceived primarily in terms of the French experience before the rise of the Capetian monarchy in the thirteenth century. It was a society characterized by political fragmentation (from the monarch's point of view), a ruling warrior aristocracy, and a subject peasantry. Lordship and the extra-familial bonds forged between men mattered as much, if not more, than the ties of kinship. But fiefs and feudal tenure figured almost incidentally in Bloch's "feudal" society. More important for that period, as French scholarship has since demonstrated, was the emergence of castles as the pivot of social organization and the development of new forms of lordship by the aristocratic families. That restructuring, however, can be understood without recourse to "feudal," a term which in fact most researchers have shunned.[2] For how can a society in which fiefs played a relatively minor role be termed feudal?

1. Marc Bloch, *Feudal Society*, trans. L. A. Manyon (Chicago: The University of Chicago Press, 1961), pp. xvii–xxi and chap.32 ("Feudalism as a Type of Society"). That tradition continues in recent works by Georges Duby, *The Three Orders: Feudal Society Imagined*, trans. Arthur Goldhammer (Chicago and London: The University of Chicago Press, 1980), and Jean-Pierre Poly and Eric Bournazel, *The Feudal Transformation, 900–1200*, trans. Caroline Higgitt (New York and London: Holmes & Meier, 1991). For the unfortunate consequences of such broad conceptions of "feudal" and "feudalism," see Elizabeth A. R. Brown, "The Tyranny of a Construct: Feudalism and the Historians of Medieval Europe," *American Historical Review* 79 (1974): 1063–1088.

2. There is a vast bibliography which is most readily accessible in Timothy Reuter, ed., *The Medieval Nobility: Studies on the Ruling Classes of France and Germany from the Sixth to the Twelfth Century* (Amsterdam-New York-Oxford: North Holland, 1979), and Poly and Bournazel, *The Feudal Transformation*.

Had Bloch focused less on the formation of medieval society and more on the mature period of the twelfth and thirteenth centuries—in which fiefs are abundantly evident—he might not have so easily discarded an earlier historiographical tradition that employed "feudal" in a more restrictive manner. For the sixteenth-century humanists like Dumoulin and Pithou, among others, and later Chantereau-Lefebvre and Brussel, "feudal" described a type of tenure and the laws governing it.[3] That usage is much closer to the medieval than is Bloch's, for it links a complex of terms like homage, fidelity, and liegeance (which related to persons) with *mouvance*, escheat, and relief (which related to property). These were not abstract concepts; they described specific practices and relationships deriving from feudal tenure. It is in this sense that "feudal" is used here: as an attribute of fief, the form of tenure that became the defining feature of French society in the High Middle Ages.

Fiefs were created in a number of ways. Some were carved out of great private estates and granted to knights in return for military service. Others were assigned by powerful laymen from appropriated church land, often in cooperation with ecclesiastical authorities. Feudal tenure also was created when lords imposed their control over allodial property (land which was held in outright ownership): that land was then said to "move" or be in the *mouvance* of the superior lord. The widespread feudalization of land, and with it the extension of feudal customs, had repercussions in virtually every sphere of life of the landholding families. Although the pace of feudalization varied by region, as did the specific feudal customs, three general characteristics of mature feudal society will be evident in this collection.

First, it was the territorial princes, in the absence of a direct royal presence, who shaped the character and institutions of the French provinces. Their policies regarding castle-building, the disposition of fiefs, and the rights of widows and younger sons profoundly influenced both the nature and the fortunes of the fief-holding families. The feudal customs that coalesced under the aegis of the princes in the twelfth century produced quite diverse regional societies, to the extent that in the thirteenth century the Parlement of Paris recognized discordant definitions of what constituted nobility (one noble parent or two).

Second, written records came into general use by laymen for both

3. See Donald R. Kelley, *Foundations of Modern Historical Scholarship: Language, Law, and History in the French Renaissance* (New York: Columbia University Press, 1970), chaps. 7–11.

administrative and personal needs. By the end of the twelfth century, the chanceries of the most powerful princes were keeping internal administrative records on fiefs, homages, and military service, as well as financial accounts. At the same time, laymen increasingly resorted to written records for their own personal affairs. Those administrative and private documents involving only laymen permit us to view the secular affairs of feudal tenants directly, without having to pass through the filter of ecclesiastical documents drawn up for quite different purposes.

Third, women became active participants in the world of feudal matters that had been created by and for men. As they acquired fiefs by inheritance, dowry, and dower, women assumed the obligations (including homage) and rights (such as feudal lordship) hitherto reserved for men. Although the rights of women varied widely by region, the codification of feudal practices and the survival of court decisions in the thirteenth century allow us to examine in some detail the role of women in feudal society.

## The County of Champagne

The broad open country (*campania*) east of Paris was known as Champagne long before it acquired political cohesion. Unlike Normandy and Flanders, which had early acquired strong territorial identities, Champagne remained a highly fragmented frontier zone between the royal domain and the German Empire; it was dominated by powerful prelates (of Reims, Châlons-sur-Marne, Langres, Sens, and Meaux), as well as a large number of virtually independent local counts and barons. Only in the course of the twelfth and thirteenth centuries did the counts of Troyes, who assumed the title "count of Champagne," tame those barons, create a sophisticated and well-run government, and make their principality one of the wealthiest and most powerful of the realm.[4]

The counts stimulated the economic development of their lands by encouraging rural immigration, founding new villages, and enfranchising

4. The most complete narrative remains Henri d'Arbois de Jubainville, *Histoire des ducs et des comtes de Champagne*, 7 vols. (Paris-Troyes: Aug. Aubry, Dufey-Robert, et al., 1859–1869); a brief account is in Theodore Evergates, "Champagne," in *Dictionary of the Middle Ages*, ed. Joseph R. Strayer, 13 vols. (New York: Charles Scribner's Sons, 1982–1989), 3:243–250. The formative period is analyzed in Michel Bur, *La formation du comté de Champagne, v.950–v.1150*, Mémoires des Annales de l'Est, no. 54 (Nancy: Université de Nancy-II, 1977).

their most populous towns. They sponsored trade fairs that made Champagne the center of international trade and finance for over a century. They supported the reformed monasteries, most notably the Cistercians who became omnipresent in the county, and they patronized writers, of whom Chrétien of Troyes was the most illustrious and the very symbol of the region's cultural achievements. Finally, the comital family established intimate, though not always amicable, ties with the Capetian royal family, ties that led ultimately to the county's attachment to the royal domain and to its inevitable economic and political decline by the fourteenth century.

Beyond its courtly culture and its fairs, Champagne is best known as a classic example of a feudal society in the strictest sense of the term "feudal." The county itself consisted of an assortment of lands that the counts held in fief from a dozen lay and ecclesiastical lords (only one-quarter of the county was held directly from the king in the twelfth century). Over these disparate lands the counts imposed a uniform administration, ruling some areas (domain) directly through their own officials, while granting the rest as fiefs to barons and knights in return for homage, loyalty, and service. The barons, bishops, and some monasteries likewise created fiefs on their own lands. In all, the fief-holding class in Champagne comprised between 3,500 and 4,000 tenants in 1200.

The counts, with the greatest number of direct feudal tenants, generated a large volume of records on feudal matters. In about 1178 and seven times during the next century, they ordered countywide inquests to verify the names, obligations, and holdings of their feudal tenants. Information obtained by sworn testimony was recorded on parchment rolls that became known collectively as the "Fiefs of Champagne" (*Feoda Campanie*). The count's officials also kept annual accounts for the disbursement of money-fiefs or fief-rents which they paid out from the rents, taxes, and duties collected during the trade fairs. Indeed, fiefs consisting of revenue rather than revenue-producing land were common in Champagne.

In addition to generating those internal records, the comital chancery processed thousands of letters it received from the count's vassals dealing with their fiefs. The letters range from simple requests, declarations of homage, and receipts of fiefs to proposed marriage contracts and dower assignments (in which fiefs were involved). These feudal letters were stored with internal copies of the count's own letters in the chancery archives, where on several occasions between 1211 and 1271 they were systematically copied into codex volumes (cartularies) for ease of consultation. The best known of the cartulary-registers was the last, the "Book of

Princes" (*Liber Principum*), which contained about one thousand letters from laymen.[5] It was precisely that volume which the early historians of feudal institutions, particularly Chantereau-Lefebvre and Brussel, scrutinized most carefully in seeking to understand the feudal practices of medieval France.[6]

Another body of evidence pertaining to feudal customs was produced by the High Court of Champagne. From the mid-twelfth century it decided questions of feudal law in sessions known as the "Days" of Troyes, although most of its decisions come to us from 1270 to 1290, when they were routinely registered. They survive in two forms: as extracts which give the particulars of the cases, and as summaries which simply state the relevant customs. Although we lack a theoretical presentation of the customs in Champagne like the one written by Beaumanoir for the nearby Beauvaisis,[7] the High Court's decisions are invaluable because they are grounded in actual cases brought to it, and thus reveal the questions at issue in the last three decades of the thirteenth century.

In sum, the oversight of feudal affairs consumed a significant administrative effort in Champagne and produced a substantial and varied collection of written records. Together with the private documents exchanged among laymen and the large volume of records retained by religious houses, they represent an exceptionally rich collection of documents for the study of feudal practices.

## The Documents

The documents presented here represent a very small sample from one region. They vary in form and origin, and include some texts not directly related to feudal practices, such as personal correspondence, papal bulls, chronicles, inquests, court decisions, and even the constitution of a religious order. Most of the documents pertaining to fiefs fall under the rubric of "charters," a generic category covering primarily title deeds and sealed letters. Customarily, a donation or property transfer was arranged

5. See Theodore Evergates, "The Chancery Archives of the Counts of Champagne: Codicology and Historiography of the Cartulary-Registers," *Viator* 16 (1985): 159–179.

6. Louis Chantereau-Lefebvre, *Traité des fiefs et de leur origine* (Paris: L. Billaine, 1662); Nicolas Brussel, *Nouvel examen de l'usage général des fiefs en France*, 2d ed., 2 vols. (Paris: C. Prud'homme-C. Robustel, 1750).

7. Philippe of Beaumanoir, *The* Coutumes de Beauvaisis *of Philippe de Beaumanoir*, trans. F. R. P. Akehurst (Philadelphia: University of Pennsylvania Press, 1992).

orally before witnesses and relatives whose consent (*laudatio*) was required for full title to pass; that legally constitutive act was later commemorated in a document validated by the seal of the initiator—if he had one—or of a recognized officeholder such as the count, a baron, a bishop, or an abbot.[8] In the thirteenth century, sealed letters became themselves constitutive acts and often displaced oral transactions altogether, as personal seals replaced living witnesses as legal authenticators.

The largest number of extant charters pertain to church property, since ecclesiastics were most conscientious in recording and preserving the proofs of their privileges and possessions. Although not intended to shed light on lay society, those charters contain irreplaceable information on individual laymen, their families, and activities. Despite the technical difficulties in "reading" charters, their sheer volume makes them an indispensable source for understanding medieval society. Although less voluminous, documents involving only laymen are even more valuable in their explicit depiction of secular affairs. The counts issued a variety of charter-like documents to their feudal tenants and townsmen, while the barons and knights after 1200 put to parchment virtually all of their transactions, including notifications, requests, permissions, dower assignments, marriage contracts, mortgages, sales, donations, and testaments. The barons often had their documents drawn up by their chaplains, while ordinary knights commissioned theirs from monastic scribes, episcopal chanceries, or literate clerics who were being produced in overabundance by the burgeoning schools and universities from the late twelfth century.

Few of the original private documents survive today, as they were either lost or discarded after their purpose had been served. Some survive because they were deposited for safekeeping in local monastic or episcopal archives; others were preserved when ecclesiastical institutions acquired fiefs and took possession of the earlier titles which otherwise would have been destroyed. But the most important repository for feudal documents was the comital chancery archives, where all incoming correspondence was stored and later copied into cartulary-registers; those cartularies remain today, as they did in Brussel's time, one of the finest collections of texts on the feudal practices of medieval France.

The generalized use of written records for all sorts of feudal matters in the thirteenth century naturally raises the question of whether the lay-

---

8. See Stephen D. White, *Custom, Kinship, and Gifts to Saints: The* Laudatio Parentum *in Western France, 1050–1150* (Chapel Hill: The University of North Carolina Press, 1988).

men who commissioned, received, and retained the documents could in fact read them. Ralph V. Turner has convincingly argued that in contemporary England "most knights were at least pragmatic readers, functional literates in today's terms."[9] The feudal class in Champagne also seems to have possessed such a "pragmatic" or "practical" literacy,[10] which is to say a rudimentary knowledge of Latin combined with an understanding of the critical contemporary terminology: fief, allod, homage, liegeance, *mouvance*, baron, lord, knight, and so on. Like most moderns, who understand the gist but not necessarily the legal locutions of the property deeds and testaments in their possession, members of the feudal class understood the essence of the dower letters, marriage contracts, letters of credit and debt, sales contracts, and various other documents pertaining to fiefs that they routinely handled.

We are fortunate that so many feudal documents survive from the High Middle Ages, for they reveal in detail how a feudal society functioned. Although most texts are official or legal in some sense and composed according to formal conventions, they all—read closely—reveal a human dimension behind their formulaic style.

9. Ralph V. Turner, "The *Miles Literatus* in Twelfth- and Thirteenth-Century England: How Rare a Phenomenon?" *American Historical Review* 83 (1978): 931.

10. M. T. Clanchy, *From Memory to Written Record: England, 1066–1307* (Cambridge, Mass.: Harvard University Press, 1979), chap. 10.

# Chronological Table

**Hugh (1093–1125)**

| | |
|---|---|
| 1103 | Assassination attempt (Doc. 96) |
| 1115 | Clairvaux founded |
| 1118 | Knights Templar founded (Doc. 78) |
| 1125 | Hugh joins the Templars |

**Thibaut II (1125–1152; IV of Blois, 1102–1152)**

| | |
|---|---|
| 1127 | Vauluisant founded (Doc. 102) |
| ca. 1130 | *In Praise of the New Knighthood* (Doc. 79) |
| 1137 | Fairs of May established in Provins (see Doc. 20) |
| 1147–49 | Second Crusade (see Docs. 81–82, 86–87) |
| ca. 1147 | Heloise founds La Pommeraye (Doc. 44) |

**Henry I (1152–1181)**

| | |
|---|---|
| 1157 | Saint-Etienne of Troyes founded (comital chancery) |
| 1164 | Henry expands the Fairs of May in Provins (Doc. 20) |
| 1171 | A new village is dismantled (Doc. 74) |
| 1171–72 | Henry resists the archbishop of Reims (Doc. 97) |
| 1175 | Henry's first community franchise (Doc. 16) |
| 1178 | First feudal inquest (see Doc. 2) |
| 1179 | Henry's pilgrimage to the Holy Land (Doc. 92) |

**Marie (regent: 1181–1187)**

| | |
|---|---|
| 1185 | Villehardouin as marshal (see Doc. 98) |

**Henry II (1187–1190)**

| | |
|---|---|
| 1188 | Fire in Troyes (Doc. 99) |
| | Saladin Tithe (Doc. 88) |
| 1190 | Third Crusade |

### Marie (regent: 1190–1197)

1196          The Paraclete is downsized (see Doc. 46)

### Thibaut III (1197–1201)

1198          Trinitarians founded (Doc. 93)
1199          Thibaut marries and dowers Blanche (Doc. 40)
1200          Sainte-Menehould castle acquired (Doc. 2)
1201          Brienne county mortgaged (Doc. 65)

### Blanche of Navarre (regent: 1201–1222)

1202–4        Fourth Crusade
1212          Statute on the female inheritance of castles (Doc. 35)
1216–19       Civil war (see Doc. 55)

### Thibaut IV (1222–1253; king of Navarre, 1234–1253)

1222          The Champagne Jews are taxed (Doc. 19)
1222          Blanche founds Argensolles (Doc. 104)
1230–32       Communal franchises (Doc. 18)
1232          Thibaut remarries (Doc. 29)
1234          Thibaut becomes king of Navarre
1239          The great heretic burning (Doc. 100)
1243          Merchants of Piacenza banned from the fairs (Doc. 24)
1248–50       Saint Louis's crusade (see Docs. 52, 90)
1249–50       The great feudal inquest (Doc. 10)

### Margaret (regent: 1253–1256)

1255          Restrictions on Templar acquisitions (Doc. 12)

### Thibaut V (1256–1269)

1257          Thibaut taxes his feudal tenants (Doc. 15)
              Thibaut's testament (Doc. 53)
1265          Nuns attack Saint-Urbain (Doc. 101)

### Henry III (1270–1274)

1270          High Court's decisions enrolled
1271          Chancery archives copied into the *Liber Principum*

**Jeanne (minor: 1274–1284)**

**Philip IV, king of France (1285–1314)**

1. The Counts of Champagne

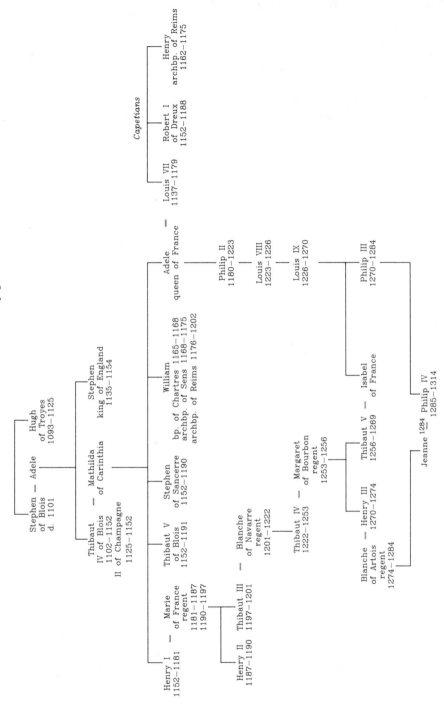

## 2. The Joinville

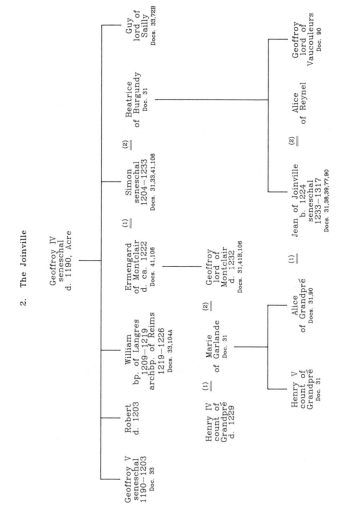

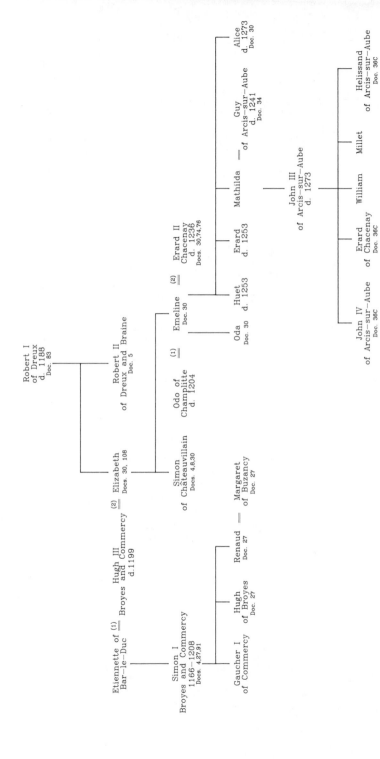

3. The Broyes–Commercy–Châteauvillain, Dreux, and Chacenay

# Table of Measures

| | |
|---|---|
| *l. s. d.* | *libra* (pound), *solidus* (shilling), *denarius* (penny), were related at the standard 12*d*. = 1*s*., and 20*s*. = 1*l*. Only pennies existed as coins; pounds and shillings were used for purposes of calculation (they were "moneys of account"). The annual revenue produced by feudal property was often expressed in *libratus terre* (translated here simply as "annual revenue"). Unless otherwise indicated, coins are assumed to be the count's coins minted in Troyes or Provins. |
| *arpent* | A measure of land (approximately an acre) which varied by locality. |
| *modius* | Unit of dry or liquid measure (the French *muid*) consisting of about twelve *sextarii* (the French *setier*) dry or about twice that in liquid. A *sextarius* consisted of about twelve bushels. The precise measure varied by locality; the "measure of Troyes" was different from the "measure of Vitry." |
| *census* | A nominal rent (the French *cens*) paid in recognition of the landlord's superior right to a property; a "recognition rent" rather than a "land rent" (*terragium*) which reflected the value (productivity) of the land. The *census* was usually paid in coin, whereas the land rent was often paid in kind. |

# The County of Champagne

Legend:

- ■ Comital castle-town
- ● Baronial castle
- ☩ Episcopal city
- △ Monastery

# 1 The Governance of a Feudal State

In the course of the twelfth and thirteenth centuries the counts forged a highly fragmented region dominated by largely independent barons and prelates into a cohesive and prosperous province. It is no exaggeration to say that comital policies account for the distinctive features of Champagne in the High Middle Ages. In three particular areas the counts left an indelible imprint on the county: its feudal aristocracy, its villages and towns, and its international fairs.

## Feudal Policies

The counts and their barons routinely granted fiefs of modest rents or small parcels of land to knights in return for military service. Since fiefs in the twelfth century were granted orally, without written title deeds, they are rarely detectable in contemporary sources except when later transferred to monastic houses, which kept records of their acquisitions. In fact, monasteries acquired substantial amounts of feudal property, as lords generously granted them open-ended licenses to acquire fiefs from their vassals (Doc. 1). By the late twelfth century, the count's chancery began to record information on fiefs before they were alienated to the church: feudal registers listed the feudal tenants and their military obligations within each castellany (Doc. 2B), and title deeds describing new fiefs and the conditions of tenure were often presented to the recipients (Doc. 3).

Count Thibaut III (1197–1201) initiated the feudal policies that his successors pursued through the thirteenth century. Using their considerable financial resources accruing from the Fairs of Champagne, the counts imposed liege homage directly on all the sons of powerful barons (Doc. 4), effectively dismantling the clans in which younger brothers, nephews, and cousins had escaped direct comital authority. The counts also regulated the construction of new fortifications, which henceforth had to conform to their specifications and be renderable on demand (Docs. 5, 6). At the same time, baronial castles built on allodial lands were either incorporated into the count's domain (Doc. 2A) or forcibly feudalized (Doc. 7).

In the 1230s, in response to the widespread alienation of feudal property by impecunious knights and indebted barons, Count Thibaut IV confiscated unauthorized alienations (Doc. 8) and purchased many fiefs that he and his predecessors had granted earlier (Doc. 9). His feudal inquest of 1249–1250 (Doc. 10) reveals a feudal aristocracy profoundly different from what it had been a century earlier: almost half of the feudal tenants were women or nonknighted men, and feudal incomes ranged from pittances to substantial fortunes. The inquest also exposed the extent of unauthorized alienations to religious institutions, which saw their recent acquisitions confiscated (Doc. 11).

Despite the personal benefit (prestige) and practical advantages (tax-exemption) conferred by feudal tenure, the alienation of fiefs continued unabated in the second half of the thirteenth century. The counts first attempted to restrict the largest purchasers of fiefs, such as the Templars (Doc. 12), then set quotas on the amount of feudal property which each religious house could acquire (Doc. 13). But those attempts failed in Champagne as they did elsewhere, and in 1291 King Philip IV imposed a retroactive sales tax on all fiefs sold or otherwise alienated to churches and townsmen (Doc. 14). By that time, however, feudal tenure had lost its enviable standing as nontaxable property, for in 1257 Count Thibaut V had enacted the first noncrusade tax on fiefs (Doc. 15).

### 1. Permission to Clairvaux to Acquire Fiefs, ca. 1145

*Count Hugh and his nephew and successor, Count Thibaut II (IV of Blois), were friends of Bernard of Clairvaux and generous supporters of Cistercian monasteries. Here Thibaut confirms Hugh's gifts to Clairvaux and authorizes the abbey to acquire fiefs from his own lands as well as from those he inherited from Count Hugh.*[1]

Be it known to all, present and future, that I, Thibaut, count of Blois, with the approval of my [eldest] son Henry and of my other sons, have confirmed to Clairvaux abbey, for the salvation of my soul and the souls of my predecessors, whatever my uncle Hugh, count of Troyes, granted [as gifts] from his lands. I have also granted that Clairvaux may acquire

---

1. Text in Jean Waquet et al., eds., *Recueil des chartes de l'abbaye de Clairvaux*, fascicules 1–2 (Troyes: Archives Départementales de l'Aube, 1950, 1982), 1:48, no. 22. See also Hugh's permission to Avenay in 1104 (Doc. 96A).

[without further permission] fiefs held from Hugh [by his vassals in Champagne] and from me [in Blois]. So that neither the passage of time nor malice may alter this grant, I have confirmed it in perpetuity with my seal.

## 2. THE COUNT ACQUIRES A CASTLE AND GRANTS FIEFS FOR CASTLE-GUARD, 1200

*In September 1200 Count Thibaut III acquired the castle and castellany of Sainte-Menehould by exchange with Count Hugh II of Rethel. Count Hugh sent Thibaut a small letter with his pendant seal as title to the castellany (Doc. A).[2] Since Thibaut needed knights to man the castle, he assigned rents and grain revenues as fiefs to support those performing that service. The count's officials added the names of the recipients to the feudal rolls (Feoda Campanie) created ca. 1178 by Count Henry I (Doc. B).[3] These new fiefs worth about 5l. annual income were quite modest; by comparison, a prebend for the support of one canon in the chapter of Saint-Etienne of Troyes yielded twice that amount.*

(A) Hugh, count of Rethel, to his dearest lord Thibaut, count palatine of Troyes, greeting. Be advised that this letter confirms to you [our oral agreement] that for the fief of Inaumont which you have given me, I gave you in exchange the fief of Sainte-Menehould. In testimony of which I send you this letter confirmed by my seal. Done in the year of our Lord 1200, in the month of September.

(B) [Knights owing full-time castle-guard at Sainte-Menehould, 1200/1201:]

Dudo of Bussy-le-Château: the lord count gave him 7l. annual revenue and one carucate of land [enough for one plow].

Adam of Thibie: 5l. annual revenue from land.

Adam's brother Milo: 5l. annual revenue from land.

Droco of Sainte-Menehould: two *modii* of oats, measure of Vitry, annually [worth about 4l.].

Peter "la Berce": the same.

Baldwin of Saint-Jean: 160 chickens annually at Suippes.

---

2. Document in AN, J 193, no. 2.

3. Texts in Auguste Longnon, ed., *Documents relatifs au comté de Champagne et de Brie (1172–1361)*, 3 vols. (Paris: Imprimerie Nationale, 1901–1914), 1: 113, nos. 2974–2980; 1: 85, no. 2305.

Clarembaud of "Fengnon": 50*l.* [cash] with which he must purchase [rent-producing] land that will be a liege fief [yielding about 5*l.* annually].

[After Count Thibaut's death in May 1201, his widow Blanche continued to reinforce the new castle:]

Lucans of "Triaus" and Gervais of Vienne must be in full-time residence (*estagium*) at the castle of Sainte-Menehould from the Feast of Saint-Remi [January 13] 1201 for two entire years, and thereafter each of them must render six weeks castle-guard (*custodia*) annually. I, Blanche, countess, gave each of them 60*l.* [cash] for constructing houses there.

### 3. THE ASSIGNMENT OF A NEW FIEF, 1201

*In granting this fief to a knight who already held fiefs from three other lords, Count Thibaut III was trying to obtain influence over a Burgundian knight who had married into a local knight family. The count did not require castle-guard in return for this new fief, only loyalty, and then only when it did not conflict with the knight's prior loyalty to his other lords.*[4]

I, Thibaut, count palatine of Troyes, make known to all, present and future, that I have given in fief to Jocelin of Avallon and his heirs the village of Gillancourt, which is in the castellany of La Ferté-sur-Aube.[5] I have also given him permission to enlarge that fief with whatever he and his heirs can acquire there; that additional property will be counted as an augmentation of fief (*in augmento feodi*). Also I have agreed not to allow any tenants of this village [to settle] in any of my own franchised villages.[6]

On account of this grant, Jocelin became my liegeman, save his liegeance [for other fiefs] to Girard of Arcy, to [Odo III] the lord duke of Burgundy, and to Peter, count of Auxerre. Done at Chaudun in my [Thibaut's] presence, in the year of our Lord 1200, in the month of January [1201]. Given [to Jocelin] by the hand of my chancellor Walter. Written by Milo [chancery scribe].

[Ten years later, Jocelin's son sold this fief to Thibaut's widow, Countess Blanche.]

### 4. LIEGE HOMAGE IS IMPOSED ON A YOUNGER BROTHER IN 1201

*Count Thibaut III began the policy of imposing liege (primary) homage on the younger brothers of baronial families who possessed fortifications that escaped his*

4. Text in Maximilien Quantin, ed., *Recueil de pièces pour faire suite au Cartulaire général de l'Yonne* (Auxerre-Paris: Durand, Pédone-Lauriel, 1873), 1–2.
5. Gillancourt is near Lignol. Jocelin's wife Marie was the sister of Josbert of Lignol (see Doc. 10C, n. 23).
6. See also Doc. 4 on tenant migration.

*direct control. Here the lord of Châteauvillain recounts how he was coerced into*
*becoming the count's liegeman.⁷ The text also illuminates another important*
*social event: the migration of tenants from one lordship to another, in the di-*
*rection of more liberal lords. Here a well-off lord forfeits part of an annual*
*revenue in order to stem the flow of tenants from his lands.*

I, Simon, lord of Châteauvillain, make known to all, present and future, that I had a dispute with Count Thibaut who wished me to hold
Châteauvillain—which I admitted was a fief held from the count of Champagne—in liege tenure from him. I, however, wished to hold that castle
directly from my eldest [half-] brother Simon, lord of [Broyes and] Commercy. But then I relented and agreed to hold it directly from the count,
who in compensation promised to assign me 30*l.* annual rent. Since his
death [in May 1201] prevented the assignment of that revenue, his wife,
my dearest lady Blanche, countess of Champagne, wished to assign me
that [rent-producing] land. Complying with his directive, she assigned me
the 30*l.* revenue on whatever the count had at Silvarouvres, Saint-Léger,
and Dinteville.

But since the prior of Silvarouvres possesses a charter in which the
count promised never to alienate his protection of that abbey and its possessions, the countess and I agreed as follows: I quit her and the lord of
Champagne in perpetuity of the custody over that priory [which she had
assigned to Simon as part of his rent], and will have instead only what the
count had at those three places except that custody, which will remain in
the count's hand. She conceded to me, in return, that she would not accept
[as immigrants] into her lands any men living in Châteauvillain and its
castellany over whom I have rights (*servicium*). If any of my men does
emigrate to her land and I can prove by legitimate witnesses—but not
through a judicial duel—that I used to have his service, I can freely reclaim
that man.

The countess and I agreed to all this, preserving the rights of the prior
of Silvarouvres as stated in the count's charter. So that this remain in force,
I have had my seal appended to this document. Done in the year of our
Lord 1208, in the month of May.

## 5. Authorization to Build a Castle, 1206
*Robert II, lord of Dreux (a royal fief) and of Braine (a comital fief) occupied a*
*powerful position on the border between Champagne and the royal domain,*

7. Text (slightly condensed here) in A. Teulet et al., eds., *Layettes du Trésor des chartes*,
5 vols. (Paris: Henri Plon, 1863–1909), 1:320, no. 848. See Genealogical Table 3.

*partly because of the location of his fiefs but primarily because he was cousin of both King Philip II and the count of Champagne. Here Robert obtains permission to build a castle on his allodial land at Fère, which he converts into a Champagne fief: in effect, he attached this land and its new castle to his preexisting fief of Braine.*[8]

I, Robert, count[9] and lord of Dreux and Braine, make known to all, present and future, the agreement between me and my dearest lady Blanche, countess of Champagne, regarding my house (*domus*) of Torcy: it will remain in the state it was on the day that this agreement was reached at Provins; that is, I acknowledge that I may not make it higher or encircle it [with a wall] until the countess's son Thibaut [five years of age] reaches his majority [in 1222]. If by chance, God forbid, Thibaut dies before then, that house will remain in its present state until an heir of Champagne comes of age and succeeds to the county.

The countess has allowed me to build a fortress (*fortericia*) on my allodial land at Fère, that is, in my enclosure there or at another suitable place closer to my house on the same allodial land there. I have converted that enclosure, the fish pond, and the forest of Dôle into a fief that I attached to my fief of Braine in order to constitute a single liege fief to be held from the countess and her son Thibaut or—if he dies—the count of Champagne. Also, I have joined to that liege fief all my allodial land in the lordship of Braine and Fère, that is, the allod that I hold from no lord. Be it known that I am liege to the countess and her son for this entire allod that I have placed in liege fief, and that henceforth my heir who will be lord of Braine and Fère will also be liege for this fief.

Within this [newly enlarged] fief I may build one fortress which will be held on oath and renderable (*jurabilis et reddibilis*) to the countess and her son, at great force or small force, so that whenever they ask to occupy that fortress for their own affairs, I will hand it over without delay to their seneschal, constable, butler, or marshal, on the understanding that they will return it to me forty days after they have finished with it, in full possession and in the same state that I gave it to them.

Be it known also that by this agreement neither I nor my heir will be

---

8. Text (repetitive legal phrases omitted here) in Brussel, *Nouvel examen*, 1:386. See Genealogical Table 3.

9. An honorific, as his mother by her first marriage had been countess of Bar-sur-Seine; neither Dreux nor Braine was a county.

able to construct any other fortification between Braine and county of Champagne unless by permission of the countess and her son.

I have sworn in good faith and without malice that I will forever abide by the agreement described in this document. The countess had one of her knights swear an oath to me and my heirs that she would observe this agreement.

So that this agreement be valid and remain in force, I have had this document drawn up and confirmed by my seal. Done at Provins, in the year of our Lord 1206, in the month of April.

### 6. AN EXEMPTION TO THE CASTLE POLICY, 1223

*Since the mid-twelfth century, the counts required every fortification—defined as any building enclosed by a wall—to be held in fief directly from them. Rear-fief tenants, consequently, were prohibited from erecting walls around their residences. Here Thibaut IV grants an exemption to that policy as a favor to a supporter to whom the count had already given a substantial fief. This abbreviated text is the copy retained in the count's archives; the original, presented to the beneficiary, would have been written out in full.*[10]

I, Thibaut, etc., make known, etc., that when Henry of Mirvaux erected walls around his house at Givry near Mirvaux, my loyal and faithful Thomas of Mirvaux [Henry's direct lord] objected on the grounds that the custom in Champagne was that every fortress, no matter what kind, must be held [directly] from the count of Champagne.

I have allowed the said Henry and his heirs to build a wall around his house fifteen-and-one-half-feet high and two-and-one-half-feet thick, but without towers and a moat, and only with loopholes for bows and crossbows appropriate to a plain wall. He may not, on account of this exemption, discontinue his [feudal] obligations to Thomas, in whose fief this house is located, etc. [Done] in the year of our Lord, 1223.

### 7. AN ALLODIAL CASTLE IS FEUDALIZED, 1221

*After the civil war of 1216–1219, the victorious Countess Blanche and Thibaut IV placed the barons of Champagne under intense pressure to convert their important allodial lands into fiefs: such feudalized lands were said to "move" or be in the* mouvance *(feudal dependency) of Champagne. Contracts establishing*

---

10. Text in Edmond Martène and Ursin Durand, eds., *Thesaurus novus anecdotorum*, 5 vols. (Paris: F. Delaulne et al., 1717), 1:903–904.

mouvance *usually contained reservation clauses for prior homages, as explained here. The result was a tangle of feudal ties that reflect an increasingly legalistic approach to homage and liegeance.*[11] *Note also Roger's close attention to the mechanics of payment of his feudal rent.*[12]

I, Roger, lord of Rozoy-en-Thiérache, make known to all, present and future, that I have received in fief and liege homage from my dearest lady Blanche, illustrious countess of Troyes, and her son, my dearest lord Thibaut, count of Champagne, my castle of Chaumont-Porcien and its entire castellany with its appendages—except for Thin-le-Moutier—all of which had been my allod located within the borders of the county of Champagne.

I have become their vassal (*homo*), save my liegeance [for other fiefs] to the king of the French, to the lord bishop of Laon, and to the lord abbot of Saint-Denis. I must swear in good faith to the countess, to her son the count, and to their heirs for the castle of Chaumont-Porcien and its entire castellany—except Thin-le-Moutier—against all creatures who can live and die.[13] I must personally swear good faith to the countess, to her son the count, and to their heirs against all creatures who can live and die except against the above named three—the lord king, the lord bishop, and the lord abbot. My heirs who hold this castle will be required to give the same homage to the said countess and her son and heirs in perpetuity.

For this [allodial conversion and homage], the countess and her son have given me and my heirs 500*l.* in pennies and a [fief-] rent of 60*l.* to be paid from the revenues collected at the gates of Provins during the fairs of Saint-Ayoul [September 14-November 1], payable to me and my heirs during the fairs by whoever collects the revenue at the gates. If the payment is not made, the said count [Thibaut would succeed in May 1222] and his heirs will be responsible for paying me and my heirs directly in coin at the end of the fair, when accounts are cleared. I and my heirs are specifically prohibited from transferring that 60*l.* rent from the hand of whoever holds the castle of Chaumont-Porcien.

If it ever happens that my heir who holds Chaumont-Porcien does not also hold a fief from the lord king of the French, that heir will be

---

11. For a similar case (with translated text), see John F. Benton, "Written Records and the Development of Systematic Feudal Relations," in his *Culture, Power and Personality in Medieval France*, ed. Thomas N. Bisson (London: The Hambledon Press, 1991), 275–290.

12. Text in Chantereau-Lefebvre, *Traité*, 2:15–16.

13. He will not take an oath against spiritual creatures.

required to give liege homage to the said countess and her son Count Thibaut and his heirs against all creatures who can live and die.

The said countess and count and their heirs may not prevent me from acquiring—if it should happen—the fief that my brother Nicholas holds from the lord of Marle according to the customs of the royal domain.[14]

So that all this remain known and be held firmly, I have confirmed this letter by my seal. Done at Epernay in the year of our Lord 1220, in the month of January, on the eighteenth kalends of February [January 15, 1221].

## 8. CONFISCATION OF AN UNAUTHORIZED ALIENATION, 1234

*Any alienation of feudal property, in whole or in part, required the authorization of the lord from whom the fief was held. Here Count Thibaut IV regrants a fief he confiscated because it had been sold without his license.*[15]

I, Thibaut, by the grace of God, king of Navarre and count palatine of Champagne and Brie, make known to all who examine this letter that since my loyal and faithful Simon of Clefmont sold to my loyal and faithful lord [Simon] of Châteauvillain all that he had at Coupray and in the appurtenances of that village—which he should not have done without my consent and approval—I had it seized and placed in my hand.

Later I gave that village to my loyal and faithful lord Peter of Jaucourt and his heirs to possess in perpetuity. I also gave to Peter and his heirs [the tenants] Dolandin of Longchamp and his family, as well as the widow of Christian.

In testimony of which I have sealed this letter. Done in the year of our Lord 1234, in the month of March.

## 9. THE REPURCHASE OF A FIEF, 1244

*Distressed by the widespread alienation of feudal property by impecunious knights to ecclesiastical houses, Count Thibaut IV began to repurchase fiefs that he and his predecessors had granted. In the 1230s and 1240s, his officials acquired a substantial number of fiefs, especially feudal rents disbursed from the comital treasury. Here a modest feudal rent is sold back to the count for the conventional price of ten times its annual revenue (Doc. A).*[16] *The seller issued a receipt of payment to the count's chamberlain (Doc. B).*[17]

14. That is, it was a non-Champagne fief.
15. Text in "Cartulary-Register" no. 7, vol. 3, fols. 238v–239r.
16. Text in ibid., fol. 117r.
17. Text in ibid., fol. 117v.

(A)  I, Renaud of Grancey, lord of Larrey, make known to all who examine this letter that I have sold and quit in perpetuity to the illustrious Thibaut, by the grace of God, king of Navarre and count palatine of Champagne and Brie, and to his heirs the 20*l.* [fief-] rent which he owes me each year at the fairs at Bar-sur-Aube for 200*l.*, which I have received. I am held to guarantee this sale in perpetuity against all claimants, and I have promised that to the lord king and his heirs. In testimony of which, I have affixed my seal to this letter. Done in the year of our Lord 1244, in the month of June.

(B)  I, Renaud of Grancey, lord of Larrey, make known to all who see this letter that for the sale of my 20*l.* [fief-] rent, I have received in full the 200*l.*, money of Provins, that was owed me from [the hand of] Master Renaud, my cleric, who received it from the venerable [John of Voisines] dean of Saint-Quiriace of Provins and Robert of Aulnay [chamberlain of Champagne]. In testimony of which I have affixed my seal to this letter. Done in the year of our Lord 1244.

### 10.  THE GREAT FEUDAL INQUEST, 1249–1250

*The sell-off of fiefs in the 1230s and 1240s seriously eroded the financial well-being of the aristocracy, jeopardizing in particular the knightly families at the lower income levels. In order to determine the current state of his feudal tenants, Count Thibaut IV ordered a comprehensive inquest in 1249–1250. Feudal tenants were convened at the count's castle-towns to testify about their current holdings, military obligations, and recent alienations. Here Thibaut announces the inquest (Doc. A),[18] typical feudal tenants give their testimony (Docs. B, C),[19] and a knight unable to appear sends a letter-report (Doc. D).[20]*

(A)  Thibaut, by the grace of God, king of Navarre and count palatine of Champagne and Brie, to all barons, castellans, knights, and other feudal tenants in the county of Champagne and Brie, greeting and warm regards. Be advised that I am sending my trusted Giles of Villenauxe, knight [bailiff of Provins], and Master James [of Rebais], my cleric,[21] through my land to inquire about my fiefs. Therefore I firmly order you, by the fidelity

---

18. Text in Teulet, *Layettes* 3 : 122–123, no. 3931.
19. Text in Auguste Longnon, ed., *Rôles des fiefs du comté de Champagne sous le règne de Thibaud le Chansonnier (1249–1252)*, (Paris: Henri Menu, 1877), 141, no. 668; 4, no. 14.
20. Text in "Cartulary-Register" no. 7, vol. 3, fol. 100r.
21. Treasurer of Saint-Quiriace of Provins, which served as the count's bureau of accounts.

which you owe me, that when you are asked you will name truthfully, on your oath, all the fiefs and rear-fiefs that you hold from me. Given at Bourges, in the year of our Lord 1250.

(B) [Feudal register for the castellany of Nogent-sur-Seine, 1249:] Henry of Ferreux, knight, liegeman, on oath [said that] he holds the [fortified] residence of Ferreux, lands, land rents, woods, vineyards, and rents: worth about 20*l.* annually. [His rear-fief tenants:] (1) Girard of Clesles, knight, holds from Henry about one *modius* of wheat annually at Ferreux on behalf of his wife [as dowry or inheritance]. (2) Anselm of Foissy holds from him revenues worth about 60*s.* annually. (3) Thibaut of Fontaine-Saint-Georges, squire, holds from him an annual rent of one *modius* of wheat. Henry owes two months castle-guard.

(C) [Feudal register for the castellany of Bar-sur-Aube, 1250:] Lady Lucy, widow of lord Jocelin of Lignol,[22] holds the house and whatever she has in the village and parish of Lignol [as dower], as well as her houses within the castle of Bar-sur-Aube [as inheritance]. Huguenin of Louvières holds from her [a rear-fief worth] about 60*s.* annually. She [Lucy] must report back within eight days the amount of castle-guard her fief owes. [Added later by a scribe:] that fief owes all-year guard duty, according to the old feudal register.[23]

(D) I, Guichard of Passavant, knight, make known to all who see this letter that I have done liege homage to Thibaut, by the grace of God, king of Navarre, and I have become his liegeman against all creatures who can live and die for the 30*l.* annual rent which he gave my father, who did homage for it in 1221 in the month of April.[24] The king is to pay me those 30*l.* each year at the fair of Bar-sur-Aube. On account of this, my father and I [in 1221] sold to the king what we had at Montigny.

I, Guichard, did another liege homage to the king, save my homage to the lord Gobert of Apremont, for another 30*l.* annual rent at the fair of Bar-sur-Aube which the king had given to Lord Drogo of Apremont. That 30*l.* rent came to me by escheat from Drogo, with the consent of Drogo's heir.

22. See Doc. 28.
23. A feudal roll of ca. 1178 states: "Josbert of Lignol is liege and owes all-year guard duty" (Longnon, *Documents* 1 : 4, no. 94). That Josbert was the grandfather of Jocelin, whose widow Lucy here is holding the fief for her minor son.
24. Guichard is quoting from his father's letter.

If I have two heirs, they will be liable for two homages [one each] to the king or his heirs, as explained above. Done at Orges, the first Wednesday after the first Sunday of Lent [March 8], in the year of our Lord 1251, in the month of March.

## 11. Unauthorized Alienations to the Church, 1250–1252

*One result of the great feudal inquest (see Doc. 10) was a list of all alienations made by feudal tenants within the past forty years (Doc. A).*[25] *The count's officials quickly and vigorously confiscated all recent acquisitions by religious institutions which lacked written authorization (Doc. B).*[26] *Those confiscations brought a loud protest from the province's prelates (Doc. C).*[27]

(A) Lord Renaud of Luxémont, under oath, said that Girard of Saint-Vrain and his brother sold to the [Cistercian] monks of Trois-Fontaines some land in the parish of Luxémont, Vauclerc, and elsewhere nearby which they held in fief from Lord Aubert of Le Plessis, who approved [of the alienation] about eight years ago [1242]. Lord Renaud also said that two years ago [1248] Lord Aubert gave a wine press in Vitry to the convent of nuns there.[28]

(B) I, Thibaut [IV], by the grace of God, king of Navarre and count palatine of Champagne and Brie, make known to all who see or hear this letter that the abbot and monastic community of Cheminon made peace with me over their [unauthorized] acquisitions from my land, fiefs, and nonfeudal rents during the regency of my dear mother [1201–1222]. As I have heard from trustworthy men, I gave the monks a letter describing my agreement with the monastery. William, abbot of [the Cistercian monastery of] Hautefontaine and Brother Alous, monk of Cheminon, appeared before me and have sworn on the Bible and on the cross, at the peril of their souls, that Cheminon abbey paid me 300*l.*, heavy money of Provins,[29] for my peace with them. But the abbot and community of Cheminon, through carelessness, they said, have lost that letter describing our agreement.[30]

25. Text in Longnon, *Rôles des fiefs*, 348, no. 1614.
26. Text in Edouard Barthélemy, ed., *Recueil des chartes de l'abbaye de Notre-Dame de Cheminon* (Paris: Champion, 1883), 120–121.
27. Text in Teulet, *Layettes* 3:170, no. 4029.
28. See Doc. 69.
29. That is, the heavier coin minted from 1225; see Doc. 68.
30. The count's chancery did, in fact, have a copy of this letter of 1223 but perhaps was unable to locate it among the thousands of letters on file in the chancery archives.

For the love of our lady Mary and for the salvation of my soul and the souls of my ancestors, I hereby approve of all of Cheminon's acquisitions of fiefs and nonfeudal rents made during my mother's regency. So that this endure forever, I have had this letter sealed by my seal. It was presented at Villefranche in Navarre on the eve of Saint Nicholas [December 6] in the year of grace 1251, in the month of December.

(C) Giles, by the grace of God, archbishop of Sens, and the bishops Matthew of Chartres, Renaud of Paris, William of Orléans, Guy of Auxerre, Peter of Meaux, and Nicholas of Troyes, to the most blessed in Christ, Thibaut, by the grace of God, king of Navarre and count palatine of Champagne and Brie, greeting and true affection in the Lord. During the recent ecclesiastical council we held at Sens, we sent you a letter asking you to release the ecclesiastical property held for over forty years, which you had your agents seize. Our prayers and request have not been answered. Rather, each day your men unremittingly confiscate more and more property, causing great injury to the church, to the clergy, and to their tenants, all of which is contrary to the church's immunity and to ecclesiastical liberty.

We are sending our representative, Master John of Verneuil, to you to explain fully our cause; on behalf of our council he will ask you to release the confiscated lands, to desist from these abuses, and to order your agents to stop.

We wish to defer to your honor and your person as much as we can, but we cannot, nor ought we, overlook oppression of the church. We do not wish to infringe on your rights but only to safeguard the church from injury, inasmuch as we can, with God's help. Given at Paris, the Friday after the Feast of Saint Martin [November 16], in the year of our Lord 1252. [The seven seals of the prelates were appended.]

12. RESTRICTIONS ON TEMPLAR ACQUISITIONS, 1191, 1255
*As William of Tyre reported, the Templars became very wealthy in the second half of the twelfth century.*[31] *After Count Henry II prohibited their acquisition of property in the towns and castles of Champagne (Doc. A),*[32] *they shifted their sights to undeveloped rural lands and within a generation had accumulated vast tracts of forests. A number of villages, deprived of their traditional forest*

31. See Doc. 78.
32. Text in Arbois de Jubainville, *Histoire*, 3:477, no. 160.

*rights, reacted violently against the Templars. Count Thibaut IV also clashed with the Templars over their acquisition of feudal property, and in 1255 his widow prohibited them altogether from acquiring feudal land within the county (Doc. B).* [33]

(A) I, Henry [II], count palatine of Troyes, make known to all, present and future, that I, for the salvation of my soul and the souls of my relatives and ancestors, concede and confirm by my seal to the Knights Templar all the donations granted them by my grandfather, Count Thibaut [II] of good memory, and by my father Lord Henry [I], count palatine of Troyes. Also I take under my protection all that the Templars possess in my lands. I grant further this privilege: that they may possess freely and quietly whatever they have acquired by alms, purchase, or any other means; however, they are not permitted to obtain the lordship (*dominium*) of any town or castle in my land.[34] So that this grant may endure, I have confirmed this letter by my seal. Done during the siege of Acre, in the year of our Lord 1191. Written by Ralph [chancery scribe].

(B) I, Bother Renaud of Vichier, master of the poor knights of the Temple of Jerusalem, and the community of those knights make known to all who will see or hear this letter that we had a dispute with Margaret, by the grace of God, [regent-] queen of Navarre and countess palatine of Champagne and Brie, Thibaut V [her son], and Isabel [his wife], daughter of the king of France, over what we claim to be able to acquire and hold within the lordship of Champagne and Brie in land and property of all kind outside the count's cities and castles, as is permitted by a letter we have from the count's predecessor [Henry II's letter of 1191 above].

That earlier understanding is modified here to allow us to acquire only from the fiefs, rear-fiefs, and nonfeudal rents (*censives*) that are already held from us and over which we have jurisdiction. Henceforth we may not acquire any of the count's fiefs, rear-fiefs, nonfeudal rents or anything that derives from these, nor anything under his jurisdiction, except by his permission.

If we do receive any of these [prohibited] types of property in alms or bequest, we must regrant them to the appropriate type of tenant: a barony must be regranted to at least a baron; a castellany to at least a

---

33. Text (abbreviated here) in Teulet, *Layettes* 3:246–249, no. 4184.
34. Henry must have seen how the possession of towns and castles in the Holy Land made the Templars an independent power.

castellan; a vassal's fief to at least a vassal (*vavasseur*); a simple fief to at least a gentleman (*gentil home*); and things held by townsmen or peasants, to townsmen or peasants. That is to say, if we receive anything from the count's men, we must regrant it to his men; if it comes from ecclesiastical tenants who are not ours, we must regrant it to ecclesiastical tenants; if anything comes to us from a knight or gentleman, we will regrant it to a knight or gentleman; but if it comes from our [own] men, we can regrant it to our men or to whomever we wish.

If we receive in alms or bequest a fifteenth, sixteenth, or seventeenth part of a barony or castellany, we must regrant it to a gentleman; if we receive a fourteenth, thirteenth, twelfth, or greater part of a barony or castellany, we must regrant it to a baron or a castellan; and this must be done within one year and one day by the master of the house in charge of alms and bequests or, if there is no master, by one of the senior brothers of the house. Until these alms or bequests have been regranted, the person in whose hands they are held temporarily is accountable to the count for their revenues and obligations.

We are allowed to acquire and hold rents and fiefs that move either of the count or of us that pertain to our own granges, ovens, mills, houses, and rents, and the use of woods that are completely ours. . . . We are allowed to acquire tithes throughout the county and lordship of Champagne and Brie, whether they move of the count's fiefs or rear-fiefs. . . . The count may not confiscate our horses or draft animals without our consent. . . .

[Notwithstanding this future prohibition,] we retain the inheritances, property, rents, and other rights that we acquired in the lordship of Champagne and Brie by alms, escheat, gift, and other means before the death of Count Thibaut IV, who died on July 14, 1253, who had approved of those acquisitions, that is, of all we acquired in the previous twenty-five years.[35]

13. AUTHORIZATION TO ACQUIRE FEUDAL PROPERTY, 1260
*The counts adopted several policies aimed at discouraging the transfer of feudal property to religious houses, including outright prohibitions (as in Doc. 11), taxation of varying severity, prescribed annual limitations, and restrictions against acquiring entire fiefs. In this act Count Thibaut V rewards a cousin, the younger brother of the powerful Count Thibaut II of Bar-le-Duc, who had been*

35. That is, from Thibaut's accession in 1222 to the great inquest of 1249–50; see Doc. 10.

*a loyal companion: he allows a specific feudal alienation and grants license for limited feudal acquisitions by the recipient monastery.*[36]

I, Thibaut, by the grace of God, king of Navarre and count palatine of Champagne and Brie, make known to all who examine this letter that in appreciation for the fidelity and friendship (*amicitia*) that my loyal and faithful Renaud of Bar-le-Duc [lord of Ancerville], knight, has long shown me, I grant that he may give to whichever religious house he chooses: his house at Troyes called the "house of the count of Bar"; 30*l*. annual rent that he collects from the sales tax on furs at the two annual fairs of Troyes; and all that he has within the suburb of Troyes.

In addition, I grant to whichever religious house he gives the above: permission to acquire [property worth] up to 80*l*. annual revenue from my fiefs and rear-fiefs, free and quit of all taxes, the fifth penny,[37] and any other obligation (*servitium*), provided that it does not acquire any fief in its entirety.

In testimony and in perpetual memory of which I, as lord of these fiefs, approve and have had my seal appended to confirm this letter. Presented [to Renaud] by the hand of my loyal and faithful vice-chancellor, Brother Peter of Roncevaux; written by my cleric Richard of Montierender, in the year of our Lord 1260, in the month of May.

## 14. ROYAL TAXATION OF ALIENATED FIEFS, 1291

*In 1275 King Philip III, realizing that alienations of feudal property to the church could not be halted, decided to tax unauthorized feudal transfers. In 1291 Philip IV extended taxation to all recent feudal alienations—whether transferred by gift or sale, whether authorized or not—and sent out agents to assess and collect the tax (Doc. A).*[38] *The agents, usually a cleric and a royal officer, examined ecclesiastical acquisitions within their districts, assessed a tax, and sent their report to the king.*[39] *A small Hospitaller house in Reims, for example, paid about three years' worth of revenue for the donations it had received and the purchases it had made since 1255 (Doc. B).*[40]

36. Text in Chantereau-Lefebvre, *Traité*, 2:249.
37. That is, the 20 percent sales tax.
38. Text in Eusèbe de Laurière et al., eds., *Ordonnances des rois de France de la troisième race*, 22 vols. (Paris: Imprimerie Royale, 1723–1849), 1:322–324.
39. See John F. Benton, "The Accounts of Cepperello da Prato for the Tax on *nouveaux acquêts* in the Bailliage of Troyes," in *Order and Innovation in the Middle Ages: Essays in Honor of Joseph R. Strayer*, ed. William C. Jordan, Bruce McNab, and Teofilo R. Ruiz (Princeton: Princeton University Press, 1976), 111–135, 453–457, reprinted in his *Culture, Power and Personality*, 255–274.
40. Text in J. Delaville le Roulx, ed., *Cartulaire général de l'Ordre des Hospitaliers de S. Jean de Jérusalem*, 4 vols. (Paris: E. Leroux, 1894–1906), 3:616–617, no. 4208.

(A) For the benefit of the church and the peace of my subjects, I [Philip IV] have enacted this decree: that seneschals, bailiffs, provosts, viscounts, and my other judicial officers cease and abstain from harassing churches over their acquisitions in the lands of my barons whose ancestors, as well as mine, have recognized through long forbearance to have been useful. I grant that both gifts to churches and their legitimate acquisitions—at least those for which authorization was requested—shall be free from any claim by me and my barons, saving only my right and my barons' right in the future.

[1] But for property which churches have acquired from my lands, fiefs, rear-fiefs, nonfeudal rents, and allods *without* my or my predecessors' authorization during the thirty years preceding my father King Philip's decree [1275], I wish a tax to be assessed and collected according to the schedule below.

[2] For acquisitions made since my father's decree—which did not address future acquisitions—up to the present day, I decree that churches may keep the property they have acquired freely [as gifts] from my fiefs and nonfeudal rents *without* my or my predecessors' authorization, provided they pay a tax of four years' revenue from those properties. For similarly unauthorized gifts from my rear-fiefs and rear-nonfeudal rents, the tax is three years' revenue.

[3] For unauthorized acquisitions not made freely [that is, purchases] from my lands, nonfeudal rents, and fiefs, the tax is six years' revenue. For similarly unauthorized acquisitions from my rear-fiefs and rear-nonfeudal rents, the tax is four years' revenue.

[4] Allods given freely to churches are taxed at two years' revenue; allods purchased by churches are taxed at four years' revenue.

[5] If nonnobles (*persone ignobiles*) have acquired fiefs or rear-fiefs outside my barons' lands without my authorization—and if there are not at least three feudal lords (*domini*) between myself and the seller—the tax is three years' revenue if the acquirer is not competent to perform the [feudal] service; if he *is* competent to perform the service, he is not liable for the tax; but if the fief is abridged, he is liable for damages assessed by my agents.

I wish that those whom I have delegated to collect these taxes render at least the amounts of this schedule, never less.

I have enacted this decree for past cases, not for future ones. I do not wish this decree to cover alienations which are so manifestly damaging [to my interests] that they cannot be tolerated. And because property is more expensive in the seneschalcies of Périgord, Carcassonne, Beaucaire, Toulouse, and Rouergue, I wish the above rates to be doubled for those areas. This decree was enacted in the Parlement on All Saints' Day [November 1], in the year of our Lord 1291.

(B) To all who see this letter, greeting and goodwill from Hugh of Noirecourt, canon of Rozoy in the diocese of Laon, and John of Saint-Vrain, bailiff of Vitry, commissioned and delegated by the most illustrious prince Philip, by the grace of God, king of the French, to deal with and collect the taxes owed by religious persons, religious houses, corporations, and nonnobles in the *bailliage* of Vitry who acquired his fiefs, rear-fiefs, nonfeudal rents, and allods during the past forty-six years.

Be it known that we have received from Brother Nicholas of Rieux, preceptor or master of the house of the Hospital of Saint-John of Jerusalem in the city and diocese of Reims, 11*l.* 6*d.* and 1 *obol*, money of Tours, [as tax] for these acquisitions:

• Four *sextarii* each of grain and oats which the deceased lord Giles of Rieux, knight, and his wife, Lady Isabel, gave as a gift: they used to collect that grain each year at the Hospitallers' grange at Grand Champ

• A modest land rent which the lord Engerran of Rumigny, knight, gave as a perpetual gift

• One-half of a field in the territory of Tours-sur-Marne which was a gift to the Hospitaller house at Crilly in the diocese of Reims

• These lands and fields were not gifts: four pieces of arable in the territory of Grand Champ worth thirteen *sextarii* of produce; one piece of arable and a field in the same place worth six *sextarii*; three measures of arable in the same place called La Fontaine-Anselme.

All of the above acquired by gift or otherwise were from the lord king's rear-fiefs and produced altogether about 4*l.* 4*s.* 4*d.*, money of Tours, annual revenue. Wherefore, we concede in the name of the king and on his behalf that the said Hospitallers may keep the above named acquisitions without being required to sell or otherwise dispose of them, saving the lord king's right. In testimony of which, we have appended our seals to this letter. Given in the year of our Lord 1292, in the month of February [1293].

15. COUNT THIBAUT V TAXES HIS FEUDAL TENANTS, 1257
*When Count Thibaut V attained his majority, his mother assumed her dower lands comprising at least one-third of his total revenues in Champagne. Since the young count's succession to the kingdom of Navarre was uncertain, he*

*faced heavy financial needs at the start of his reign. In taxing his feudal tenants one percent of their income in each of three years, Thibaut imposed the first noncrusade tax upon the Champagne feudal aristocracy.*[41]

Thibaut, by the grace of God, king of Navarre and count palatine of Champagne and Brie, to all the barons, castellans, and vassals (*vavasur*) of the county of Champagne, and to all who hold in fief and rear-fief from me and from you [the barons, castellans, and vassals], greeting and good-will. Be it known that according to our mutual agreement reached at Sézanne regarding my needs, those who hold fiefs and rear-fiefs from me and from you barons, castellans, and vassals must pay a one-hundredth income tax (*centenne*) in each of the next three years. The first payment will be due the Sunday after All Saints' Day [November 4], 1257.

If this tax is paid during the next three years, I promise you that neither I nor my heirs will ask anything more from you or your heirs, nor from your men, nor from those who hold in fief and rear-fief [from you], and that henceforth you and your heirs will be quit of this tax and will be as you were before we talked about it.

If peace [in Navarre] is made within the next three years, anything remaining from the collected tax beyond my needs will be returned to you barons, castellans, and vassals, and to your men, according to what each has given.

So that memory of this may be preserved, I have affixed my seal to this letter which was drawn up at Orléans, on Thursday of All Saints' Day [November 1] in the year of our Lord Jesus Christ 1257.

## Rural and Urban Policies

From the middle decades of the twelfth century the counts encouraged peasant migration into their lands by founding villages with favorable terms of residence and tenure (Doc. 16). These new villages (and re-founded old ones) drew immigrants both from outside the county and from the Champagne lands of less enlightened lords, who often tried to halt the emigration of their own tenants (see Docs. 3, 4). Monasteries with large tracts of undeveloped land tried to tap the current of rural migration

41. Text in Gustave Saige, Henri Lacaille, and L. H. Labande, eds., *Trésor des chartes du comté de Rethel*, 5 vols. (Monaco: Imprimerie de Monaco, 1902–1916), 1: 287–288, no. 126.

by contracting partnerships (*pariages*) with the counts to establish jointly sponsored communities (Doc. 17).

The towns of Champagne also experienced rapid growth. The twin capitals of Troyes and Provins became the largest: they not only hosted the international fairs but acquired vigorous indigenous industries as well (see Doc. 23). The counts preferred to rule their towns directly, however, granting very few urban franchises before 1230. In that year Thibaut IV granted a communal franchise to the townsmen of Troyes (Doc. 18), and in the next two years awarded similar charters to at least a dozen of his most important towns. Since the grants applied to all his tenants living within the surrounding castellanies as well as in the towns, Thibaut effectively franchised most of his tenants who became, consequently, a privileged class liberated from the hated tallage (*taille*) and other personal constraints. Those who lacked the franchise, primarily tenants of other lords, would later be known as "serfs."

Jewish communities had a long history in Champagne, where the counts and their barons protected and taxed them. Recognizing the importance of Jewish businessmen to the county and the international fairs, the counts did not succumb to the royal policies of expulsion and confiscation of property; instead, the Jews of Champagne were saddled with exorbitant taxes as the price of remaining in the county (Doc. 19).

### 16. COUNT HENRY FRANCHISES A NEW VILLAGE, 1175

*In this grant to the new community of Villeneuve-au-Châtelot, Count Henry I franchises the residents, regulates violence, and establishes a simple administrative organization. Several of the clauses are explained by the fact that the residents were immigrants, in some cases dissatisfied tenants of neighboring lords. The original document was preserved in the village for at least one hundred years, for in 1276 the villagers produced it for an inquest into the count's rights there. This is the earliest extant franchise granted by the counts.*[42]

I, Henry, count palatine of Troyes, make known to all present and future, that I have founded a new village between the road to Pont-sur-Seine and Perigny-la-Rose with these customs (*consuetudines*):

[1] Each man living in this village shall pay 12*d.* and one *mina* [about six bushels] of oats annually as a residence tax. He will owe 4*d.* in annual rent for each *arpent* of arable and meadowland he cultivates.

---

42. Text in Longnon, *Documents*, 2:21–22. See the analysis in Theodore Evergates, *Feudal Society in the Bailliage of Troyes under the Counts of Champagne, 1152–1284* (Baltimore and London: The Johns Hopkins University Press, 1975), 44–45.

[2] Houses, vineyards, and cultivated lands and fields may be purchased and sold at will [without tax].

[3] For misdeeds assessed at 60s., there will be a 5s. fine; for those assessed at 5s., the fine will be 12d. Appeal to the provost will cost 4d.

[4] Men living in this village will not be required to perform military service unless I appear in person [to summon them].

[5] For a judicial duel, after sureties are given to the provost, the parties may still reach an accord without the provost, but in that event each must offer him 2s. 6d. [for his trouble], which he may accept if he chooses. Even if hostages are exchanged [between the parties], an accord may be reached without the provost, but in that case, each party must offer the provost 7s. 6d., which he may accept. If a duel takes place, the victor must pay 100s.

[6] If on market day an unarmed person strikes another so violently that blood flows, the perpetrator is to be fined 60s. And if an armed person strikes someone down in anger, for that crime he will be at the count's mercy.

[7] Residents will be free from tolls and sales taxes in all my lands.

[8] I also allow the men of this village to have six councilmen (*scabini*) who will manage the common affairs of the village and who will be present at the provost's pleas.

[9] No knight nor anyone else may challenge a resident on account of a prior contract or for any other cause except if that resident has been the knight's dependent tenant (*homo de corpore*) and subject to the old and taxable commendation,[43] for which the knight ought to have his right.

Present at this enactment were these witnesses: Lord Anselm of Traînel [butler of Champagne]; Matthew "the Red," Hugh of "Purreyus," Thecelin of Clérey, and Hugo "Rage" [the count's knights and advisers]; Artaud, chamberlain [of Champagne]; Matthew, provost of Pont-sur-Seine; and Benedict of Pont-sur-Seine [a wealthy townsman and adviser to the count].

Done at Provins, in the year of our Lord 1175. [This charter was] presented [to the villagers] by the hand of William, chancellor [of Champagne].

## 17. A JOINT SPONSORSHIP (*PARIAGE*) OF A NEW COMMUNITY, 1223

*A* pariage (pariagium) *was a contract between two lords to develop and share the administration of certain lands belonging to one of them, usually a religious*

---

43. *Antiquam et talliabilem commendacionem.*

*house. The count or other powerful lay lord was "associated" over the land and was granted half of the revenues. In most cases, as here, the land in question was distant from the monastic owner, and thus difficult to administer. Since such arrangements were mutually beneficial, they were quite numerous from the mid-twelfth through the mid-thirteenth century, a time of sustained agrarian expansion. This contract, abbreviated slightly when it was copied into the count's cartulary, was typical.*[44]

I, Thibaut, count palatine of Champagne and Brie, make known to all, present and future, who see this letter that the venerable abbot Gilbert, the community of Saint-Bénigne of Dijon, and their prior, Galcher, associated me and my heirs over the entire territory of Montreuil in this manner:

[1] I must attract men there and construct a [new] village.

[2] I and my heirs will have one-half of all the revenues, fines, and justice from the men who reside in this village after it is constructed; the prior of Saint-Bénigne will have the other half of the revenues. I will have jurisdiction over theft, homicide, adultery, and rape.

[3] If any man decides to leave the village, I and the prior each will take one-half of that man's remaining movables and land.

[4] I or my heirs may build a residence there, if we wish.

[5] The prior of Saint-Bénigne will have [sole possession of] his grange there with lands and fields sufficient to be farmed by one plow; and he will have the church and the entire tithe of the village for himself.

[6] None of Saint-Bénigne's men may settle in this village, nor will I accept them there; likewise, no man living in my domain or on the lands of my feudal tenants or on [monastic] lands under my protection may settle there without my permission.

[7] I and my heirs may not bestow this village on anyone else nor grant it in alms, in homage, in fief, or in custody, except to the prior of Saint-Bénigne; nor may I tax or trouble the men there without the prior's consent. Nor may I compel those men to give me military service unless I appear in person.

[8] Neither a provost nor a mayor may be installed there without the consent of the prior of Saint-Bénigne, and whoever is installed in those offices must give an oath of fidelity both to the prior and to me or my heir.

44. Text in Estienne Pérard, ed., *Recueil de plusieurs pièces curieuses servant à l'histoire de Bourgogne* (Paris: C. Cramoisy, 1664), 330–331. See also Doc. 75.

So that this remain permanent, I have had this letter sealed with my seal. Done in the year of our Lord 1223, in the month of June.

### 18. THE COMMUNAL FRANCHISES OF 1230–1232

*After northern French barons, angry with Thibaut IV, invaded Champagne in 1229–1230, a number of the count's towns lay in ruins. The count decided to compensate the townsmen who had rallied to his defense by granting charters of franchise to his largest and most important towns, including his twin capitals of Troyes and Provins. The franchises lifted the old and burdensome personal obligations, taxes, and restrictions from his tenants in both the towns and their surrounding castellanies. They further instituted internal self-administration by a local mayor and councilmen, a self-assessed tax on wealth, and several other privileges.*

*The charter for Troyes was the first and served as a model for the other grants, which the count presented in person as he traveled through the county.*[45] *The charters were written in the French vernacular so as to be readily comprehended by townsmen not learned in Latin. It should be noted that only the count's men, not all residents, of these towns and their districts were franchised: residents who lived within ecclesiastical jurisdictions did not enjoy the privileges. Nevertheless, by creating a large, privileged class of nonnobles, the communal franchises were a milestone in the social history of the county.*

I, Thibaut, count palatine of Champagne and Brie, make known to all, present and future, who see this letter that I franchise and quit all my men and women of Troyes of all tolls and tallages (*tailles*) in this manner: those from whom I have had the right to collect tallage, as well as immigrants who have come to live in Troyes, will pay 6*d.* annually for each pound value of their movable possessions—excluding their weapons, clothing, and ordinary household furnishings. But wine goblets and all gold and silver objects are to be counted with the taxable movables. Each pound value of real property will be taxed at the rate of 2*d.* annually.

[1] If any of my tenants, or the tenants of my fief-holders, or tenants from lands under my protection, come to live in Troyes, the townsmen (*borjois*) of Troyes may accept them only with my consent. And if any of these seek admission to the community (*comunete*) of Troyes, claiming not

45. Text in Dominique Coq, ed., *Chartes en langue française antérieures à 1271 conservées dans les départements de l'Aube, de la Seine-et-Marne, et de l'Yonne*, Documents linguistiques de la France, série française, 3 (Paris: Editions du CNRS, 1988), 3–6, no. 1. For an analysis, see Evergates, *Feudal Society in the Bailliage of Troyes*, 47–59.

to be from my lands or the lands of my feudal tenants or from lands under my custody, it will be my decision whether to admit them or not; and if I refuse them admission, they will have a fifteen-day safe-conduct in which to leave.

[2] Anyone who wishes to pay a 20*l.* annual tax will be exempt from the property assessment and its tax that year.

[3] I grant [to the community] the provostship and the justice of Troyes and of its lands and vineyards within the district of Troyes, as I have them on the day of this document, for 300*l.*, money of Provins, which will be paid to me annually at Pentecost. All fines [assessed by the provost] on the men and women of the community and on those who reside there temporarily—fines which I used to collect—henceforth will go to the townsmen of Troyes. The community will also collect all fines up to 20*s.* imposed on foreigners; the rest will be mine. I will retain jurisdiction over murder, rape, and larceny in cases where the facts are well known. And I will keep the fine imposed on the victor of a duel, whom I will assess according to the customs of the city. I also retain jurisdiction over false weights and measures, for which I will collect a 40*s.* fine for myself and 20*s.* for the townsmen.

[4] I retain jurisdiction over churches under my protection, my knights (*chevaliers*), my feudal tenants (*fievez*), and my agents, so that if anyone of the community of Troyes injures any of these, that is, a cleric, a knight, a feudal tenant, or my agent who brings suit to me, I will collect the entire fine, although the amount will be determined by the mayor and councilmen of Troyes according to the customs of the city.

[5] Each year I or my representative will choose thirteen men from the community who will, within fifteen days, select one of themselves as mayor. If they do not select a mayor within that period, I myself will choose one of them as mayor. And the thirteen men will swear on Scriptures that they will preserve my rights and those of the commune (*comune*) of Troyes, and that they will govern the town and its affairs in good faith. These twelve councilmen (the *juré*) and the mayor will act in good faith and may not be criticized [for their decisions]. If their judgment or oversight is inadequate in some instance, that will be brought to my attention, according to the customs of Troyes, but they shall not be accountable nor fined for their judgment or lack of attention.

[6] These twelve councilmen and the mayor will collect the taxes assessed at 6*d.* per pound value of movable property and 2*d.* per pound value of real property, to be assessed according to the oaths of those who must

pay. If the mayor and at least three councilmen suspect anyone of a false declaration, they may increase the assessment to what they consider appropriate, but on no account will anyone who has taken an oath be fined [for false declaration]. The tax is to be paid on the Feast of Saint Andrew [November 30].

[7] All members of this community may sell and buy real estate and other things as they have in the past,[46] and will retain the privileges and the customary practices which they have had in the past. If anyone wishes to bring suit against anyone of the commune, I may not hear the case outside the city unless I am a party to the case; in any event, the case must be decided according to the customs of Troyes.

[8] Each man owes me military service (*ost et chevauchiee*), as before. Men over sixty years of age are exempt but should send a replacement if they are able to. If I summon men to military service during the fairs, the money changers and merchants necessary for the operation of the fairs may send replacements. Anyone not responding to a military summons will be fined. And I promise in good faith not to abuse this obligation, and to summon men only for my essential needs.

[9] Horses and weapons needed for military use may not be confiscated from members of the commune for debts, pledges, or other reasons. If I or my agents need horses and carts [for military purposes], we will ask the mayor of Troyes to find and lease them, paying out of my own revenues. If horses are destroyed [in service], the mayor and the councilmen will decide what will be paid in compensation from my revenues. Each member of the community who is worth 20l. [annual income] must keep a crossbow with fifty bolts in his house.

[10] The townsmen will bake at my [banal] ovens, and mill [their grain] at my [banal] mills. If those are inadequate, the mayor and councilmen will decide where they must bake and mill, providing always that my own ovens and mills are used to capacity.

[11] The [current] mayor and councilmen are responsible for all decisions and debts undertaken by the preceding mayor and councilmen.

[12] I agree not to alienate [to someone else] any of the provisions stated here.

[13] If anyone of the community is arrested or seized for my debts, I promise to obtain the release of him and his possessions. If anyone is arrested for another reason, I promise in good faith to seek his release.

46. That is, they are not restricted by mortmain; see Doc. 39.

[14] If any newcomer enters the community but decides not to remain, he may freely leave with my fifteen-day safe-conduct. If any of my
sergeants or other men who have charters [of individual franchise] from
me or my ancestors wishes to be part of the commune, he may; if he does
not, he will remain under my jurisdiction.

I have sworn to all the provisions contained in this charter both for
myself and for my heirs and their heirs in perpetuity. So that this remain
secure, I have had this letter sealed with my seal. Done in the year of grace
1230, in the month of September.

19.  A TAX ON THE JEWS, 1222

*Jewish communities had long flourished in Champagne, not only in the city of
Troyes, a well-known center of Jewish teaching, but also in a number of smaller
towns and villages, some even under local barons.*[47] *Despite popular hysteria
against the Jews during the great crusade recruitments, the counts protected
"their" Jews in return for substantial annual taxes from each community.
Champagne became a haven for Jews when King Philip Augustus expelled Jews
from the royal domain (1182) and confiscated their lands; although the king's
Jews were readmitted in 1198, they suffered periodic confiscations and expulsions
thereafter.*[48]

*In the early thirteenth century the counts resisted royal and papal attempts
to restrict Jewish money-lending, although Countess Blanche, dependent on royal
support early in her regency, was forced to join King Philip (1206) in fixing a
maximum 43 percent annual interest rate on Jewish loans. Within a week of
Thibaut IV's accession to the county (May 1222), he and his mother reaffirmed
the traditional comital policy of taxing the Jews very heavily but without any
threat of expulsion or confiscation of property. Their decree also describes the taxes
which Jews ordinarily paid to the counts.*[49]

I, Blanche, countess, and I, Thibaut, her son, make known that since
we are able to tax our Jews at will, they are obligated to pay us 70,000*l.*,
money of Provins, according to this schedule: 15,000*l.* at Troyes one year

47. See Robert Chazan, *Medieval Jewry in Northern France: A Political and Social History*
(Baltimore and London: The Johns Hopkins University Press, 1973), chap. 3.

48. See William Chester Jordan, *The French Monarchy and the Jews: From Philip Augustus to the Last Capetians* (Philadephia: University of Pennsylvania Press, 1989).

49. Text in Solomon Grayzel, *The Church and the Jews in the XIIIth Century*, 2d ed.
(New York: Hermon Press, 1966), 353–354, no. 9.

after the next fair of Saint-Remi[50] [1223]; 15,000*l*. at the following fair of Saint-Remi [1224]; 15,000*l*. at the next fair [1225]; and 15,000*l*. at the next [1226]. They will pay the remaining 10,000*l*. in the fifth year [1227].

[1] We will [collect and] turn over to those Jews the remainder of the loans now due to them but not yet paid, up to 30,000*l*. Anything over that amount [turned over to them] will be added to the 70,000*l*. tax owed and will be payable to us according to the above prescribed schedule; if the unpaid loans amount to less than 30,000*l*., the amount less than 30,000*l*. will be deducted from the 70,000*l*. tax.[51]

[2] Thereafter, all debts owed to the Jews, both due and outstanding, will be in their hands.

[3] During that five-year period the annual tax (*censive*) owed to us by the Jews will be paid to the community of our Jews.

[4] All Jews who come to dwell in our lands in that period will be liable to the tallage of the Jews (*tallia Judeorum*).

[5] All Jews of our lands will be exempt from tolls and road taxes during that time.

[6] The tax on seals by which the letters of the Jews are sealed will go to the community of the Jews during that period.

[7] All personal property of our Jews who die or who depart our lands, which ought to be ours, will go to the community of the Jews of our lands during the five-year period in order to help pay the tax.

[8] We will not seize for our use bedding[52] and horses from our Jews within that five-year period.

So that this decree be known and held firmly, we have corroborated this letter with our seals. Given [to the Jewish community] at Nogent-sur-Seine, the Tuesday after the week following Pentecost [May 31], in the year of grace 1222.

50. The fair of Saint-Remi, or the "cold fair" of Troyes, lasted from November 2 through December 20.

51. The Jewish community must have estimated its outstanding loans to Christians at about 30,000*l*. Comital officials would collect those loans and turn over the proceeds to the Jewish representatives, who would use that money to pay the 70,000*l*. tax. Outstanding loans beyond the 30,000*l*. amount were in effect forfeited, while the Jews were not penalized if they had less than 30,000*l*. in outstanding loans. Thus the tax consisted of all outstanding loans plus 40,000*l*., some of which would come from the exemptions from ordinary taxes described in succeeding clauses.

52. The manuscript (BN, Latin 5992, fol. 306r-v) reads *culcitra* (erroneously transcribed by the editor as *calcate*). This clause pertains to wartime, when the count customarily could expropriate private goods for his troops; a similar clause is in the communal charters (see Doc. 18, par. 9).

## The Fairs of Champagne

The trade fairs established by Thibaut II and nourished by Henry I emerged as the center of international trade and finance by the end of the twelfth century, when they were held alternately at Troyes, Provins, Bar-sur-Aube, and Lagny.[53] The earliest extant regulation is for the May fair of Provins in 1164 (Doc. 20). Until that time, the counts seem not to have foreseen the extraordinary success of the fairs, for they earlier had given away substantial rights and revenues generated by the fairs (Doc. 21). Among the most important items exchanged was cloth produced by northern French cities (Doc. 22), for which the Italian merchants offered more exotic goods such as spices and silk. In the thirteenth century both Troyes and Provins became important cloth-producing centers (Doc. 23), as their local economies became inextricably tied to the fairs.

The fairs succeeded because the counts vigorously enforced the "customs of the fairs," the regulations governing the conduct of all participants. The cardinal rule of the fairs was that every merchant and his goods—for merchants traveled with their goods until the late thirteenth century—came under the count's protection as soon as he set out for the fairs. The threat of exclusion from the fairs was a powerful one, which merchants ignored at their peril (Doc. 24).

The increasing flow of revenue from taxes, fees, and rents produced by the fairs furnished the counts an important resource for "money-fiefs" or "fief-rents" (see Docs. 10D, 67). Countess Blanche created fief-rents to procure or reaffirm the loyalty of the barons during her regency, and Count Thibaut IV used them to obtain the conversion of important allodial properties into fiefs. Fief-rents were usually collected at the end of the fairs during the clearing of accounts (see Doc. 7). Since they often were supplementary revenues, fief-rents were readily sold off in times of need (see Docs. 9, 89).

20. REGULATIONS OF THE FAIRS OF MAY, 1164

*In 1137 Count Thibaut II established an area within Provins for merchants, both local and foreign, to trade their goods in security. Here Henry I enlarges*

---

53. See O. Verlinden, "Markets and Fairs," in *The Cambridge Economic History of Europe*, vol. 3 (Cambridge: Cambridge University Press, 1963), 126–137, and Rosalind Kent Berlow, "The Development of Business Techniques Used at the Fairs of Champagne from the End of the Twelfth Century to the Middle of the Thirteenth Century," in *Studies in Medieval and Renaissance History* 8 (1971): 3–31.

*the boundaries of the trading area (new walls had been erected as the town*
*expanded) and sets the conditions for the conduct of the fairs.*[54]

In the name of the holy and indivisible Trinity, I, Henry, count palatine of Troyes, to the churches, clerics, knights, townsmen, and all men
who have houses within the boundaries of the Fairs of May. In order to
assure memory of past acts into the future, it is fitting that letters be carefully drawn up so that malicious purposes do not contravene good in-
tentions. Therefore, since my father, Count Thibaut of good memory,
gave you a document establishing the Fairs of May [in 1137], which has
unfortunately been lost in a fire, I have revised and reestablished them after
hearing the truthful testimony of men who were with my father when he
established the fairs.

That most noble prince Thibaut established the boundaries of the
fairs which I describe here and order to be retained and not changed
by anyone, either through force or presumption: from the tower of [the
seneschal] Girard and the houses of Peter "the Purse" [the chamber-
lain] and Anselm "the Fat" (both of which are within the fair boundaries)
extending down the street to the old [town] gate of Jouy (which is located
between the house of Saint-Quiriace and the house of Peter "the Devil")
and from there directly through the new town to the church of Notre-
Dame. Again, from the same tower [of the seneschal] going along Saint
John Street, then from the house of Richard of Verdun to the new
[town] gate of Chauvigny, passing in front of the prison and through
the vacant lot. Whatever is within both the new and old walls and
bounded by these streets was established by my illustrious father Count
Thibaut, with the consent of your ancestors and of his council of faithful men [his barons], as the location of the Fairs of May. These are the
regulations:

[1] No merchant may lodge or transfer his goods or pack horses beyond those boundaries until all the lodges there are filled; at that time,
merchants may lodge in the new market where dry-goods merchants are
allowed to store and display their goods for sale. The money changers
must continue to reside in the old market where they have been residing.
If a newly arrived merchant lodges outside the prescribed area before it is
filled, he must purge himself by proving that he did not know of this

54. Text in Elizabeth Chapin, *Les villes de foires de Champagne* (Paris: Honoré Champion, 1937), 282–284, no. 2.

regulation; if he cannot prove his innocence, all his goods, as well as the person who subverted this regulation by renting him lodgings, come under the count's mercy without any [legal] recourse. If the count does not wish to implement this prescribed penalty against transgressors, all of the [confiscated] goods will go for the common use of those to whom the fairs are conceded [the townsmen within the fair boundaries] as compensation for the loss of lodging revenue.

[2] No obstacles may be placed in front of any merchant lodge—not scales, tables, stalls, or chests. The place must be open to allow free passage at night.

[3] Half of the rent of all houses located within the fair boundaries went to my father, and now comes to me, as you and your ancestors conceded. Exception is made for: (a) the houses owned by the hospital which my father exempted so that they could help the poor; (b) the houses which I gave to the chapter of Saint-Jacques for the use of those canons and the poor; and (c) the houses of the chapter of Saint-Quiriace which I have exempted from all customary payments—one is next to the butchers' hall and the other, formerly owned by Roger "the Leaf," is half owned by Milo, son of the deceased Gerold of Rozay-en-Brie.

My father granted this ordinance to your ancestors, and I likewise have granted it to you and your successors in perpetuity, and I have sealed this letter in order to guarantee its stability. These are the witnesses from Saint-Quiriace: William [canon], my brother; Matthew, dean; Renaud, treasurer; Haice of Plancy; and Master Stephen. These are the witnesses for me: Geoffroy of Joinville, seneschal; Odo of Pougy, constable; Anselm of Traînel, butler; Peter "the Purse," chamberlain; William [of Provins], marshal; Drogo [of Provins] and his brother Peter "the Purse"; Daimbert of Ternantes; and Artaud, chamberlain. Done at Provins in my palace in the year of our Lord 1164. Given [to the townsmen] by William, chancellor.

21. THE OFFICIAL WEIGH STATION, 1174

*The counts required all merchandise sold by weight (including raw wool, silk, and spices) to be weighed and taxed at designated weigh stations. The right to weigh and tax certain goods was a lucrative one, which the counts often granted to religious houses as a benefaction. Here Count Henry reaffirms the monopoly of the weigh stations of Troyes and Bar-sur-Aube which his ancestor, perhaps Count Hugh early in the century, had granted to the monastery of Saint-*

*Pierre-le-Vif of Sens. This document contains the earliest reference to the wardens of the fairs.*[55]

I, Henry, count palatine of Troyes, make known to all, present and future, that since the monastery of Saint-Pierre-le-Vif of Sens controls the weigh stations of Bar-sur-Aube and of Troyes as a gift from me and my ancestors, the lord abbot, Odo, complained to me about the large amount of merchandise which ought to be weighed but which did not come to his scales as required by custom; rather it was taken elsewhere to avoid his tax.

In order to redress this situation, I hereby order that no one may take merchandise that by custom must be weighed to any place but the abbot's scales. If anyone is discovered to have bypassed the abbot's scales, he will pay me a fine assessed by my agents, plus a 2s. fine to the abbot, in addition to the tax itself.

I also ordered my agents and the wardens (*custodii*) of the fairs who receive this letter that they have this requirement cried out at the beginning of the fairs: that anyone violating the monopoly (*bannum*) of the abbot's scales will have to pay not only the tax but also a fine to me and a fine to the abbot.

Henceforth, neither a franchised house nor other franchised place [where goods are sold without the sales tax] carries with it an exemption from Saint-Pierre's scales: all merchandise liable to the weighing tax must be taken to Saint-Pierre's scales.

So that this remain established and be held unswervingly, I have confirmed this letter with my seal. These witnesses were present: Drogo of Provins, Daimbert of Ternantes, and Girard Eventat [the count's advisers]; Salo [viscount] of Sens; Milo, son of Daimbert of Ternantes; Josbert "Siccus" [provost] of Provins. Done at Troyes, in the year of our Lord 1174. Presented [to the abbot] by William, chancellor.

## 22. Cloth Merchants Must Pay the Sales Tax, 1175

*Count Henry I here assigns the sales tax paid by the cloth merchants at the fair of Provins to the chapter of Saint-Etienne of Troyes, which he founded next to his palace in 1157 and which served as his chancery.*[56]

---

55. Text in Maximilien Quantin, ed., *Cartulaire général de l'Yonne*, 2 vols. (Auxerre: Perriquet, 1854, 1860), 2 : 257–258, no. 240.
56. Text in "Cartulary of Saint-Etienne of Troyes," fol. 35r.

I, Henry, count palatine of Troyes, make known to all, present and future, that all cloth merchants from Reims, Paris, Rouen, Etampes, and Limoges, as well as all other cloth merchants who sell at the fair of Provins, must pay a sales tax to Saint-Etienne of Troyes. That was my gift to Saint-Etienne.

So that this remain established and secure, I have affixed my seal to this letter. Present as witnesses were: Lord Anselm of Traînel [butler]; William [of Provins], marshal; Drogo of Provins and his brother Peter; Daimbert of Ternantes; and Girard Eventat [the count's advisers]; and Artaud, chamberlain. Done at Provins in the year of our Lord 1175. Presented [to Saint-Etienne] by William, chancellor. Written by William [his notary].

### 23. CLOTHMAKERS AT PROVINS MUST BE RESIDENTS, CA. 1223
*Provins was, in addition to being a fair town, an important cloth-making center in the thirteenth century. Foreign merchants, realizing the possibilities of producing cloth locally for sale at the fairs, must have threatened the native producers. Here Count Thibaut IV imposes a residence requirement on all clothmakers; this abbreviated text was the copy made by his chancery clerks.*[57]

I, Thibaut, etc., make known, etc., that my townsmen of Provins asked me whether it was permitted to anyone who was neither my man (*homo*) nor a resident (*mansionarius*) of Provins to make cloth there. At their request, and for the common good of the entire town of Provins, I granted that henceforth no one may make cloth in Provins unless he resides there or is my man. [Rest of document omitted by copyist.]

### 24. THE MERCHANTS OF PIACENZA ARE BANNED FROM THE FAIRS, 1243
*The protection of merchants and their goods on the roads to Champagne was a major factor in the success of the fairs. In obtaining the cooperation of princes along the main land routes to eastern France, the counts were able to assure merchants of safe travel far beyond the county. Of course, the counts had to enforce that protection, as the following incident demonstrates.*[58]

*Letter no. 1* (October 1242): Thibaut [IV], by the grace of God, king of Navarre and count palatine of Champagne and Brie, to the discreet men

---

57. Text in "Cartulary-Register" no. 5, fol. 323v.
58. Text in "Cartulary-Register" no. 7, vol. 2, pp. 333–341.

and his friends, the *podestà* and commune of Piacenza, greeting and regards. The merchants of Siena, Florence, Pistoia, Lucca, and Pisa, and
certain others who come to my fairs, have brought to my attention a serious charge: that certain men from your city despoiled them of all their
goods and held them in captivity. Therefore I ask that you, after careful
inquiry, have those merchants and all their goods released, and everything
seized from them returned, which I have heard they value at a minimum
of 12,000*l.*, money of Provins.

If you refuse to take action, I will not be able deny these merchants
the justice and law of the fairs which, as I remember, I imposed against
the merchants of Marseilles at your request, for the benefit of your own
merchants at my fairs.

I remind you that you may not disturb merchants coming to the fairs
of Champagne, no matter who they may be, nor their goods; if they are
molested while under your jurisdiction, I am obliged to intercede with
you to do what is right.

So that you may act on this request, you may send your reply with
the bearer of this letter. Done at Provins, in the year of our Lord 1242, in
the month of October.

*Letter no. 2* (February 1243): Thibaut, by the grace of God, king of
Navarre and count palatine of Champagne and Brie, to his dear and discreet men in Christ, the *podestà*, council, and commune of Piacenza, greeting and warm regards. Some time ago the merchants of Florence, Siena,
Pistoia, and Lucca brought to my attention a serious complaint: that while
on their way to my fairs, they were despoiled of their goods on the road
between Lodi and Pavia heading to Piacenza; they estimate that they lost
a large quantity of coins, which I asked you in my sealed letter to have
returned to them. But from your letter of reply, I take your excuse to be
neither valid nor relevant,[59] since the merchants swore that they were
robbed by your men who took their goods to your city. Therefore, I ask
you again to have the stolen goods returned just as, if you recall, I restored
the goods taken by the merchants of Marseilles from your merchants.

Be assured that if you do not do this, I will not be able to deny those
merchants their right according to the custom of my fairs, which by law I
am bound to uphold. If you are remiss in this, I shall proceed against you
as I did against the men of Marseilles on your behalf. I ask you especially

59. Piacenza probably claimed to lack jurisdiction in the matter.

to do this in view of the fact that the count of Burgundy, who was holding the goods of your merchants in Lyons, released them at my request; unless you do the same, I will not fail to proceed against you.

*Letter no. 3* (December 9, 1243): John, castellan of Noyon and Thourotte [and governor of Champagne],[60] to the prudent and discreet men, *podestà*, commune, council, and consuls—citizens as well as merchants—of Piacenza, greeting and regards. My most excellent lord Thibaut, by the grace of God, king of Navarre and count palatine of Champagne and Brie, wrote to you, not once but twice, asking you to have returned to certain merchants of Florence, Siena, Pistoia, Lucca, and Pisa what was stolen from them by certain robbers who despoiled them of their goods as they were coming to the fairs. Five of those merchants and their goods were taken in captivity to your city, detained publicly, and forced to ransom themselves.

Be advised that unless you act in this matter, the count will not be able to ignore it, as the custom of the fairs, which he is obliged to enforce, requires him to proceed against you, just as on another occasion, at your request and for your benefit, he acted against the merchants of Marseilles. I likewise, acting at his request while he travels to his kingdom of Navarre, was instructed by him to write to you about this matter, since apparently you gave both him and me an inadequate response, and those merchants have been complaining forcefully to him that, according to the customs of the fairs, your merchants should be excluded from the fairs, just as your own merchants and certain others invoked those customs against other cities.

On behalf of my lord, I ask and advise you to carry out what he requested so that I may spare your merchants. If you have not taken care of this matter by the next fair of Saint-Ayoul of Provins [September 14], I will have to carry out the regulations of the fairs. So that you may not plead ignorance about the complaint of the injured merchants and about what the lord count asked of you, I have attached a copy of their petition and of his letters to you.

Asking your discretion in these matters, I have sent a special envoy, the bearer of this letter who represents the count, Erard "le Pescon" of Sézanne, to whom you may give your letter of reply within the time speci-

60. The governor of Champagne acted as the count's chief executive officer whenever the count was absent from the county, in this case in Navarre.

fied, or else the lord count or I or another representative will be compelled to act against you and your merchants of Piacenza.

This is the complaint of the merchants: that when they left their houses to come to the fair of Saint-Ayoul of Provins, some men of Piacenza violently assaulted them, seizing them and their goods with 14,000*l.*, money of Tours, in coin. This occurred while the merchants were traveling under the protection of the king of France and of the lord count palatine of Champagne and Brie. The merchants and their goods were taken into captivity in the city of Piacenza, where they were publicly incarcerated until they paid a ransom and were released with [only] 155*l.* of their own money. For that reason, those merchants petitioned the lord count and asked him to warn the men of Piacenza to return their goods in full and to pay for damages and losses, which they estimated at 6,000*l.*; and that if the perpetrators did not comply, the lord count should exclude them from all his lands, from the fairs of Champagne, and from his safe conduct, and that he should ask his friends [that is, other princes] to do the same—as the law and practice of the fairs of Champagne provide— just as the count excluded certain merchants of Toulouse and Metz for seizing the merchants of Lyons, Marseilles, Piacenza, Bologna, Florence, and Siena.

For the law and practice (*ius et usuagium*) of the fairs of Champagne are that if a merchant complains of theft or violence to his person or his goods while either coming to the fairs or returning from them, the count of Champagne must require the malefactors to make restitution; if the latter do not wish to do so, they should be excluded from the fairs and from the land of Champagne and denied its safe-conduct. If the malefactor later wishes to make compensation, he may do so only at the fairs in the presence of the count or of his delegate, just as the law and practice of the fairs declare.

The merchants' petition also asked that the exclusion [of Piacenza] begin with the next fair of Saint-Ayoul [September 14]. The count immediately sent a letter to the men of Piacenza, then another letter, and finally even I sent a letter, to which your reply was unsatisfactory both to me and my lord.

My lord's first letter is as follows [Letter no. 1].

This is my lord's second letter [Letter no. 2].

In testimony of which, I affixed my seal to this letter.

[The governor appended this note to be sent to the count, who was still in Navarre:] Be it known that when the sealed letter of the commune of Piacenza arrived in response to my letter mentioned above, it was read at Provins in the presence of the merchants of Florence, Siena, Pistoia and their legal representatives. The latter said that they did not wish to refute the reply of Piacenza regarding their losses unless the law required them to, but if they were required to respond, they would [missing text]. After taking counsel, I decided to notify the king about the matter. Done in the year of our Lord 1243, on the Wednesday after the Feast of Saint Nicholas [December 9], in the month of December.

# 2 Family Affairs

Chroniclers who often noted the familial and domestic affairs of kings and princes rarely mentioned those of the barons and knights, whose own affairs must be gleaned from the fragmentary information contained in monastic title deeds.[1] From the late twelfth century, however, laymen increasingly used written documents for their private affairs and thus have left us with precious information on intimate aspects of their lives.

## Marriage and Divorce

Most marriage agreements were reached orally between the parents of the couple, an arrangement that could result in later disputes over the terms of the marriage (usually the dowry), the premature death of a spouse, or even the validity of the marriage itself (Doc. 25). Church law was not entirely clear about whether a legitimate marriage began with the mutual consent of the partners or at the consummation of the marriage. Theologians in northern France generally adopted the first view, which became church law under Pope Alexander III (1159–1181).[2]

As church law became more precise, families too paid closer attention to the practical consequences of marriage in written marriage contracts. Prenuptial agreements (Doc. 26) and marriage contracts (Docs. 27–29) became increasingly complex, as they specified the dowry, dower, and contingencies in the event of a spouse's death without heirs (primarily the return of the dowry). Divorce and remarriage produced even more com-

1. For the exceptional accounts of the Amboise and Guines families, see Georges Duby, *The Knight, the Lady and the Priest. The Making of Modern Marriage in Medieval France*, trans. Barbara Bray (New York: Pantheon, 1983), chaps. 12–13.
2. For discussions of medieval marriage and the family, see David Herlihy, *Medieval Households* (Cambridge, Mass.: Harvard University Press, 1985), Christopher N. L. Brooke, *The Medieval Idea of Marriage* (Oxford: Oxford University Press, 1989), and James A. Brundage, *Law, Sex, and Christian Society in Medieval Europe* (Chicago and London: The University of Chicago Press, 1987), chaps. 5–8.

plicated settlements (Docs. 30, 31), not to mention outright spiteful situations (Doc. 32).

### 25. AN UNCONSUMMATED MARRIAGE IS UNDONE, 1153

*In this well-known case, Anselm II, lord of Traînel (1152–1185) and close companion of Count Henry I, married the daughter of Geoffroy of Donzy. The marriage, however, was not consummated, perhaps because the bride was too young. Shortly afterward, Count Henry's own brother, Count Stephen of Sancerre, took advantage of the situation by marrying the girl himself. Deprived of both his wife and her dowry, Anselm complained to Count Henry, who in turn appealed to King Louis VII to right the wrong by force. Although the dispute was resolved, sixty years later Geoffroy of Donzy's grandson, Hervé IV, reopened the case, prompting the inquest reported here in 1217.[3]*

I, Odo [III], duke of Burgundy, and I, Gaucher [III] of Châtillon-sur-Marne, count of Saint-Pol, make known to all, present and future, who see this letter that we and Robert of Courtenay [cousin of King Philip II] arranged a compromise in the dispute which arose [in 1213] between the countess [Blanche] of Champagne and the count [Hervé IV of Donzy] of Nevers over the latter's claim to Oulchy and Neuilly. Having undertaken an inquest [to determine the facts of the case], we ordered Guy Gasteblé, knight [now a monk at Preuilly abbey], to make a sworn statement, which is as follows:

"Geoffroy of Donzy gave his daughter [Alice] in marriage to Anselm of Traînel and their marriage[4] was celebrated at Donzy on a certain Friday [in 1153]. As dowry, Geoffroy gave Anselm [the castle of] Neuilly and whatever else he had there, as well as one-half of the town of Oulchy, since Geoffroy did not possess the castle there.[5] In return, Anselm gave Geoffroy about 500*l.*, or even more, Guy believes.[6]

"Anselm, however, did not sleep with his bride that night after the marriage but abruptly returned to his own lands. Afterward, Count Stephen [of Sancerre] married the girl and took her to [the castle of] Saint-Aignan, which he received [from her father] as dowry. When An-

---

3. Text in Martène and Durand, *Thesaurus novus anecdotorum*, 1:863. A genealogy of the Donzy is in Constance Brittain Bouchard, *Sword, Mitre, and Cloister: Nobility and the Church in Burgundy, 980-1198* (Ithaca: Cornell University Press, 1987), 327–328.

4. Guy calls this unconsummated marriage a *sponsalia*; see also Doc. 45.

5. The castle of Oulchy belonged to Count Henry.

6. This payment was a "reverse dowry" or "counter dowry" given by the husband to the bride's family. Since Justinian it was known as the "donation for reason of marriage" (*donatio propter nuptias*) and was expected to be equal in value to the dowry (see Doc. 29B and Herlihy, *Medieval Households*, 16).

selm heard about that, he complained to Count Henry that since Henry had arranged Anselm's marriage, he ought to guarantee it. Henry immediately appealed to King Louis, explaining how his own brother Stephen had injured and disgraced Lord Anselm, whom Henry esteemed above all his knights. So insistent was Henry's representation that the king went with him to besiege Saint-Aignan. Guy Gasteblé was present at that siege.[7]

"After the castle fell, Geoffroy of Donzy, his wife, and Count Stephen made peace with Anselm of Traînel in this manner: for the injury and dishonor done to Anselm, and in compensation for the money he had given to Geoffroy of Donzy, Anselm was given both Neuilly and half of the town of Oulchy [the original dowry]. This was approved by all who had the right of approval (*laudatio*).

"Anselm and his [second] wife Hermesend[8] held those properties for fifteen years or more, then exchanged them with Count Henry for half of the count's tolls at Pont-sur-Seine and at the gate [of Villecran] of Provins. Later Anselm gave 30*l*. from that annual revenue at Pont-sur-Seine to his brother Garnier, who had contributed part of the 500*l*. that Anselm had paid to Geoffroy of Donzy."

That was the sworn testimony of Guy Gasteblé. Since Guy was infirm and of advanced age, and feared that he might die before giving his testimony in person,[9] we have had his deposition drawn up and sealed with our seals. Done in the year of our Lord 1217, in the month of July, on Sunday after the week following the Feast of the Apostles Peter and Paul [July 6].

## 26. A PRENUPTIAL AGREEMENT, 1205

*When Milo, lord of Chaumont, died on the Fourth Crusade (1202), Countess Blanche retained his mortgaged castle and quickly bought off the claims of his widow Chaumonde and his younger brother Josbert by granting them other lands in exchange.[10] Josbert gave those newly acquired lands to his own son on the occasion of the latter's marriage in 1205. In order to retain the lands within his own lineage, Josbert obtained this quitclaim from his son's father-in-law, Renier II of Nogent-en-Bassigny, a powerful local baron.[11]*

---

7. This remark by the scribe appears in a preliminary draft of the testimony (printed in *Recueil des historiens des Gaules et de la France*, ed. Dom Bouquet et al., 24 vols. [Paris, 1737–1904], 12:128, note a) but was omitted in the final act translated here.

8. Daughter of Guy, count of Bar-sur-Seine.

9. He must have been about eighty years old in 1217.

10. Milo had mortgaged his castle once before to the count, to go on the Third Crusade, but returned to redeem it.

11. Text in Teulet, *Layettes*, 1:298, no. 789.

I, Renier of Nogent-en-Bassigny, make known to all, present and future, that when the son of Lord Josbert of Chaumont marries my daughter, he will become liegeman to my lady the countess [Blanche] and the counts of Champagne, and will owe one month's castle-guard annually at Chaumont for the land of Ageville, the oven and mill of Aubepierre, and whatever else he has at Aubepierre which my lady the countess of Champagne gave Josbert and his heirs in exchange for the escheated land of Lady Chaumonde and [the castle of] Chaumont.

If Josbert's son should die without an heir by my daughter, or if my daughter should die without an heir by Josbert's son, that land will revert to Lord Josbert and his heirs. So that this agreement remain valid in the future, I have affixed my seal to this letter. Done in the year of our Lord 1205, in the month of December.

[Ultimately Renier did acquire this fief; see Doc. 68.]

### 27. A BARONIAL DOWRY, 1223

*When Renaud, a third son of the baronial family of Broyes-Commercy, married the daughter of a substantial knight family, he received 500l. in cash as his wife's dowry.[12] The cash was to be invested in income-generating land (which would have yielded about 50l. annually), since the principal itself had to be preserved for his wife's children. But since Renaud pocketed the cash instead, he had to convert his own inheritance into the dowry, in the event that he and his wife Margaret did not produce an heir and the dowry had to be returned to her family.*

I, Thibaut [IV, count of Champagne, make known, etc.][13] that Renaud, [third] son of Simon, the deceased lord of Commercy, has affirmed in my presence that when he married Margaret, sister of Henry, lord of Buzancy, the said Henry and his brothers gave their sister 500l. as dowry with which Renaud was to purchase [income-producing] property. But since Renaud was not able to find suitable land, he instead assigned that sum to Margaret and Lord Henry and her other brothers on his own village of Mondement, on these conditions:

[1] If Margaret dies and Renaud remarries, his children by the second marriage will have no right to inherit that village; likewise if Renaud dies

---

12. Text in Martène and Durand, *Thesaurus novus anecdotorum*, 1 : 904. See Genealogical Table 3.

13. The chancery scribe who made this file copy abbreviated the formal address.

and Margaret remarries, the children of her second marriage will have no right to that village.

[2] If Margaret dies without any children by Renaud, he may retain that village for his lifetime, after which it will revert in full to Henry and Margaret's other brothers as their inheritance.

[3] Renaud's brother Hugh, lord of Broyes, from whom Renaud holds that village in [rear-] fief, consented to this agreement in my presence, save his [feudal] rights. And I, from whom the village is ultimately held in fief, likewise approved, saving my [feudal] rights over it. Done in the year of our Lord 1223, in the month of June.

## 28. A CONTRACT OF MARRIAGE BETWEEN KNIGHTLY FAMILIES, 1231

*This rather complicated marriage contract between two knightly families provides for a dowry yielding about 10l. annually and the groom's assumption of half of his inheritance (his parents are to hold the rest for their lifetimes).*[14] *However, since that entire inheritance has been leased for seven years, the marriage may take place only after the lease expires. The groom, Herbert II of Bayel, was a cadet whose older brother had received the family homestead at Bayel. The bride, one of six daughters (and three sons) of Jocelin of Lignol,*[15] *received a very modest dowry. The young couple together would have had just enough income to maintain a simple life-style.*

I, Thibaut [IV], count palatine of Champagne and Brie, make known to all, present and future, that my loyal and faithful Guy of Bayel and his wife Clementia have made a marriage contract in my presence with Jocelin of Lignol for the marriage of their son Herbert with Jocelin's daughter Emeline. These are the clauses:

[1] Guy has given to his son whatever he had at Bayel, at the village called Les Mez, and at Bar-sur-Aube and within those village districts, including tenants, woods, lands, and in all other things.

[2] Jocelin has given his daughter Emeline an annual rent of 5l. [from his property] that will be assigned by two other men, one to be named by Guy and the other by Jocelin. And Jocelin will give his daughter 100l. cash [as dowry], which is to be invested in [income-producing] property by the two appointed men within one year after the marriage.[16]

[3] Peter Guin [of Bar-sur-Aube, chamberlain of Champagne and

14. Text in "Cartulary-Register" no. 7, vol. 1, fols. 146v–148r.
15. See Doc. 10C.
16. It would yield about 10l. annually.

Jocelin's father-in-law] and his son Guy affirmed in my presence that they gave whatever they had at Les Mez to Emeline or to Jocelin's other daughter Lucy, whom Herbert [earlier] had engaged to marry.

[4] Herbert will hold the above mentioned 5*l.* rent, the property purchased with the 100*l.* cash, as well as the land at Les Mez, in fief and liege homage from Guy, son of my faithful chamberlain Peter Guin, save liegeance to me and save the liegeance contracted to anyone else before the marriage.

[5] Guy of Bayel and Clementia agreed that if Emeline dies before the marriage, they will have Herbert marry another of Jocelin's daughters when she becomes nubile, under the same terms.

[6] Guy of Bayel and Clementia leased to Peter Guin all they have at Bayel—except one garden that Guy chooses to keep—and all they have at Les Mez and Bar-sur-Aube and in their districts, for seven years during which they may not take any of the produce or rents, although Guy may fish in Bayel's waters without paying a tax.

[7] If Herbert dies within these seven years, Peter Guin or his heirs may extend the lease for two more years.

[8] If Herbert marries Emeline or another of Jocelin's daughters after the seven-year period, Guy of Bayel and Clementia will retain for their lifetimes one-half of all the property at Bayel, Les Mez, and Bar-sur-Aube, but they will not be allowed to sell, mortgage, donate, or alienate any of it in any manner because it must revert to Herbert and his wife.

[9] Guy, Clementia, and Herbert have agreed in my presence that they will not seize or judge any men or women [tenants] of Bayel except for murder or theft. Peter Guin and his heirs are likewise constrained.

At the request of Guy of Bayel and Clementia and of Jocelin, this contract passed through my hand so that if anyone of them contravenes it, I will have the right to seize his property. Done in the year of our Lord 1231, in the month of June.

29. COUNT THIBAUT IV'S MARRIAGE CONTRACT, 1233
*Thibaut IV married three times. The first marriage, forced upon him by his mother Blanche, to Gertrude of Dabo (1220–1222), ended in divorce. The second, to Agnes of Beaujeu (1222–1231), ended with her death. The third, to Margaret of Bourbon, was celebrated on September 22, 1232. Two months later, the bride's father formalized her dowry payment (Doc. A),[17] and Thibaut assigned his*

---

17. Text in Martène and Durand, *Thesaurus novus anecdotorum* 1:971–972.

*bride her dower. The next spring, in March 1233, the count and his father-in-law, who also was the constable of Champagne, appeared before the bishop of Troyes to record the details of the marriage contract (Doc. B).*[18]

(A) I, Archambaud [VIII], lord of Bourbon [and constable of Champagne], make known to all that I owe the noble Thibaut, count palatine of Champagne and Brie, 36,000*l.*, good legitimate money of Paris, for the marriage of my dearest daughter Margaret, payable at these terms: 16,000*l.* at the next fair of Lagny [January 1233] and 5,000*l.* at each of the next fairs of May [at Provins, 1233], of Saint-Ayoul [at Provins, September 1233], of Lagny [January 1234], and of May [at Provins, 1234]. And if, God forbid, I do not meet these terms, Count Thibaut will collect damages and penalties which I, without any complaint or legal recourse, will pay to Giles of Acy and Itier of Brosse, knights [the count's officers]. If either of them dies, the count will choose another man from his council in place of the deceased man.

Moreover, I promise that if I am otherwise deficient, I will place myself in captivity in Provins, where I will spend each night and not leave the town without the count's permission until I have rendered him full satisfaction. That captivity will not relieve me or my pledges from that payment [of 36,000*l.*], nor from damages or penalties which I am obligated to pay according to the above-stated terms. And I promised by the oath I gave personally to observe the above agreement. In testimony of which I have confirmed this letter with my seal. Done in the year of our Lord 1232, Wednesday after the Feast of Saint Martin the apostle and evangelist [November 18].

(B) Robert, by the grace of God, bishop of Troyes, to all who receive this letter, greeting in the Lord. Be it known that the noble Thibaut, count palatine of Champagne and Brie, and the noble Archambaud, lord of Bourbon, appeared before me to confirm the [oral] marriage agreement they made and which is described below.

[I] Thibaut, count of Champagne, having contracted a legitimate marriage[19] with Archambaud's daughter Margaret, gave to Margaret in

---

18. Text (redundant phrases condensed here) in Teulet, *Layettes* 2 : 245–246, no. 2231.

19. *Per verbi de presenti*, that is, consent given in the present time, as opposed to a promise of a future marriage (a betrothal). Examples of court cases over consent are in Charles Donahue, Jr., "The Canon Law on the Formation of Marriage and Social Practice in the Later Middle Ages," *Journal of Family History* 8 (1983): 144–158.

her presence this dower: [20] [the castellanies of] Sézanne, Lachy, Barbonne, Nogent-sur-Seine, Pont-sur-Seine, Méry-sur-Seine, Payns, Chantemerle, and Semoine with all their annexes and appurtenances.[21]

[2] Thibaut stated that he made this donation of his free will, without deception or guile, and promised that he, his heirs, and successors would not in any way jeopardize it. He pledged himself and all his goods, both what he now possesses and what he might possess in the future, as well as those of his successors and heirs, under pain of excommunication by the bishop of Langres and interdict of all his possessions within the diocese of Langres. Thus he renounced, for himself and his successors, all benefit, aid, privilege over things or persons, and all rights there, whether written or not and whether ecclesiastical, customary, or legal.

[3] The said Archambaud recognized that he promised the count 36,000*l*., money of Paris, [as dowry] for the marriage of his daughter, on this condition: that 4,000*l*. will be accounted for each full year that Margaret lives with Thibaut. If she should live nine years, the count will keep the entire 36,000*l*. But if, God forbid, Margaret should die within that nine-year period, Archambaud will hold her dower until he collects 4,000*l*. for each year less than nine years she did not live. If those [dower] revenues are not sufficient, Thibaut will make up the difference; if those revenues are more than required, Thibaut will have the surplus.

[4] If Margaret dies within that nine-year period but leaves an heir, the count will retain the entire 36,000*l*., providing the heir survives to that ninth year. For each year the heir lives up to nine years, 4,000*l*. will be accounted, just as for Margaret herself. If the heir happens to die [after Margaret's death], Archambaud will take from Margaret's dower lands 4,000*l*. revenue for each year remaining in the nine-year period.

[5] If by chance, may God forbid, Count Thibaut and Margaret divorce, for whatever reason, Thibaut will repay Archambaud the entire dowry without Archambaud's having to ask for it: within one year of the divorce, Archambaud will take the count's entire income, from whatever source, except for 7,000*l*. that Thibaut will retain for his own expenses. Archambaud will deduct that income from the 36,000*l*. owed him, and if he does not collect at least 20,000*l*. within one year of the divorce, Thibaut will make up the difference; and if Thibaut does not make up the differ-

20. *Donatio propter nuptias*, that is, the traditional reverse dowry; but here it constitutes the bride's dower and is assigned to her rather than to her family (compare Docs. 25, 27, 63).

21. Several of these castellanies had been part of Countess Blanche's dower lands until her death in 1229; see Doc. 40.

ence, the count must give pledges for the rest. If the count's income is more than 20,000*l.* that first year, anything over that amount that Archambaud takes from it will be deducted from the total amount owed him.

[6] For the repayment of the rest of the 36,000*l.* after the first year following the divorce, Thibaut will place himself in captivity in Sens, where he must spend each night until he has repaid Archambaud in full.[22] While Thibaut remains in Sens, Archambaud may not seize the count's pledges; but Archambaud may seize them if Thibaut does not place himself in captivity in Sens, as provided for here. Count Thibaut swore to observe fully the agreement described in this letter.

At the count's request, I [Robert, bishop of Troyes] promised to Archambaud that if the count or his heir or successor ever violates this agreement, I will excommunicate him and place all his lands within my diocese under interdict. I have sealed this letter, excepting only my rights at Méry-sur-Seine.[23] Given [to Archambaud] in the year of grace 1232, in the month of March [1233].

30. A PROJECTED DIVORCE SETTLEMENT, 1224

*When Erard II, lord of Chacenay (1191–1236) and a baron of some importance in southern Champagne, returned from the Fourth Crusade, he married the widow of a war hero, Odo of Champlitte, who had died in Constantinople in 1204. By the time Erard went on crusade again in 1218, he and his wife Emeline had a family of two sons and two daughters, in addition to her daughter by Odo. In 1224 Erard sold his wife's dowry for a substantial sum of money, effectively dispossessing his stepdaughter who was in her early twenties and ready for marriage. Whether this sale led to talk of divorce after almost twenty years of marriage, we do not know, but Erard quickly agreed to repay his wife and to provide a dowry for her daughter.[24] This document is unusual in that it provides for contingencies in the event of a divorce, which does not seem to have occurred.[25]*

I, Erard, lord of Chacenay, make known to all who see this letter that I sold to the Knights Templar the village of Courban, which I possessed

22. Sens was in the royal domain, although adjacent to Champagne. Thus Thibaut would have to place himself in forced confinement outside his own lands.
23. The bishop is protecting his right to episcopal lands within a castellany assigned as Margaret's dower.
24. Text in Ernest Petit, *Histoire des ducs de Bourgogne de la race capétienne*, 9 vols. (Paris: Picard, 1885–1905), 2:460–462, no. 695.
25. See Doc. 29B, pars. 5–6, for the divorce clauses in Count Thibaut IV's marriage contract.

[as dowry] through my wife Emeline, for 840 marks of silver,[26] with the consent of Elizabeth [Emeline's mother], lady of Châteauvillain, and her son Simon [Emeline's brother].[27]

[1] If by chance I or anyone else raises the question of divorce between me and my wife Emeline, and if we do in fact divorce, I will be required to repay that entire sum and place it in the hands of the cellarmasters of Clairvaux within two years of our divorce: that is, 420 marks of silver payable in the first year and the remaining 420 marks the following year. If I do not make the first payment on time, Emeline may take possession of [his village of] Bligny with all its appurtenances. If I make full payment to the cellarmasters of Clairvaux within the second year, she will use that money to purchase land with the approval of [her brother] Simon, lord of Châteauvillain, from whom she will hold it [in fief]. Her eldest daughter [by her first marriage], Lady Oda, will receive from that land as much as she should have been assigned [in dowry] at Courban. Bligny then will revert to me and my heirs. If Simon dies before this transaction is completed, Emeline ought to carry out these provisions with the help of her mother.

[2] If I do not make the payment of 840 marks in full within two years, Emeline will have Bligny and its appurtenances as her inheritance just as she had possessed Courban, on this condition: if I or my heirs repay in full within five years, we may repossess Bligny. But if we do not repay within five years, Emeline will possess Bligny for life as her inheritance. And if she and I are divorced within that period, and if she then remarries and has children, they will have no right to Bligny—only my children by her have that right—but they may have a share of Emeline's other lands and anything beyond what should have been assigned at Courban.

[3] If Emeline and I do not divorce, she will have [as dower] after my death whatever I have at Loches-sur-Ource and Landreville which I purchased from Philip, lord of Plancy, as well as what I inherited at Essoyes. But if I happen to exchange my property at Essoyes with my uncle, Lord James of Durnay, Emeline will be compensated [with other property], and I will be quit of the 840 marks of silver. If Emeline predeceases

26. The contract of sale equates that sum with 2,030*l.*, money of Provins; see Petit, *Histoire*, 2:462, no. 696 (September 1224).

27. Elizabeth was the sister of Robert II of Dreux (see Doc. 5). In ca. 1178 she became the second wife of Hugh III of Broyes-Commercy (d. 1199) and had two children, a son Simon, who became lord of Châteauvillain (see Doc. 4), and Emeline. See Genealogical Table 3.

me, her daughter Oda will have the same share of my inheritance as she would have had from Emeline's own land at Courban.

[4] I especially wish to concede to Emeline the revenues and duty-taxes of Meurville,[28] worth 30*l*., money of Provins, annually; I will henceforth take nothing from this revenue either directly myself or through my agents. This compensates her for her land at Marcilly, which I gave [as dowry] to Count Guigues [of Forez] when he married my daughter Alice.

[5] Regarding the above, Emeline is not to make any transfer without the permission of her brother Simon or of her mother. If I in any way fail to execute this accord, I wish and even require that my lord Hugh, bishop of Langres, or his successor compel me by imposing ecclesiastical censure on my lands.

In testimony of this act, I have appended my seal to this document in the year of our Lord 1224, in the month of September.

31. A MARRIAGE DEPENDS ON A DIVORCE, 1231

*Marie of Garlande, widow of Count Henry IV of Grandpré (d. 1229), remarried in 1230 to Geoffroy of Joinville (lord of Montclair), eldest son of the seneschal Simon of Joinville. Within a year, however, she obtained a divorce from the archbishop of Reims, apparently against Geoffroy's wishes. Shortly thereafter she negotiated a marriage for the daughter of her first marriage, Alice, with Geoffroy's seven-year-old half-brother Jean, the future seneschal and biographer of Louis IX (see Genealogical Table 2). In order to secure a canonically valid marriage for her daughter, Marie had to obtain Geoffroy's consent to their own divorce.[29]*

I, Thibaut [IV], count palatine of Champagne and Brie, make known [to all who see this letter] that the following agreement was made in my presence between Simon, lord of Joinville and seneschal of Champagne, and Marie, countess of Grandpré: for the marriage of her daughter Alice to Jean, Simon's eldest son by his [second] wife Beatrice, who was the daughter of Stephen, count of Burgundy. These are the clauses:

[1] Countess Marie and her son Henry [V, count of Grandpré] will give to Jean and Alice an annual revenue of 300*l*., money of Paris, [as dowry] on condition that Jean and Alice not claim anything more from

---

28. See Doc. 108.

29. Text in Ambroise Firmin Didot, *Etudes sur la vie et les travaux de Jean, sire de Joinville* (Paris: Typographie de Ambroise Firmin Didot, 1870), 191–192, no. "O."

Countess Marie and her son Henry, from either the paternal or maternal inheritance.

[2] If the marriage does not take place, the said Alice will be returned in liberty to a safe place by the countess and Henry.

[3] The said Jean must dower Alice according to the custom of Champagne.[30]

[4] And most important of all, Lord Simon of Joinville must make his son Lord Geoffroy [of Montclair] accept the final divorce decree between himself and the said countess of Grandpré as it was promulgated by the archbishop of Reims in the presence of the papal judges who were delegated to hear the case. If Geoffroy is unable to appear in person before those judges, he must send a sealed letter to the lord archbishop of Reims stating his acceptance of the divorce decree. Simon, lord of Joinville, will also guarantee all the debts owed by Geoffroy if anyone tries to collect them from Countess Marie and Henry.

I, Count Thibaut, at the request of both parties and as [feudal] lord, promised in good faith to respect this agreement, and in order that it remain valid, I have sealed this letter with my seal. Done in the year of our Lord 1231, in the month of June.

### 32.  A WOMAN TAKES HER ESTRANGED HUSBAND TO COURT, 1284
*The High Court of Champagne decides in favor of a woman who brought suit against her second husband: he had abandoned her, she claimed, deprived her and her children of her own rents, and then tried to intimidate her by taking her to an ecclesiastical court.*[31]

Lady Agatha of Damery testified that her [second] husband holds all the property that she and the children of her first marriage inherited and did not allow them to have any of its revenues. He further brought suit in an ecclesiastical court against those who administered the property for her, causing her great trouble and expense. Thus she petitioned [this court] on behalf of herself and her children so that they might use those revenues for their own needs.

The court ordered the bailiff of Vitry to summon the parties and attempt to reach a settlement between them by which the husband would reconcile with his wife and children and administer the revenues for their

---

30. See Doc. 43.
31. Text in John F. Benton, "Philip the Fair and the *Jours* of Troyes," *Studies in Medieval and Renaissance History* 6 (1969): 305–306, no. 2; reprinted in his *Culture, Power and Personality*, 215–216, no. 2.

benefit. If the bailiff cannot arrange an accord, he is to seize the revenues and administer them so that the lady and her children are sufficiently provided for.

## Inheritances

Champagne was a region where partible inheritance practices (roughly equal shares among all children) conflicted with the principle of feudal tenure (indivisible fiefs transmitted to sons only). Although two separate tenurial systems (feudal and allodial) coexisted through the thirteenth century, feudal customs changed profoundly as siblings demanded an equitable share of inheritances (Doc. 33). Paternal fiefs might be preserved intact, however, when younger sons inherited their mothers' dowries or newly acquired fiefs (Doc. 34).

While castles and large estates were becoming feudalized (see Docs. 4, 5, 7), the question of female succession to castle-fiefs arose. In 1212 a baronial council which met to resolve that issue (Doc. 35) established two cardinal principles that later were extended to male successions as well: castles could not be divided among heirs, but all other property had to be divided equally among all brothers or, in the absence of male heirs, among all sisters. Although the eldest son was privileged among brothers, sisters received only half of a brother's share of a feudal inheritance (Doc. 36).

Aristocratic women received dowries when they married, and young men took a small share of their future inheritances when they came of age, usually at twenty-one. On the death of the father, the sons would divide only half of the inheritance, since according to the custom, a widow ordinarily retained the other half as her dower (see Doc. 43). If the father died leaving minor children, however, heirs could assume their feudal properties at a very young age: eleven for girls and fifteen for boys (Docs. 37, 38). Thus the age at which tenants assumed feudal land varied greatly according to familial circumstances (see Doc. 41B). A mixed marriage, moreover, could complicate not only inheritance but even the status of the children, especially when the mother was noble but the father was not (Doc. 39).

### 33. A YOUNGER SON CONTESTS HIS INHERITANCE, 1215
*Guy was the fifth son of Geoffroy IV of Joinville, seneschal of Champagne, and only an infant when his father died at Acre on the Third Crusade (see Genea-*

*logical Table 2). After Guy's two older brothers, Geoffroy V (seneschal, 1190–
1203) and Robert perished on the Fourth Crusade, both the lordship of Joinville
and the seneschalcy of Champagne passed to the fourth brother, Simon (1204–
1233).*[32] *Although Guy had been assigned a small cash settlement by his father
in 1190 and later acquired the lordship of Sailly, which had passed successively to
younger brothers, he decided ca. 1214 to challenge his brother Simon's inheritance
which was, technically, an escheat from their eldest brother and thus liable to
the custom of equal division among the surviving brothers. Guy and Simon asked
their brother William, bishop of Langres (1209–1219), to arbitrate the dispute.*[33]
*Although Guy received half of the Joinville properties in Champagne, Simon
retained all his father's fiefs in the German Empire.*

I, William, by the grace of God, bishop of Langres, make known to
all who see this letter that in the dispute which arose between my brothers
Simon, lord of Joinville and seneschal of Champagne, and Guy, lord of
Sailly, over his inheritance, this settlement was reached: Simon, lord
of Joinville, gave and conceded to the said Guy one-half of all his land in
Champagne, in addition to 40*l.* of annual revenue to be assigned from his
own land, to possess in perpetuity. Guy, in return, acquitted Simon and
his heirs of all that he claimed from: (1) the escheat of our brother Geoffroy [V] of good memory; (2) the seneschalcy of Champagne; and (3) the
cash settlement that was devised [but not yet paid] to Guy by our father.
In testimony of which I have sealed this letter. Done in the year of grace
1215, in the month of September.

### 34. FIEFS ARE ALLOTTED TO FUTURE HEIRS, 1230
*Comital policy since ca. 1200 required younger sons with substantial fiefs to be-
come the count's liegemen (see Doc. 4). Consequently, when vassals acquired new
fiefs by purchase or grant, they often promised to keep those fiefs as distinct entities
and to pass them to younger sons (see Doc. 10D). Here a castellan of some importance submits a typical letter promising to abide by the count's wishes. In this
case, however, the two fiefs eventually were merged, as only a single son survived
to inherit.*[34]

I, Guy, lord of Arcis-sur-Aube, make known [to all] present and future that my dearest lord Thibaut, count of Champagne, gave me the fief

32. See Doc. 41.
33. Text in BN, Français 11559, fol. 391r-v (seventeenth-century copy of the original,
with abbreviated address).
34. Text in "Cartulary-Register" no. 7, vol. 3, fols. 78v–79r.

which Lord William of Vertus, son of the deceased Josbert of Vertus, used to hold from him—except for the gate next to William's house, which the count retains in his own hand. I promised the count that as soon as I have two heirs, the one who receives this fief will be the count's liegeman before all other men for this fief; the other heir who receives [the castle of] Arcis-sur-Aube also will be the count's liegeman before all other men for that fief. In testimony of which I have sealed this letter with my seal. Done in the year of the Lord 1230, in the month of December.

35. THE STATUTE ON THE FEMALE INHERITANCE OF CASTLES, 1212
*With the feudalization of allodial castles from the late twelfth century,[35] a thorny issue of succession arose: in the absence of a direct male heir, should a castle pass to a daughter or to the closest male relative? A baronial council summoned by the regent countess of Champagne in 1212 established fundamental legislation on that point by reconciling the principle of feudal descent (and the need to preserve the integrity of castles as military structures) with the custom of familial partibility: the eldest daughter would inherit the castle, but her sisters would share all other assets of the inheritance equally.[36]*

I, Blanche, countess palatine of Troyes, make known to all, present and future, that with the common counsel and consent of my barons and vassals,[37] I have decreed that when any baron or vassal of Champagne and Brie dies without a male heir but leaves several daughters, the eldest daughter will inherit his castle; the other daughters will have plain land, each receiving a share equal in value [annual income] to the value of the castle, but excluding: the value of the lordship and the fortress itself, the jurisdiction inside the castle, and the value of the fiefs attached to the castle.

If, after an equitable settlement among the daughters, there is plain land left over, it will be divided equally among all of them. If, however, the plain land is insufficient to provide each daughter with the same revenue as the eldest daughter who takes the castle, all the daughters will share some of the castle revenues.

If there are two or more castles, the eldest daughter may take the best one, the second daughter the next best one, the third daughter the third best, the fourth daughter the fourth, and so on. The remaining daughters

35. See Docs. 4, 5, 7.
36. Text in Teulet, *Layettes* 1: 385–386, no. 1031.
37. *De communi consilio et assensu baronum meorum et vavassorum.*

will have plain land in such a manner that if it does not yield revenue equal to that of the castles, the revenues from the castles will supplement those from the plain land.

This statute (*stabilimentum*) I have enacted for castellans and vassals who have castles and fortified houses. [An unrelated provision on duels follows.] So that all this remain permanent, I have confirmed this letter with my seal. Some of my barons and vassals also have affixed their seals to this statute [thirty-four seals were appended]. Done in the year of our Lord 1212.

[In 1224 these principles were extended to male heirs.[38]]

### 36. THE CUSTOM REGARDING FEUDAL INHERITANCES, CA. 1270, 1287

*Two principles governed inheritances: (1) men were preferred to succeed to feudal property (women had only half of men's shares of direct inheritances and none of collateral ones), and (2) strict partibility was maintained for allodial and other nonfeudal property. These customs are explained in three decisions of the High Court of Champagne (Docs. A–C).[39] Such inheritance divisions could seriously fragment patrimonies, as is illustrated by the Couture family, in which the eldest son retained only one-third of the paternal estate in 1250 (D).[40]*

(A) It is the custom in Champagne among noblemen and noble-women, that is, vassals (*vauvassour*), who have several children and several residences, that after their deaths their eldest son may choose [as his share of the inheritance] the residence he prefers, particularly if it is enclosed by a moat or wall [that is, a fortified house], according to his right as the eldest. The next oldest brother will have the next house and attached lands, and the rest of the brothers will follow suit [each choosing the next most valuable residence with attached lands]. If there are houses for all of them, they shall divide the remaining property [plain land] equally.

If there are sisters, each will have one-half a brother's share of the plain land, but if there are more houses than brothers, the sisters will take their share of the houses in addition to plain land [so that each child would have a residence]. If there are only sisters, they will share the inheritance equally.

38. Text in Paulette Portejoie, ed., *L'ancien coutumier de Champagne (XIIIe siècle)* (Poitiers: P. Oudin, 1956), 142–144, note. See Doc. 36A for the High Court's summary of these principles ca. 1270.

39. Texts in ibid., 142–146, art. 2; 221, art. 56; 221–222, art. 57.

40. Text in Longnon, *Rôles des fiefs*, 25, no. 108.

If there are [rear-] fiefs held from the family, the eldest son will choose which of those will be held from him, and the other children will divide the remaining [rear-] fiefs among themselves. This is generally the custom in Champagne [ca. 1270].

(B)  It is the custom in Champagne that sisters do not have a share of a fief passing collaterally to their brothers. Sisters have an equal share of collateral inheritances only for allodial property and nonfeudal rents [ca. 1270].

(C)  It is the custom that for property descending from a father and mother, a son has twice the share [of feudal property] as a sister, unless the property is allodial or a nonfeudal rent [which is shared equally]. This custom was determined by an inquest at Troyes in the suit brought by Lady Helissand of Arcis-sur-Aube, wife of Monsieur Gautier of Merrey, who claimed a share of the escheated castle of Chacenay against [her brothers] Monsieur John of Arcis-sur-Aube, Monsieur Erard [of Chacenay], and their brothers. The court announced eight days after Pentecost [May 25] in the year 1287 that she did not have any right in this case except for allodial property and nonfeudal rents.[41]

(D)  [Feudal register for the castellany of Bray-sur-Seine, 1250:] Milo of Couture, knight, under oath, said that he holds [in fief from the count] his house at Couture, lands, tenants, a vineyard, and the right of justice there, all of which produces about 40*l.* annually. His sister Lady Gila holds [in rear-fief] from him about 25*l.* annual revenue at Bray-sur-Seine and at Couture. His second sister, Margaret, holds about 22*l.* annual revenue at those same places. His brother William holds about 40*l.* annual revenue at Couture. Milo owes forty days castle-guard annually.

## 37. THE AGE OF FEUDAL MAJORITY, 1278

*In Champagne, families retained very strong control over feudal property, except in cases of unauthorized alienations. A widow assumed the full rights and responsibilities of her husband as guardian for their children, without interfer-*

---

41. Helissand was the great-granddaughter of Erard II of Chacenay (see Doc. 30) whose two sons died overseas in 1253. The Chacenay estate passed to Erard's daughter Alice and, on her death in 1273, to her four nephews and niece (Helissand). Since this was a collateral transfer, the feudal property was divided equally among the four nephews only. See Genealogical Table 3 and Portejoie, *L'ancien coutumier,* 163, n. 4.

*ence by the feudal lord. The High Court of Champagne here states the widow's rights and the point at which her children were required to assume legal responsibility for their father's fiefs.*[42]

It is the custom in Champagne that a widowed lady: (1) has wardship over her minor children; (2) may claim her husband's movable goods if she agrees to settle his personal debts; and (3) must do homage to the lord from whom she holds the property in custody for her children. Her male heir must do homage to that lord on reaching his fifteenth year; if she has only a daughter, the latter must do homage at eleven years of age. If the heir does not do homage at the prescribed time, the lord may take the fief into his own hands until homage is done, for a man is out of wardship at fifteen years and a woman at eleven years.[43]

This judgment in favor of the lady of Molins was reached at Troyes in the year 1278 by these judges: Lord John of Acre, governor of Champagne, with Master Anselm of Montaigu, Florent of Roye, the lord of Broyes, Master Vincent of Pierrechastel [chancellor], William of Châtelet [bailiff], Hugh of Chaumont [former provost of Troyes], and William Pusvilains, bailiff. This is the general custom.

### 38. AN INQUEST ON THE AGE OF COUNTESS JEANNE, 1284

*Even though the customary age of feudal succession was generally known, the precise age of the heir in question was not always clear. In this case, the point was of considerable importance, as Jeanne had become heiress of Champagne in 1273 after the childhood death of her older brother. Jeanne spent her childhood at the royal court in Paris betrothed to Prince Philip. The royal family, anxious to have her secure full possession of Champagne before the marriage, sought recourse in the practice by which eleven-year-old heiresses assumed their feudal possessions. This inquest determined both Jeanne's age and the relevant custom regarding heiresses. The introductory and concluding paragraphs are in Latin, but the testimony is recorded as it was spoken in French.*[44]

An inquest regarding the age of Jeanne. In the year 1283, on the Saturday after the second Sunday of Lent [March 11, 1284], an inquest was conducted by [John of Nesle] the lord of Falvy-sur-Somme, former count

---

42. Text in Portejoie, *L'ancien coutumier*, 148–150, art. 5.
43. See Docs. 38, 41B.
44. Text in Paul Viollet, ed., *Les Etablissements de Saint Louis*, 4 vols. (Paris: Renouard, 1881–1886), 165–168, n. 8.

of Ponthieu,[45] and Master William of Poil, provost of Isle-Aumont, regarding: (1) the age of the heiress of Champagne and (2) the custom of Champagne as to the age when a young woman (*domicella*) may do homage.

These witnesses were heard regarding the age of the countess: The archdeacon of Blois said under oath that he believes she has begun her twelfth year, and he believes that because eleven years ago, between Christmas and Epiphany [January 6, 1273], the king of Navarre [Count Henry III] directed him to go to Lyons and at that time the queen [Countess Blanche of Artois] gave birth to this girl at Bar-sur-Seine. The marshal of Champagne [Hugh III of Conflans] said on his sworn oath that she was eleven years old on the past Feast of Saint Hillary [January 13], and he knows that because he raised her from the baptismal font. James of Ervy [financial receiver of Count Henry III] said on his sworn oath that the young lady (*damoisele*) was eleven years old on the eighth day after Christmas [January 2], and he knows that because he was the first man to see her [after her birth]. Adam of Servigny, knight, said on his sworn oath that the young lady was eleven years old on the fifteenth day before Candlemas [January 17], and he said that he saw her baptized. Alice, lady of Le Moulin-du-Bois, said on her sworn oath that between Christmas and Candlemas [February 2] eleven years ago she was at Troyes and heard the news that the young lady was born at Bar-sur-Seine. Micheau of Bar-sur-Seine said on his sworn oath that he believes the young lady was eleven years old on the twentieth day after Christmas [January 14] or on Candlemas [February 2], and he knows that because the abbot of Montiéramey said to the marshal of Champagne in the latter's house: "We have a beautiful girl." John "Becars" of Essômes said on his sworn oath that she was eleven years old the twentieth day after Christmas [January 14], and he said that she was born in 1272 in the second week of January [1273]. Renier Accorre [financial receiver of Champagne] said on his sworn oath that the young lady was eleven years old on the twentieth or twenty-first day after Christmas [January 14 or 15], and he knows that because at the time King Henry sent him to find out about it. Gombez of Sézanne said on his sworn oath that the young lady was eleven years old at the beginning of the twentieth day after Christmas, and he knows that because he saw her baptized. Belossiers of Ormay said on his sworn oath that the

45. John's wife Joan, the heiress of Ponthieu, died in 1279. John was active in the Parlement of Paris from 1264 to 1290, and thus represented royal interests in Champagne during this inquest.

young lady was born around the twentieth day after Christmas eleven years ago, and he knows that because he was with Count Henry at Troyes when he heard the news that the queen [of Navarre] had delivered a child.

These testified regarding the custom of Champagne: the marshal [Hugh III of Conflans], the lady of Le Moulin-du-Bois, Monsieur Gilo of Bricon, the lord [Jean IV] of Arcis-sur-Aube, Master Anselm of Montaigu, the provost of Paris, the viscount of Châlons, Goulart, Monsieur Peter of Malmaison, James of Ervy [financial receiver], Master Stephen of Asnières, the dean of Bar-sur-Seine, John "Becars" of Essômes, the provost of Villeneuve, the knights Monsieur Girard of Anguissy and Milo of Ferreux, Renier Accorre [financial receiver], the knights Monsieur William of Loisy, Monsieur Guy of Blois, and Adam of Servigny, Master John (clerk of the bailiff of Sens), Master Stephen "Becart," John of Vernon, Simon of Courtisols, Monsieur Robert of Thourotte, the archdeacon of Auxerre, the seneschal of Champagne [Jean of Joinville], Master John of Taillefontaine, and Florent of Roye.

They were asked whether it was the custom of Champagne that a woman who completes her eleventh year and begins her twelfth may do homage and receive homage from her vassals (*vassalis*). Monsieur Gilo of Bricon, knight, speaking for all the sworn and in their presence, said that it is the custom of the region of Champagne, and for the county itself, that a woman who has completed her eleventh year and begins her twelfth may do homage to her lords (*seigneurs*) and may receive homage [from her vassals]. So it has been in many cases without challenge, even though the woman has not completed her twelfth year.[46] All who were sworn testified to this and agreed to it by their oaths.

In testimony of which I, John, lord of Falvy-sur-Somme, former count of Ponthieu, and I, Master William of Poil, provost of Isle-Aumont, carried out this inquest at the request of Bishops Guy of Langres and William of Auxerre, of Robert, duke of Burgundy, and of the venerable Matthew, abbot of Saint-Denis, who raised the issue in respect to their fiefs [held by the counts of Champagne]. We announced these findings in the presence of the abbot of Saint-Etienne of Dijon, of Hugh of Montarmet, canon of Auxerre, and of Hugh of "Castrum," canon of Brioude, masters of law, and we have sealed this finding with our seals. Done in Paris in the year and day stated above.

[Philip and Jeanne were married four months later, on August 16, 1284, and in October 1285 they became king and queen of France.]

---

46. See Doc. 37.

### 39. WHEN A NOBLEWOMAN MARRIES A COMMONER, CA. 1270

*Mixed marriages could complicate feudal tenure, especially when a noblewoman who was married to a commoner wished to pass her feudal property to her children. The issue became acute in the thirteenth century, as feudal tenure became more a reflection of social class than of an ability to perform military service. The tendency to equate social and property status was reinforced by the customs requiring the transfer of property inappropriate to one's status.[47] In the case decided here by the High Court of Champagne, the children of noble mothers and commoner fathers[48] were compelled to choose their social-tenurial status: either they could do homage for their mother's presumably minor rear-fief and retain her aristocratic standing, or they could choose their father's more substantial nonfeudal property and with it his non-noble standing. The children here tried to keep both inheritances.[49]*

It is the custom in Champagne that when a noblewoman marries a commoner (*homme de poeté*), the lord from whom she holds her fief [as inheritance or dowry] does not have to accept her husband's homage for that fief if he does not wish to do so. If she has heirs, they are disinherited [of that fief] after her death, and her feudal lord may incorporate her fief into his own domain because the children assume the lower condition (*la peour condicion*) [of their father] and become liable to tallage and mortmain,[50] if their father was liable for them, unless the heirs repudiate their father's inheritance.

That custom was invoked in the case of Lady Beatrice of Poissons near Joinville who had married a commoner from Vaucouleurs; her [feudal] lands reverted [after her death] to the lord [Jean] of Joinville. In a second case, Erard of Dinteville took back the lands of Durant of Copies who had married a lady from Dolancourt.

The lord [Jean] of Joinville[51] and Erard of Dinteville offered the heirs to do right according to the custom of Champagne [that is, to return their mothers' lands if they renounced their fathers' nonfeudal inheritances].

---

47. See Doc. 12B.

48. The standing of the fathers (*homme de poeté*) might be freely translated as "serf," were it not for the pervasive modern impression that serfs were "tied to the land" and virtually slaves. In this case, "commoner" represents someone of peasant stock who did not live in a franchised community (see Docs. 16–18) and consequently was liable for heavy tenurial and residential obligations to his landlord.

49. Text in Portejoie, *L'ancien coutumier*, 150–152, art. 6.

50. Tenants liable to mortmain (*mainmorte*) could bequeath their tenancies only to adult children living in their households, a restriction imposed to discourage emigration. Most community franchises abolished mortmain; see Doc. 16, par. 2.

51. See Genealogical Table 2.

But the men did not stay [after the court decision] to do that, so the children were disinherited [of their mothers' fiefs].

## The Dower Custom

Dowers—revenues assigned by husbands for their wives' support during widowhood—had long been common in aristocratic families, but only from the 1170s was feudal property, hitherto reserved for men, designated as dower land.[52] Thibaut III is the first count known to have granted his bride a dower letter (Doc. 40), an example that was followed by barons and knights in the next few decades. Like the count, the wealthiest lords assigned their wives specific dower lands for which the women did homage to the feudal lord, usually as widows when they took possession but occasionally at the initial assignment of the dower (Doc. 41). It became customary, however, for men to designate half of their property as dower land, which would pass to their heirs only after the death of their wives (Doc. 42).

An important aspect of the dower custom in Champagne is that women who lacked written dower letters were considered to possess half their husbands' lands by common law (Doc. 43). This custom had an enormous impact on successions, since heirs often had to wait many years to obtain their entire inheritance: Elizabeth of Châteauvillain outlived her husband by almost thirty years, while Beatrice of Joinville remained a widow for at least twenty years.[53] In the thirteenth century about 20 percent of the feudal tenants at any time were women, mostly widows holding their dowers.

40. COUNT THIBAUT III DOWERS COUNTESS BLANCHE, 1199
*On July 1, 1199, the twenty-year-old Count Thibaut III was married to Blanche of Navarre, sister of King Richard I's queen, Berengaria, in the presence of distinguished company at Chartres. After the ceremony, Thibaut assigned Blanche, as her dower, seven castles and castellanies in central and southern*

---

52. One of the earliest dowers assigned on feudal lands dates from ca. 1151: Ivo II of Nesle dowered his wife Yolande with one-half of Nesle and its castle, which was held in fief from the count of Vermandois; see Ivo's testament of 1157 in William Mendel Newman, *Les seigneurs de Nesle en Picardie (XIIe-XIIIe siècle)*, 2 vols. (Philadephia: The American Philosophical Society, 1971), 2:84–86, no. 30.

53. For Elizabeth of Châteauvillain, see Docs. 30, 108, and Genealogical Table 3; for Beatrice of Joinville, see Doc. 90 and Genealogical Table 2.

*Champagne which provided at least one-third of his annual income.*[54] *She would eventually enjoy those revenues for seven years (1222–1229) after her retirement as regent for their son Thibaut IV.*

In the name of the holy and indivisible Trinity, I, Thibaut, count palatine of Troyes, by this document make known to all, present and future, that I have given in dower to my wife, Countess Blanche, daughter of the king [Sancho VI] of Navarre, seven of my castles with all their appurtenances and dependencies, namely Epernay, Vertus, Sézanne, Chantemerle, Pont-sur-Seine, Nogent-sur-Seine, and Méry-sur-Seine, and all that I have in their castellanies in direct domain, in fiefs, and in the guardianship of churches, in full possession.

These were present and heard the announcement: Adele, illustrious dowager-queen of France [Thibaut's paternal aunt]; Berengaria, dowager-queen of England [Blanche's sister and Richard Lionheart's widow]; the venerable Renaud [of Bar-le-Duc], bishop of Chartres [Thibaut's first cousin]; Rotrou, bishop of Châlons-sur-Marne; Garnier, bishop of Troyes; Geoffroy, count of Perche; William [I], count of Joigny; Walter [III], count of Brienne; Geoffroy [V of Joinville], seneschal of Champagne; Gaucher of Châtillon-sur-Marne [butler of Champagne]; Geoffroy [of Villehardouin], my marshal;[55] and many others. In order to preserve this act, I have sealed this letter with my seal. Done at Chartres, in the year of our Lord 1199. Presented [to Blanche] by the hand of Walter, chancellor [of Champagne], on the kalends of July [July 1]. Written by Peter [chancery scribe].

41. THE SENESCHAL'S WIFE DOES HOMAGE FOR HER DOWER LANDS, 1209

*Shortly after Simon of Joinville, seneschal of Champagne (1204–1233), married Ermengard of Montclair (in Lorraine), he dowered her with half of his lands, for which she did homage to Countess Blanche (Doc. A).*[56] *Nine years later in 1218, following Simon's unsuccessful opposition to Countess Blanche during a civil war, the Joinville family decided to formalize succession to the Joinville lordship in the event of Simon's death, and Ermengard agreed to modify her absolute claim to her dower (Doc. B).*[57]

54. Text in Teulet, *Layettes* 1:204, no. 497. See Doc. 29B for the dower assigment of Thibaut's son.

55. Chronicler of the Fourth Crusade.

56. Text in "Cartulary-Register" no. 7, vol. 1, fol. 155r-v. See Genealogical Table 2 and, for Simon's life, Henri-François Delaborde, *Jean de Joinville et les seigneurs de Joinville* (Paris: Imprimerie Nationale, 1894), 46–67.

57. Text in "Chronique et mélanges," *Bibliothèque de l'Ecole des Chartes* 39 (1878): 561.

(A) I, Blanche, countess palatine of Troyes, make known to all who inspect this letter that my loyal and faithful Simon of Joinville [seneschal of Champagne] has affirmed in my presence that he dowered his wife Ermengard with one-half of all that he holds [in fief] from me. At Ermengard's request, and on Simon's petition to me, I have received her in liege homage (*in ligiam feminam*) for that half [of Simon's fief], saving however Simon's right [to administer it] for as long as he lives. So that this remain valid, I have had the present letter drawn up and sealed by my seal. Done in the year of our Lord 1209, in the month of June.

(B) I, Ermengard, lady of Montclair,[58] make known to all who see this letter that I will forgo my dower, that is, half of all the land of my lord Simon, lord of Joinville, seneschal of Champagne, of which I was dowered and for which I owe homage to my lady Blanche, countess palatine of Champagne, if I marry after my husband Simon's death. This I have decided on the advice of my friends and of my husband's friends. That dower includes Vaucouleurs and its castellany, Montiers-sur-Saulx, and Osne-le-Val, but excludes their woods and forests so that the villagers there may continue to enjoy the use of those woods and forests as they did before my dower was assigned.

I announce further that as long as I do not remarry, I will possess [as guardian] all my husband's lands, after the settlement of his debts, except the castle of Joinville, which his vassals (*homines et fideles*) will occupy and maintain.

Be it known that when Geoffroy, my eldest son, reaches fifteen years of age, I will relinquish his entire inheritance to him, if he wishes me to retire, and I will return to my own dower lands [as described above]. Done in the year of grace 1218, in the month of July, eight days after the Feast of the Apostles Peter and Paul [July 6].

[Ermengard died by 1222 and her son Geoffroy, lord of Montclair, died in 1232 after being divorced (see Doc. 31). Simon remarried and had four more sons of whom the eldest, Jean, succeeded as lord of Joinville and seneschal of Champagne; he later became the biographer of Louis IX (see Doc. 90).]

## 42. TWO KNIGHTS DOWER THEIR WIVES, 1221, 1223

*By the early thirteenth century it was customary for widows to receive one half of their husband's estate as their dower lands unless a marriage contract or a*

58. Her mother's inheritance.

*devised dower stipulated otherwise. Increasingly knights of even modest means recorded their dower settlements in documents sealed by the count or a prelate, thus assuring their wives secure title. The two dower letters here are typical. In the first (Doc. A), the dower is set at exactly half of the husband's lands.[59] In the second (Doc. B), the dower is described as the counterpart to the wife's dowry (they were usually of comparable value).[60] In this case the dower would produce about 20l. annual revenue (10 percent of the value). These texts are slightly abbreviated because they are the internal copies retained by the count's chancery which prepared the documents; the originals would have been presented to the wives, either directly by a chancery official or by the husbands.*

(A) I, Blanche, countess palatine of Troyes, make known to all, etc., that my loyal and faithful Thibaut of Isle has affirmed in my presence that he assigned to his wife Adeline one-half of all his land in dower. With her consent he assigned her share on: what he has at Le Corbier with its dwelling, what he has at "Fons Pipinus," and his land at "Brya." If these lands are in fact worth more than half of all his lands, Thibaut's heirs [at his death] will take the surplus [over one-half], whereas if these dower lands are worth less, his heirs will make up the difference from his other lands.[61] In testimony of which, etc. Given in the year of our Lord 1220, on the Feast of the Purification of Mary [February 2, 1221].

(B) I, Thibaut [IV], etc., notify, etc., that my loyal and faithful William of Bernon has affirmed in my presence that he gave to his wife Lucy, the daughter of Dodo of Flogny, half of all his goods in dower. In particular he assigned her half of all the land which he holds from me in fief, in return for the 200l. [cash] that he received as her dowry. I have approved this, saving my right of justice and the [military] service owed [for the entire fief]. [Done in 1223].

### 43. THE DOWER CUSTOM OF CHAMPAGNE, CA. 1270

*Whoever compiled the "customs of Champagne" from the register of High Court decisions neglected to copy the date and details of the case which resulted in this statement of the dower custom.[62]*

59. Text in "Cartulary-Register" no. 5, fol. 362r.
60. Text in ibid., fol. 314r.
61. So that his widow will receive exactly one-half of his estate.
62. Text in Portejoie, *L'ancien coutumier*, 154, art. 9.

It is the custom in Champagne that a noblewoman, if she lacks a written dower assignment and remains a widow, will have these: (1) the house she chooses from her husband's estate; (2) her husband's movable goods if she agrees to pay his [personal] debts; but if she declines to accept his movables and debts, she must pay only the debts contracted on her own lands, for a widow is not obligated to pay anything in order to receive her dower; and (3) one-half of her husband's entire estate as her dower, which she has by reason of common law (*par droit commun*). This is the practice generally.

## Ecclesiastical Placements

Although childhood oblations continued in Benedictine monasteries, the twelfth century was rather an age of adult conversion, as genuine spiritual needs induced men and women to leave their families for a monastic vocation.[63] The charismatic example of Bernard of Clairvaux made the Cistercians the largest of the new orders, with a particularly dense implantation in Champagne, and Clairvaux itself continued to attract aristocratic men through the thirteenth century (Docs. 47, 48; see also Doc. 91). But young women and widows also were drawn to the monastic life. So great, in fact, was the demand for female placements that Abbess Heloise was asked to establish daughter houses of her convent, the Paraclete (Doc. 44).

Among the most prestigious convents in Champagne was Avenay, where Countess Marie spent twelve years acquiring an education and maturity before she married Count Henry at twenty years of age (Doc. 45). Like the Paraclete and many other convents, Avenay was overwhelmed by applicants and grew beyond its resources; after falling into debt, it was forced to reduce its size (Doc. 46). Powerful families, of course, continued to place their daughters in desirable institutions (Doc. 49), and occasionally even a woman of modest means could secure admission to the convent of her choice (Doc. 50).

44. ABBESS HELOISE FOUNDS THE CONVENT OF LA POMMERAYE, CA. 1147
*Although best known for her tragic love affair with Abelard, Heloise spent thirty-four years as abbess of the Paraclete (1130–1164), which Abelard estab-*

---

63. See John Boswell, *The Kindness of Strangers: The Abandonment of Children in Western Europe from Late Antiquity to the Renaissance* (New York: Pantheon, 1988), chap. 8.

*lished for her. So many women were attracted to her convent that she sponsored six daughter houses. The first was a priory established ca. 1142 in the nearby village of a loyal benefactor, Anselm of Traînel. A few years later Countess Mathilda, whose husband Count Thibaut II had provided Abelard sanctuary in Champagne, asked Heloise to establish a new convent near Sens. Here the archbishop describes that foundation.*[64]

I, Hugh, by the grace of God, archbishop of Sens, wish it to be known to all, present and future, that at the request of religious men, Heloise, abbess of the Paraclete, with the approval of her entire convent conceded to the countess of Blois the place called La Pommeraye for the construction of a convent under the following provisions:

It was agreed that the first abbess of La Pommeraye would be Lady Gertrude, a noble and honest woman who was canonically elected to that position by the community of the Paraclete. Her successor will be canonically elected according to church law by the community of La Pommeraye, if it is able to; but if the nuns cannot agree on a successor, they are to go to the Paraclete to find an abbess, for they are not allowed to seek an abbess from outside the order of the Paraclete.

The abbess of La Pommeraye will visit the Paraclete once annually to discuss ecclesiastical affairs and to sit with its chapter as an abbess of that order. Likewise the abbess of the Paraclete will sit with the community of La Pommeraye once annually to correct any deficiencies.

In return for this grant by the Paraclete, the countess gave it three *modii* of wheat to be collected each year from the mill at Crevecoeur below Provins; this the countess did with the consent of her sons Henry [the Liberal], Thibaut [V, count of Blois], and Stephen [count of Sancerre], and she promised to guarantee it.

All this was done with the consent of the abbess and the community of the Paraclete. The abbess and the countess promised that these provisions could not be changed by the lord pope or by anyone else, and that neither of the parties will rescind the agreement. The abbess and the countess reached this accord through my good offices, and I received their goodwill promise in my hand. So that this be observed by the present and future, I have sealed this chirograph and have had it divided in two.[65]

[A few years later, Countess Mathilda was buried at La Pommeraye.]

64. Text in Charles Lalore, ed., *Cartulaire de l'abbaye du Paraclete* (Paris: E. Thorin, 1878), 71–73, no. 53.

65. Two identical texts were written on a single piece of parchment, which then was cut in two parts through the word CHYROGRAPHUM written between them.

### 45. COUNTESS MARIE AND HER TUTOR AT AVENAY, 1158

*During the Second Crusade, probably in 1148, Louis VII and Eleanor of Aquitaine promised their infant daughter Marie (b. 1145) in marriage to the twenty-one-year-old Henry, heir apparent of Champagne (see Doc. 82). After the divorce of her parents, Marie was betrothed to Henry (1153) and placed in the convent of Avenay in Champagne for instruction until her marriage, which was postponed until 1164/1165 when she was about twenty. While at Avenay she was recognized as countess of Champagne, in which capacity she was able to do a favor for her tutor.[66]*

In the name of the holy and indivisible Trinity, I, Henry, count palatine of Troyes, wish it to be known for posterity that for the love of God and at the request of Alice of Mareuil, tutor of my wife[67] the countess [Marie], I have given and conceded in perpetual possession to the nuns of Saint-Pierre of Avenay eight *sextarii* of [grain] revenue to be collected from my mills at Aubérive each year within eight days of the Feast of Saint-Remi [January 13]. So that this gift remain permanent, I have had it put into writing and I have confirmed it with my seal. Witnesses to the [oral] gift and to the confirmation were: Marie, countess of Troyes; Anselm of Traînel [butler]; William [of Provins], marshal; William, notary. Done in the year of our Lord 1158, in the reign of Louis, king of the French, and while Samson was archbishop of Reims. Given [to the nuns] at Vertus by William my chancellor.

### 46. LIMITATION ON THE NUMBER OF NUNS AT AVENAY, 1201

*The influx of aristocratic women into monasteries was so great by the late twelfth century that many institutions outstripped their resources, took on debt, and faced severe financial crises. In 1196 Pope Celestine III limited Heloise's monastery of the Paraclete to sixty nuns because it had taken in more women than it could support.[68] Here the archbishop of Reims restricts the size of Avenay because of its debts.[69]*

William [brother of Count Henry I], by the grace of God, archbishop of Reims and cardinal of S. Sabina, greeting in the Lord to all

66. Text in Louis Paris, *Histoire de l'abbaye d'Avenay*, 2 vols. (Paris: Picard, 1879), 2:82, no. 13.

67. Marie was called *sponsa* here; only after she began to live with her husband was she called *uxor* (married woman). See Doc. 25 for the case of an unconsummated marriage (*sponsalia*).

68. Lalore, *Paraclete*, 33–34, no. 20.

69. Text in Paris, *Avenay*, 2:94, no. 34. See also Doc. 104B.

who receive this letter. In order to administer my office in a praiseworthy manner, I must look after the churches and persons under my jurisdiction. Having been touched by pious compassion for Avenay abbey, which is under pressure to receive nuns yet is burdened by debts owed to creditors, I, with the consent of the abbess and the convent, have been forced to order that henceforth no one may be accepted as nun or promised to be given a prebend there until the number of nuns is reduced to forty. Under threat of a proclamation of anathema, let no one attempt to subvert this restriction, save by authority of the Apostolic See. So that this will be preserved, I have ordered the present document drawn up and I have sealed it with my seal. Done in the year of our Lord 1201. Given [to the nuns] by the hand of Matthew, my chancellor, in the month of August.

### 47. A knight becomes a monk at Clairvaux, ca. 1205

*When he became a monk at Clairvaux, Simon of Bricon gave the monastery, as his entrance gift, permission to acquire property from his fief, apparently without telling his wife Mathilda. No doubt surprised by the monastery's purchases—perhaps the fief was her dowry or dower—she came to Clairvaux to verify that license and met her former husband at the great gate of the wall surrounding the monastery, as women were not allowed beyond that point.[70]*

I, Garnier, by the grace of God, former bishop of Langres [1193–1198, resigned to enter Clairvaux], make known and testify to all, present and future, that when Lord Simon of Bricon prepared to assume the religious habit, he came to Clairvaux where, in my presence, he conceded to the brothers of Clairvaux, for the salvation of his soul, permission to purchase property from his fief at Cunfin. Later he came out to the gate at Clairvaux, where he confirmed this in the presence of his wife, who then also conceded it.

### 48. The lord of Reynel becomes a monk at Clairvaux, 1216

*We do not know why John, lord of Reynel (1212–1216), decided to become a monk four years after succeeding his father. Here he settles his affairs, giving Clairvaux an entrance gift, making small donations to monasteries near his lordship,*

---

70. Text in Jean-Marc Roger, "Les Morhier champenois," *Bulletin philologique et historique* (1978): 119–120, no. 21. The date falls between 1205 and Simon's death in 1215.

*and arranging for the payment of his debts.*[71] *John's younger brother Gautier succeeded him as lord of Reynel.*[72]

Be it known to all who see this letter that I, John, lord of Reynel, before I assumed the religious habit and took my vows, gave to the abbey of Notre-Dame of Clairvaux as a perpetual gift 20*l.*, money of Provins, to be collected each year from the toll revenues at Rimaucourt: 10*l.* of that amount is for the purchase of oil for the abbey, the remaining 10*l.* is for use at the abbot's discretion.

I gave 2*s.*, money of Provins, each week from the toll revenues at Rimaucourt to the [Cistercian] abbey of La Crête. I gave 2*s.* each week from the sales tax of Reynel—in addition to the 12*d.* [each week] I gave previously—to the nuns of Saint-Martin of Benoîtevaux. I also gave them nine shares of a field at "Brollio de Mennois." To the [Cistercian] abbey of Auberive I gave 10*l.* annually at Christmas.

I gave to my [youngest] brother, Master Thibaut, 10*l.* annual revenue for the next ten years to pay off my debts of 100*l.* which I owe Clairvaux.

I gave to the brothers of Lagenevoie three measures of wheat to be collected each year from the tithe of Signéville. To the chapel [in the castle] of Reynel I gave 12*d.* from each day's sales tax at Reynel for the lighting of that church.

In order to validate this act, I have sealed it with my seal. Done in the year of our Lord 1216.

49. THE CASTELLAN OF VITRY PLACES HIS DAUGHTER IN AVENAY, 1228
*The pressure of noble families seeking placements for their daughters in convents (see Doc. 46) resulted in more generous entrance gifts. Here the castellan of Vitry not only places his daughter but even obtains a spiritual benefit for his contribution.*[73]

I, Hugh, castellan of Vitry, make known to all who see this letter that I, with the consent of my wife Alice, have given in pure gift to my daughter Anselette, who is a nun in Saint-Pierre of Avenay, ten *sextarii* of rye from my mill at Coulommiers, collectible there each year on the eighth day after the Feast of Saint-Remi [January 21]. She is to enjoy this revenue

---

71. Document in AD, Haute-Marne, 5 H 10 (La Crête), no. 485.
72. Gautier's daughter Alice inherited Reynel; she became the second wife of the chronicler Jean of Joinville ca. 1260 (see Genealogical Table 2).
73. Text in Paris, *Avenay*, 2:113, no. 65.

for her lifetime, after which it is to pass to the convent of Avenay for the celebration of an anniversary Mass for myself and my wife, Anselette's parents. So that this remain uncontested, I have sealed this letter with my seal. Enacted in the year of our Lord 1228, in the month of August.

50. POPE URBAN IV ORDERS A CONVENT TO ACCEPT A LITERATE GIRL, 1262

*In this unusual letter, Pope Urban IV[74] fulfills the request of a young woman who apparently wrote directly to him seeking a monastic placement. Urban refers to her as a "literate" girl, who by joining a convent would lift a burden from her father, a knight, who had to provide for her many brothers. Urban must have sympathized with this enterprising young woman from his homeland, for here he orders Notre-Dame of Soissons to accept her.[75]*

Urban, bishop and servant of the servants of God, to his faithful abbess and the convent of Notre-Dame of Soissons, of the Benedictine order, greeting and apostolic benediction. Alice, a literate girl (*puella litterata*) whose father, the knight Americ of Bernoc, was burdened with many sons, desired to join your monastery as a nun, as she said.[76] Therefore I ask and exhort you by this apostolic letter, and in reverence to the Apostolic See, that you receive her as a nun and sister and treat her with sincere charity in the Lord, notwithstanding the limitation placed on the number of nuns allowed in your convent, a limitation established by the Holy See by which you are not to receive any new members without papal indulgence, under pain of interdict, suspension, and excommunication.

I have written to the provost of the cathedral chapter of Soissons to order you to accept Alice under threat of ecclesiastical censure, if you refuse to receive her. Done at Viterbo, the fifth day before the ides of March [March 11], in the first year of my pontificate [1262].

## Testaments

The prospect of imminent death often prompted ill or endangered aristocrats to distribute gifts to religious houses, friends, and relatives. Such bequests before death constituted irrevocable gifts to which legal title

74. See Doc. 101.
75. Text in BN, Collection Moreau, vol. 185, fol. 60r.
76. Presumably in her letter to the pope.

passed immediately. True testaments—bequests after death—are known in Champagne only from the last decades of the twelfth century. They contain several elements: a provision for burial; the selection of executors; donations to religious houses and charitable institutions; payments for anniversary Masses; and gifts to relatives and friends. Bequests by testament were limited to personal possessions and nonfeudal property.

The four testaments selected here range from the knight Hagan of Ervy's 60*l*. (Doc. 51) to Count Thibaut V's more than 10,000*l*. (Doc. 53). The well-to-do knight Erard of Nully (Doc. 52) distributed 400*l*. and left 300*l*. to found a chapel in his name, a gesture that clearly mimicked the barons. All testaments except the count's named close friends; the unmarried Marie of Esternay even remembered her wet nurse (Doc. 54).

### 51. The testament of the knight Hagan of Ervy, ca. 1190
*Hagan of Ervy drew up this testament before departing on the Third Crusade.[77] It is exceptionally detailed for an early testament. Hagan seems to have been unmarried at the time, perhaps widowed, but later he subsidized his two sons' journey to Constantinople (see Doc. 89).*

May all who see this letter know that Lord Hagan of Ervy made his testament in this manner: after his death, half of all his personal possessions are to go to Pontigny abbey, where he wishes to be buried.

He bestowed his palfrey worth 10*l*., money of Provins, on the abbey, and gave 100*s*. for its care. He gave to the abbey's gatekeeper 100*s*. for celebrating thirty Masses in his memory and 20*s*. for buying bread for distribution to the poor. He gave 20*s*. to the abbey's infirmary for pittances to the infirm. Each year the monks will be paid 30*s*., money of Provins, by Robert and Benedict of Chambelin and William of Dannemoine and their heirs [Hagan's tenants] for celebrating an anniversary Mass; Hagan also gave an entire vineyard at Dannemoine for that purpose.

He bequeathed: 60*s*. to the dean of Saint-Florentin; his green silk quilt, a coverlet, two sheets, a pillow, and 20*s*. to Lord Conon of Ervy; 20*s*. to his chaplain; and 10*s*. to Odo the cleric. Also, 20*s*. each to: the leper house of Ervy, the chapters of Saint-Etienne and Saint-Pierre of Troyes, the convents of Foissy and Notre-Dame-aux-Nonnains of Troyes, and the Hospital of the Count in Troyes; and 5*s*. each to the other hospitals in Troyes.

77. Text in Quantin, *Cartulaire général*, 2:424–425, no. 420.

Also: 10s. to Brother Hubert of Troyes and 20s. to the priests [of the Temple house]; 20s. to Lady Mahot; 10s. each to all of Hagan's nieces who are nuns and to his two nephews who are monks in Montier-la-Celle and Molesme, and 5s. to Parrenot [monk] of Montier-la-Celle.

Also: 20s. to the twenty leper houses on the road between Troyes and Pontigny; his all-weather cape to the priest of Sommeval; 20s. to his godson Milo [lord] of Ervy; 20s. to the dean of Saint-Etienne of Auxerre; 40s. each to Saint-Germain and Saint-Etienne of Auxerre; and 10s. to each of the forty rural churches in the castellanies of Ervy and Saint-Florentin.

For saying his anniversary Mass, he gave: 5s. annually to the church of Ervy; 10s. annually from the revenue of his oven to the leper house of Ervy, as well as one *sextarius* of oats that Clarinus owes to the church of Sommeval; three-quarters of a field to the church of Champsicourt; one-quarter of a *modius* of wine annually to the church of Dannemoine; 40s. annually to Saint-Etienne of Troyes; 10s. annually to the Hospital of the Count in Troyes; an *arpent* of land to Saint-Pierre of Auxerre, as well as an *arpent* of woods—if they wish to clear it—and one *sextarius* of oats and 27d. from the customary tax of Cheny.

I, Hagan, have confirmed by my seal the testament contained in this document and ordered it to be observed. And I asked the abbots of Pontigny and Saint-Michel [of Tonnerre] and the dean of Saint-Florentin to validate this document with their seals and to see to it that my testament is faithfully carried out as I have provided. [Three seals were appended.]

## 52. THE TESTAMENT OF THE KNIGHT ERARD OF NULLY, 1249

*Before departing on Louis IX's crusade, Erard of Nully drew up this testament to dispose of his substantial estate. He carefully spread his benefactions among important monasteries, and although he neglected neither his friends nor his domestic servants, he reserved almost half of his estate for the foundation of a proprietary chapel to his own glory.[78]*

In the name of the Father, Son, and Holy Spirit, I Erard, knight, of Nully, being of sound mind and body, for the salvation of my soul, have made this testament of my free will and wish it to be observed.

[1] I give to God and to the monks of Val-des-Ecoliers 40l. now and 40l. after my death for an annual commemorative Mass.

78. Text in Jean-Gabriel Gigot, ed., *Chartes en langue française antérieurs à 1271 conservées dans le département de la Haute-Marne*, Documents linguistiques de la France, série française, 1 (Paris: Editions du CNRS, 1974), 22–23, no. 22.

[2] I give 20*l*. to each of the following monasteries: Vaux-sur-Saint-Urbain, Ecurey, Benoîtevaux, and Boulancourt; 10*l*. each to Saint-Urbain, Clairvaux, and Saint-Etienne of Toul; and 5*l*. each to the Dominicans of Toul and to Val-de-Passey; 2*l*. to the hospital of Toul; 5*l*. to Bonnet; 1*l*. each to Sexfontaine, Luméville-en-Ornois, Tourailles-sous-Bois, Horville-en-Ornois, Bertheléville, Rachecourt-sur-Blaise, Baudignécourt, and Vesaignes-sur-Marne.

[3] I give 2*l*. to Isabel, wife of Jarre of Baudignécourt; 10*l*. to the brothers of Val-des-Ecoliers of Reims; 30*l*. to lord Villain [of Nully], knight; 30*l*. to Ermengard of Briey; 30*l*. to my lady Huode of Dienville; 20*l*. to my lord Erard, chaplain of Gondrecourt; and 40*l*. to the son of lord William of Baudignécourt.

[4] I give 8*l*. to the poor for clothing and shoes.

[5] I give 14*l*., after my death, to my domestic servants, and 1*l*. to Epizon.

[6] I give 300*l*. to found a chapel at Horville, and I invest Lord Erard, chaplain of Gondrecourt, with it. During my lifetime I will appoint the chaplain, and after my death whichever of my heirs holds Horville will have the perpetual right of appointment.

[7] For carrying out these provisions, I have chosen as executors: the prior of Val-des-Ecoliers; Lord Erard, chaplain of Gondrecourt; and Lord William of Baudignécourt. If one of the executors dies, I wish the remaining two to act as if they were three.

So that these things be firmly established, I have affixed my seal to this letter and have had the prior of Val-des-Ecoliers and Lord Erard [the chaplain] affix their seals to it as well. This was enacted in the year of our Lord 1249, in the month of August. [Three seals were appended.]

### 53. The testament of Count Thibaut V, 1257

*After attaining his majority in 1257, Count Thibaut V prepared to secure his claim to the kingdom of Navarre, which his father had inherited in 1234. Before setting out, he taxed his feudal tenants (see Doc. 15) and drew up this testament.[79] Noteworthy are the large sums he left to his household retainers, the Franciscan sisters of Provins, and the poor.*

In the name of the Father, Son, and Holy Spirit, I, Thibaut, by the grace of God, king of Navarre and count palatine of Champagne and Brie,

---

79. Text in Teulet, *Layettes* 3:391–392, no. 4387.

send greeting in the name of the Lord to all, present and future, who will see this letter. Be it known that I have made my testament in the following manner, and wish it to be observed, as testaments ought to be:

[1] First, I leave to my household, which has served me well, 2,000*l.* to be distributed by my executors at their discretion, according to the importance of service rendered to me.

[2] Then I leave to the Franciscan sisters of Provins firewood from my woods closest to Provins—as much as my executors deem appropriate to that convent's needs in perpetuity—as well as 500*l.* for the purchase of vineyards or of wine [rent]—depending on what the executors deem more useful—for perpetual use by that convent [see also item 6].

[3] Then I leave to the following monasteries: La Barre of Château-Thierry (500*l.*),[80] Saint-Maclou of Bar-sur-Aube (300*l.*), Notre-Dame-au-Jardin (400*l.*), Vitry (500*l.*), La Grace-Notre-Dame (300*l.*), Argensolles (500*l.*),[81] and to Troisy, Belle Eaux, the abbey outside Bar-sur-Aube, Ramerupt, Pré-Notre-Dame of Troyes, Le Mont of Provins, Champs-Benoît of Provins, and Le Pont-Notre-Dame (100*l.* each).

[4] To the Franciscans of Provins, Sézanne, and Troyes (100*l.* each). To the Dominicans of Troyes (100*l.*), Clairvaux (200*l.*), the chapter of Dominicans (100*l.*), the chapter of Franciscans (100*l.*), and the chapter of the Trinitarians (100*l.*).[82] To the Trinitarians of Vitry, La Soude, De la Vere, and Fontaine Jesus (50*l.* each). To the hospitals of Provins (200*l.*), Vitry (100*l.*), Château-Thierry (100*l.*), Montmirail (100*l.*), Troyes (200*l.*), Sézanne (60*l.*), and Meaux (50*l.*). To the convent of Foissy (200*l.*).

[5] To the poor commoner students at Paris (500*l.*). To the hospitals in my castles of Champagne which are not provided for already (20*l.* each). To the leper colonies in those same castles (10*l.* each). To my chapels in Champagne (10*l.* each) and to all their chaplains (100*l.*).

[6] To the Franciscan sisters of Provins for building their church (500*l.*).

[7] To the poor commoners of Champagne, for purchasing clothing and shoes on the Feast of Saint-Remi [January 13] following my death, as provided by my executors (1,000*l.*).

[8] To administer all this, I have selected as executors my very dear mother, Margaret, by the grace of God, queen of Navarre; the bishops of Auxerre, Troyes, and Meaux; the abbot of Clairvaux; the lord [John] of

80. See Doc. 105.
81. See Doc. 104.
82. See Doc. 93.

Thourotte [Thibaut's cousin and butler of Champagne]; and my lord Conon of Vitry, my chaplain. If any of these [latter] six executors is not available, five or four or three of them [with the queen] shall have the authority to act. If only two of them are available, however, those two may select a third executor to serve with them. Whenever the executors meet to handle my affairs, their expenses will be paid from my revenues that are not otherwise assigned at Coulommiers.

[9] I wish that all the revenues of my lands be placed in the hands of the executors until my successor [his brother, Henry III] has promised to carry out this testament, and that the bishop-executors enforce this provision by excommunication if my successor does not carry it out. And if the king of France objects to any of these provisions, I ask him to discuss his objection with my executors in order to work out a reasonable solution, as long as my successor is bound to follow them.

[10] After providing all these things, I decided to be buried at Clairvaux.

In witness to all these provisions, I have affixed my seal to this testament which was made in the year of our Lord 1257, in the month of November.

### 54. THE TESTAMENT OF LADY MARIE OF ESTERNAY, 1279
*Marie was a well-born young lady who seems to have spent her last days in the care of the nuns at the Paraclete. She must have died before a formal document could be drawn up, for here the abbess issues the testament in Marie's name.*[83]

In the name of the Father, Son, and Holy Spirit, amen. Marie, humble abbess of the Paraclete, of the Benedictine order, and the noble-born Lord Hugh of Romilly-sur-Seine, knight, send greeting in the Lord.

Be it known that the noble-born young lady Marie of Esternay, of the diocese of Troyes, being of sound mind, made her testament in our presence in this manner:

[1] First, for the salvation of her soul, she bequeathed 30*l.*, money of Tours, to the convent of Notre-Dame of Pieté near Ramerupt, where she wished to be buried.

[2] Then she bequeathed 30*l.* to the abbess and convent of the Paraclete and 20*l.* to the treasury of the Paraclete; 5*l.* to Agnes of Traînel and 4*l.* to Agnes of Mécringes, both nuns at the Paraclete; 1*l.* to Lord Garnier,

83. Text in Lalore, *Paraclete*, 259–260, no. 294.

the chaplain of the Paraclete, 1*l.* to the four priests at the Paraclete; and 4*l.* to the four sisters of Chappes who are nuns at Notre-Dame of Pieté.

[3] Then 6*l.*, money of Tours, for the purchase of cloth to be distributed to the poor; 1*l.* to the nuns of [Paraclete's priory of] Traînel; 2*l.* to the convent of Bois-Jardin; 2*l.* to the Franciscans of Sézanne; 1*l.* to her wet nurse who nourished her; and 5*s.* to the priest of Quincy who drew up this testament.

[4] For carrying out these provisions, she chose as her executors the noble-born lord Hugh of Romilly-sur-Seine, knight, and her own brother the noble-born John of Esternay, knight, who swore oaths to execute this testament as faithfully as possible. Given in the year of our Lord 1278, on the Feast of the Circumcision of the Lord [January 1, 1279].

# 3 Feudal Affairs and Lordship

The large-scale feudalization of land in the twelfth century resulted in the extension of extra-familial rights and restrictions over much property. The requisite permissions for tenurial changes occasioned by inheritance, sale, donation, or mortgage were handled on an oral basis initially, but with the proliferation of secular written records in the thirteenth century, those matters were routinely put to parchment. Even lordship, which was not an absolute right but rather determined by negotiation between the parties, was described with increasing precision.

## Notifications

The exchange of sealed letters became a normal part of aristocratic life in the thirteenth century, as changes in feudal tenure were routinely recorded in private documents. Each time homage was done, a sealed letter confirmed the act (Doc. 55). When the lordship of a fief changed—as by sale or familial transfer—notices informed the tenants affected (Docs. 56, 63). Very few of these strictly secular transactions survive, however, since they were discarded or destroyed after they had served their purpose. The few that do survive, such as the directive to secure a family's approval of a sale (Doc. 57) and a lord's authorization to alienate feudal land (Doc. 58), suggest a widespread use of impermanent documents for feudal affairs.

The importance of seals as authenticators of documents is illustrated by the lady of Brienne's confirmation of the validity of both of her seals, the small one for personal business and the large one for important matters (Doc. 59). A sealed letter could serve as a simple deposition regarding the facts of feudal tenure (Docs. 60–62) or as a public document of great weight, such as the sworn association of nobles who appended their seals to a carefully crafted document declaring their opposition to royal taxation (Doc. 64).

55. A RENUNCIATION AND A RENEWAL OF HOMAGE, 1216, 1219
*In 1216 a civil war broke out in Champagne following the decision of the royal court of peers to confirm the succession of Thibaut IV. A number of barons in the southeastern part of the county preferred Erard of Brienne, lord of Ramerupt (1190–1244), who had claimed the county on behalf of his wife, Philippa, daughter of Count Henry II (see Doc. 59). Before undertaking hostilities, the rebel barons renounced their current homages to Countess Blanche and Count Thibaut IV (Doc. A).¹ After being excommunicated and then defeated on the field of battle, the rebels finally made peace in the spring of 1219. As Simon IV of Clefmont (1200–1238) explains here, he has renewed his homage (it was a prerequisite for the lifting of his excommunication) and now names the fiefs for which he is liege. This sealed letter was retained by the Champagne chancery as proof of Simon's capitulation and homage (Doc. B).²*

(A) To Blanche, countess of Champagne, and her son Thibaut, greeting. I, [Simon] the lord of Sexfontaines, notify you by this letter that I formerly was your vassal (*homo*). Now, however, a more just heir [of the county of Champagne] has requested my support, and I am so attached to him, I could never abandon him. Therefore, know that I have bound myself to that more just heir, and henceforth I will not consider myself to be your vassal. I have sent Lord Erard of Chacenay,³ whom you hold captive, as my credible messenger to tell you this [1216].

(B) I, Simon of Clefmont, make known to all, present and future, that because of evil advice I withdrew my fidelity and homage from the noble lady Countess Blanche and her son Thibaut, count of Champagne. Heeding the advice of prudent men and my friends, and penitent, I returned to their fidelity and homage and I rendered them liege homage, by which I became their liegeman except for my liegeance to the count of Burgundy.

Later, in the presence of the bishop of Langres,⁴ I swore that I would swear in good faith to my lady and her son Thibaut against all living creatures except against the count of Burgundy, to whom I am liegeman be-

1. Text in "Cartulary-Register" no. 7, vol. 3, fol. 132v.
2. Text in Teulet, *Layettes*, 1:480, no. 1343.
3. See Docs. 30, 74, 76.
4. The bishop was William of Joinville, who had sympathized with the rebellious barons; see Genealogical Table 2.

fore all others. I also swore that I would swear to them to hold my castle of Clefmont against all living creatures except the count of Burgundy, from whom I hold that castle.

I quit to Countess Blanche and Thibaut the viscounty of Montigny and all I used to claim in that village and in its appurtenances, as well as all the domain I used to have in Ageville, and all else that I claimed from the countess, from lord Renier of Nogent-en-Bassigny, from Lord Haimo of Ecot, from the sons of Girard "Joute," and from Haice's sons.

Be it known that I am their liegeman for three fiefs: (1) my castle of Is-en-Bassigny, which I inherited from my father; (2) all that I have at La Ferté-sur-Aube and [rents] at the fairs of Champagne, which came from my mother; and (3) what I have at Vendeuvre, which I have [as dowry] through my wife. Each of these fiefs is a liege fief.

So that this will endure and be held securely, I have confirmed this letter by my seal. Done in the year of our Lord 1219, in the month of April.

### 56. A SALE OF THE *MOUVANCE* OF REAR-FIEFS, 1219
*The lord of Grancey sold an entire village to the Cistercian monastery of Auberive. Since half of the village was held from him by his feudal tenants, he had to arrange the transfer of their homages to the abbot, their new feudal lord.*[5]

I, Odo [II], lord of Grancey, make known to all, present and future, that I sold to the monks of Auberive and gave in perpetual free gift, without any reservation, all that I used to have in the village of Saint-Loup, that is: (1) half of the entire village in lands, fields, woods, running waters, and justice that was in my domain, and (2) those things that were held from me in [peasant] tenure, as well as those that moved [in feudal tenure] from that village, retaining nothing for myself or my heirs.

All my feudal tenants (*feodales mei*), who hold the other half of the village from me [in fief], henceforth will hold it from the abbot and brothers of Auberive. I promised the abbot and brothers that I would have those feudal tenants do homage to them, and further that I would guarantee this sale against all legal challenges arising from it. [He then makes a small gift to the abbey which is approved by his wife and six sons.]

5. Document in AD, Haute-Marne, 1 H 37 (Auberive). Bouchard, *Sword, Mitre, and Cloister*, 332–334, gives a genealogy of the Grancey.

## 57. A KNIGHT'S FAMILY MUST APPROVE HIS SALE, 1226

*Securing clear title to property remained a constant concern of proprietors, as litigation brought by unknown family members or feudal lords could be expensive (see Doc. 75). Ecclesiastics, who encountered increasing opposition to their acquisition of feudal property, paid particular attention to securing the approval of all persons who might claim a right (see Doc. 72). As these two letters illustrate, the transfer of property was a complicated process involving many persons.[6]*

(A) William [of Joinville],[7] by the grace of God, archbishop of Reims, to his dear dean of Dom-le-Mesnil, greeting in the Lord. This is to notify you that Lord Poitevin, knight, and his brother Renaud have in my presence sold their share of the tithe of Machault to the abbey of Saint-Nicaise. Since it was difficult for Poitevin's wife to appear before me with her children to approve this sale,[8] I direct you to go personally to Guignicourt to obtain from her, her children, and others who have the right of approval (*laudatio*), their sworn oath given personally[9] that they will not later claim title to the tithe as dowry or by any other reason. You are to certify that you have done so by sending me a sealed letter within eight days [undated letter].

(B) William, by the grace of God, archbishop of Reims, to all who see this letter, greeting in the Lord. Be it known that Lord Poitevin, knight of Guignicourt, and his brother, Lord Renaud, knight, have recognized in my presence that they sold to the abbey of Saint-Nicaise of Reims their share of the small and large tithe of Machault for 60*l.*, money of Paris, and have promised on their oaths to guarantee the sale and not to reclaim title. Poitevin's [eldest] son Ralph, knight, and his nephew Peter approved that sale in my presence.

Poitevin's wife Gertrude and his [younger] sons Hugh, cleric, and Simon, squire, and his daughters Alice, Gertrude, and Armelota also approved on their oaths given in the presence of the dean of Dom-le-Mesnil, as described in his letter,[10] that they will not reclaim title to the tithe as

6. Texts in Jeannine Cossé-Durlin, ed., *Cartulaire de Saint-Nicaise de Reims (XIIIe siècle)* (Paris: Editions du CNRS, 1991), 423, no. 329; 429–430, no. 340.

7. See Genealogical Table 2.

8. Poitevin and his family lived at Guignicourt-sur-Vence, which is located north of Rethel near the Meuse River and a considerable distance from Reims. Hence, only the adult men of the family and their lord traveled to Reims (see Doc. B).

9. *Fide corporali prestita*, literally an oath sworn in the hands of another.

10. It does not survive; but see Doc. 72D for a similar letter.

dowry or by any other reason and that they will swear against all other claimants that they guarantee the sale to the abbey.

Lord Gervais of Condé, who was lord of that fief, as he said, quitclaim all his right to that tithe in my presence. Then the knights Poitevin and Renaud divested themselves of their share of that tithe into my hands, and at their request I invested the abbey with it, conceding the free use of the fruits of that part of the tithe. Given [to Saint-Nicaise] by the hand of Hugh, my chancellor, in the year of our Lord 1226, in the month of May.

### 58. Permission to sell a rear-fief, 1229

*It is rare for a letter sent by one layman to another regarding a relatively minor feudal matter to survive today unless it was deposited with a monastery or registered by an episcopal chancery. In this case, the recipient gave the letter of authorization to the purchaser of his land, the monastery of Larrivour, which later made a copy of it in its charter book.*[11]

I, Walter [IV], count of Brienne, make known to all, present and future, that I have permitted Lord Clarembaud [V] of Chappes to sell up to three or four hundred *arpents* of his woods of Dosches, which he holds from me in fief, to the monks of Larrivour or to a layman, if he is able to. In testimony of which, I have given Clarembaud this letter sealed with my seal. Done at Troyes, in the year of grace 1229, in the month of December.

### 59. The two seals of the lady of Ramerupt, 1222

*Philippa, daughter of Count Henry II, had a weak claim to the county of Champagne that her husband Erard of Brienne, lord of Ramerupt,*[12] *tried to exploit against the regent countess Blanche. After failing to convince most of the barons of Champagne during a civil war (1216–1219), Erard and Philippa made peace and sealed a number of documents renouncing all claim to the county. In the very month that Count Thibaut IV attained his majority and with it full possession of the county, Philippa issued this letter in order to dispel any apprehension about her earlier renunciations.*[13]

I, Philippa, wife of Lord Erard of Brienne, make known to all, present and future, that I spontaneously and of my own free will, and with the consent of my husband, lord Erard, conceded, promised, and did all that

11. Text in the "Cartulary of Larrivour," fol. 15r, no. 20.
12. See Doc. 75.
13. Text in Teulet, *Layettes*, 3:545–546, no. 1535.

is contained in various letters which are sealed with my large seal and which are in the possession of Countess Blanche and her son Lord Thibaut, count palatine of Champagne and Brie.

For the greater security and confirmation of all that is contained in those letters, I have sealed this letter with my small seal, which I have used for a long time mostly in my private affairs, and give it to the countess and count, affirming that all my letters sealed with my large seal which they have now or might have in the future retain the same validity as if I possessed only my large seal, and that I cannot disavow those letters simply because I possessed several seals concurrently.

Done in the year of our Lord 1222, in the month of May.

### 60. THE FORMER CHAMBERLAIN DOES NOT RECALL A GRANT, 1238

*Robert of Milly retired as the count's chamberlain in 1222. Sixteen years later, Count Thibaut IV asked him whether he recalled having made a feudal grant during the count's minority, before new homages were routinely recorded in the Book of Homages.*[14]

To his illustrious lord, king of Navarre and count palatine of Champagne and Brie, Robert of Milly, his faithful knight [and former chamberlain], greeting with all respect and honor. You directed me, my lord, to confirm to you by my sealed letter whether I know anything about a grant of twenty-eight *sextarii* of wheat and 28*s.* which Humbert of Wassy claims that we gave him [in fief]. Be assured that I do not recall ever having been present at such a donation, and I do not have the least memory of it.[15] Done in the year of our Lord 1238, the Saturday before the Feast of Saint Lawrence [August 7].

### 61. THE LORD OF VIGNORY CORRECTS KING LOUIS IX, 1239

*The lack of a registry of fiefs made it extremely difficult for any prince to know for certain what lands he had assigned in fief. Specific questions were usually determined by local inquests. In this case, a baron unable to appeal to his lord, Count Thibaut IV, who was on crusade, writes directly to the king about a misassignment of feudal rights.*[16]

To his most serene lord Louis [IX], by the grace of God, illustrious king of France, Gautier, lord of Vignory, sends greeting and goodwill. I

14. Text in "Cartulary-Register" no. 7, vol. 3, fol. 67r.
15. There is no evidence that Humbert ever held a fief from the count.
16. Document in AN, J 193, no. 28.

have heard that the noble John, former count of Chalon-sur-Saône,[17] received from you the [*mouvance* of the] fief of a certain village of mine called
Colombey-les-Deux-Eglises and that he claimed I should hold it from him
[in fief]. About this, however, you should be aware, my lord, that I hold
that village with its appurtenances [directly] in fief from my dearest lord
Thibaut, illustrious king of Navarre [and count of Champagne]. I do not
hold anything else from that count [John] except the village of Ambon-
ville. Given in the year of our Lord 1239, in the month of June.

### 62.  A CADET PAYS RELIEF FOR HIS BROTHER'S FIEF, 1252

*When John, count of Rethel (1243–1251), died without children, his lands passed
to his two younger brothers. The older, Gaucher, who was archdeacon of the
cathedral chapter of Liège, took the county of Rethel, which was the more important share of the estate. Since collateral transfers were liable to an inheritance tax (relief), Gaucher had to pay the count of Champagne, from whom
Rethel was held in fief, approximately one year's revenue from the fief (see also
Doc. 63).*[18]

I, John, castellan of Noyon and Thourotte [and governor of Champagne in the count's absence], make known to all who see this letter that
Count Gaucher of Rethel has paid to the king of Navarre, count palatine
of Champagne and Brie, 2,000*l.*, money of Paris, as relief (*rachat*) for the
county of Rethel, which moves [feudally] from the said king. Rethel was
an escheat from Gaucher's brother, Count John. I paid the king those
2,000*l.*, money of Paris, on behalf of Gaucher. This was done in the year
of our Lord 1252, in the month of August.

### 63.  FEUDAL TENANTS MUST PAY HOMAGE TO A NEW LORD, 1252

*When Count John of Rethel died in 1251 and his land passed to his brothers
(Doc. 62), his widow, Marie of Thourotte, withdrew to her dower lands at Hautment.*[19] *Her two brothers-in-law, however, arranged a very complicated estate
settlement in which Marie was forced to exchange her dower for lands elsewhere.
Here she directs her feudal tenants to pay homage to the new count of Rethel.*[20]

Marie, called countess of Rethel, daughter of the noble lord John
[III] of Thourotte [and governor of Champagne], to all the feudal tenants,

17. John exchanged his county with the duke of Burgundy in 1237.
18. Text in Saige, Lacaille, and Labande, *Rethel*, 1:208–209, no. 130.
19. Hautment is located considerably beyond the northern limits of Champagne.
20. Text in Saige, Lacaille, and Labande, *Rethel*, 1:204–205, no. 126.

knights, men and communities of the castle and castellany of Hautment, greeting and affection. By this letter I notify you all, collectively and individually, that I have spontaneously and of my own will released to my brother-in-law, the noble Gaucher, count of Rethel, the dower[21] which the noble John, former count of Rethel and my lord and husband, gave me. That dower consists of all the rights I have had and that I might have in the castle of Hautment, its castellany and its annexes both in homages [for fiefs] and in all other things. Wishing, therefore, to do right to Lord Gaucher regarding both the lordship and inheritance of the said castle, castellany, and annexes, I direct you to render to him what you owe him in both homages and other obligations, and that you obey him as your lord. In testimony of which I send you this letter, sealed with my seal. Done in the year of our Lord 1252, on the fourth Sunday after the Resurrection of the Lord [April 28].

### 64. THE NOBLES OF CHAMPAGNE PROTEST ROYAL TAXATION, 1314

*The nobles progressively lost their tax-exempt standing, first to crusade taxes such as the Saladin Tithe (see Doc. 88), then to occasional needs of their count (see Doc. 15), and finally to the frequent impositions of King Philip IV. In 1314 in the last months of the king's life, after a war subsidy had been collected but not used for its designated purpose, the nobles of Champagne led a movement to create regional leagues against royal exactions.[22] Here they enumerate their griefs and swear an alliance with the noble leagues of neighboring provinces.[23]*

To all who will see or hear this letter, we the nobles and the commoners of Champagne, send greeting on behalf of ourselves as well as those of Vermandois, the Beauvaisis, Ponthieu, Corbie, and the nobles and commoners of Burgundy, and all our allies and supporters within the kingdom of France.

Know that the most excellent and powerful prince, our very dear and redoubtable lord Philip, by the grace of God, king of France, has levied several tallages, subsidies, and unreasonable exactions, has debased the coinage, and has done other things which have afflicted and impoverished us without bringing honor or profit to the king or his kingdom. Several

21. *Dotis mee sive donacionis propter nuptias.*
22. See Elizabeth A. R. Brown, "Reform and Resistance to Royal Authority in Fourteenth-Century France: The Leagues of 1314–1315," in *Parliaments, Estates and Representation*, vol. 1 (London, 1981), 109–137, reprinted in her *Politics and Institutions in Capetian France* (Great Yarmouth: Variorum, 1991).
23. Text (slightly condensed here) in Longnon, *Documents*, 2:515–516.

times we have humbly and devotedly requested that he lift these burdens from us, but he did not do so. In this very year of 1314 he imposed unreasonable taxes and subsidies on the nobles and commoners of the realm. We can no longer endure these exactions in good conscience, for they jeopardize our honor, our privileges, and our liberties and those of our descendants.

Therefore we, the nobles of Champagne named below, for ourselves and our supporters and allies within the kingdom, have sworn and promised by loyal oath and good faith to the count of Auxerre and Tonnerre, and to the nobles and commoners of those two counties, and to their allies and supporters, that we will help them at our own expense, according to our respective means, in the current subsidy and in all other unreasonable taxes levied by the lord king in the future. The amount of our aid will be determined by a commission of twelve of our knights and twelve of their knights. We also swear than none of us will withdraw from this agreement without the consent of the others.

We have sworn to observe these provisions forever, but we wish to preserve the obedience, fidelity, loyalty, and homage, sworn and not sworn, and all other obligations which we owe to the king of France, our lord, and other lords and their successors, for we do not wish in any manner to violate those.

So that this agreement remain firm, at the request of the nobles and commoners of Champagne, we have sealed this letter with our own seals: I, John, lord of Châteauvillain; William of Dampierre, lord of Saint-Dizier; John, count of Joigny; John of Guines, viscount of Meaux and lord of La Ferté; Hugh, lord of Conflans and castellan of Sommevesle; Philip, lord of Plancy; Aubert of Thourotte, lord of Chasteley; Erard, lord of Nanteuil-la-Fosse; Henry of Boys, tutor of John, count of Grandpré, for myself and for the count; William, lord of Thil and Marigny; Guy, lord of Broyes; Dreux, lord of Traînel; Dreux, lord of Chappes; Gautier, lord of Arzillières; John of Garlande, lord of Possesse; John of Joinville, lord of Jully; William, lord of Saint-Chéron; Henry of Traînel, lord of Villeneuve; Hugh of Conflans, lord of La Boutillerie; John of Saint-Florentin, lord of Jaulges; Odo, lord of Clérey; Hugh of Chappes, lord of Dienville; Henry, lord of Olizy; John of Saint-Florentin, lord of Vièvre; John, lord of Maligny; John, lord of Guerchy; William of Esnon, lord of Lasson; William, lord of Brion; John of Saint-Dizier, lord of Vignory; Hugh of Châteauvillain, lord of Pleurs and Baye; Stephen, lord of Saint-Phal; William, lord of Pougy; Guy, lord of Arblay; André of Le Plessis, lord of Thiéblement. Done in the year of our Lord 1314, on the 24th day of November. [Thirty-four pendant seals survive.]

## Mortgages, Debts, and Sales

Since most fiefs produced fixed annual revenues, feudal tenants often were forced to mortgage or sell off property to raise cash for extraordinary expenses (such as a crusade), investments, or to support an extravagant lifestyle. The main creditors were the counts themselves (Doc. 65), foreign merchants (Doc. 66), the Jews (Doc. 67), the military orders (Doc. 68), and monasteries (Doc. 69). Despite the restrictions on feudal alienations (Doc. 70), fiefs continued to pass to the church (see Doc. 11) and, to a lesser extent, townsmen (see Doc. 14).

Feudal alienations took a number of forms, including conversion to nonfeudal rents (Doc. 71) and outright sales. The complexity of such transactions is illustrated by the sale of one fief that required six different documents to complete (Doc. 72). But laymen were not alone in their financial difficulties: some monastic institutions facing similar constraints (see Doc. 46) resorted to loans from laymen (Doc. 73).

65. CASTLES ARE MORTGAGED TO THE COUNT, 1201, 1210
*Barons who needed ready cash often mortgaged their castellanies to the count (see Doc. 91). Here the count of Brienne, one of the most distinguished barons of Champagne, mortgages his castle and ancestral lands in preparation for an expedition to claim his wife's lands in southern Italy, where he died in 1205 (Doc. A).*[24] *A few years later the heiress of Beaufort mortgaged her castellany to Countess Blanche for unknown reasons (Doc. B).*[25]

(A) I, Walter [III], count of Brienne, make known to all, present and future, that I have mortgaged all my land to my lord and dearest friend Thibaut [III], count palatine of Troyes, for 700*l.* That land consists of [the county of] Brienne and all its dependencies except its fiefs and alms.

When that land has yielded 700*l.* in revenues to Thibaut or his agents,

24. Text in "Cartulary-Register" no. 7, vol. 2, pp. 68–69.
25. Text in "Cartulary-Register" no. 3, fol. 71r.

it will be returned integrally to me and my heirs. Done at Sézanne [at Count Thibaut's court], in the year of our Lord 1201, in the month of April.

(B) I, Guy [II] of Dampierre make known that I hold the castle of Beaufort and its entire castellany [as collateral] for 829*l.* with the consent of my dearest lady Blanche, countess of Champagne. However, from the twentieth day after next Christmas I will not be able to claim anything from that land. In order to validate this act, I have confirmed it with my seal. Done in the year of our Lord 1210, in the month of June.

### 66. A BARON'S DEBT TO A SIENESE MERCHANT, 1224

*Foreign merchants doing business at the fairs of Champagne often made loans to the regional aristocracy, since the count of Champagne could be relied on to enforce repayment. Here a substantial baron pledges his feudal property for a loan repayment.*[26]

I, Walter [lord] of Arzillières, make known to all who see this letter that I conceded to my dearest lord Thibaut [IV], count palatine of Champagne and Brie, that he may seize my [feudal] property without my objection and without betraying his faith to me, unless I repay 260*l.* 40*s.* to Palmerius of Siena by the deadline specified in the count's own letter [it does not survive]. If I fail to fulfill the provisions of that letter, I permit my lord Thibaut to take my property and to hold it until I have satisfied Palmerius. In testimony of which I have had this letter written and confirmed by my seal. Done in the year of grace 1224, on the Thursday before the Feast of Saint John the Baptist [June 21].

### 67. A BARON'S DEBT TO THE COUNT'S JEWS, 1231

*Like foreign merchants, the Jews who loaned money to the barons relied on their personal protector, the count, to enforce repayment. By this letter the count is given possession of a fief-rent whose revenue he will pay to the baron's creditors until the debt is retired.*[27]

I, Geoffroy, lord of Deuilly, make known to all who see this letter that I have transferred to my dearest lord Thibaut, count palatine of Cham-

---

26. Text in "Cartulary-Register" no. 7, vol. 3, fol. 182r-v.
27. Text in ibid., fols. 148v–149r.

pagne and Brie, my entire fief that I possess in his fairs, that is, a revenue of 66*l*. 4*s*. 8*d*., from which the count will repay the 246*l*. debt that I owe his Jews. When the debt is repaid [in four years], the count will return that fief to me to hold just as I held it on the day this letter was drawn up. In testimony of which I had my seal appended to this letter. Done in the year of grace 1231, on the Sunday after the Assumption of Mary [August 17].

### 68. A FIEF IS MORTGAGED TO THE HOSPITALLERS, 1231

*In 1219 Countess Blanche granted Ageville in fief to Renier II, lord of Nogent-en-Bassigny, who soon built a fortress there.*[28] *Within a decade, however, Renier experienced financial difficulties, and in 1231 mortgaged that fief for 200l.*[29] *The reference to the "heavy" coin of Provins is to the new coin minted since 1225. Since the lighter old coins remained in circulation, it was important to specify the coin of repayment.*

I, Renier, lord of Nogent-en-Bassigny, make known by this letter that I promised and guaranteed to my dear and venerable lord Thibaut, count palatine of Champagne and Brie, that within three years after the next Easter [March 23] I will redeem my village of Ageville which I mortgaged, with his approval, to the brothers of the Hospital of Jerusalem for 200*l*., heavy money of Provins. Done in the year of our Lord 1231, in the month of March.

### 69. A FIEF IS MORTGAGED TO THE CISTERCIANS, 1238

*Properties acquired by dowry or escheat and located at a distance from a knight's main possessions often were sold or mortgaged to raise cash, either for current expenses or for reinvestment in nearby properties. Here Aubert of Le Plessis, who held several fiefs from the count, mortgages one that he had acquired by escheat in the 1220s.*[30] *He continued to sell off property through the 1240s (see Doc. 11A).*

I, Aubert of Le Plessis, make known to all who see this letter that I have mortgaged to the abbot and monastery of Trois-Fontaines for 300*l*.,

---

28. See Doc. 26.

29. Text in "Cartulary-Register" no. 7, vol. 3, fol. 90v. A year later he had to mortgage another village for 200*l*. (ibid., fol. 91r: the creditor was Stephen, provost of the cathedral chapter of Langres).

30. Text in "Cartulary-Register" no. 7, vol. 3, fols. 211v–212r. This fief was listed as a recent acquisition in the Book of Homages of the 1220s (Longnon, *Documents*, 1:151, no. 3927).

money of Provins, the fief of Vavray with its appurtenances that I hold from my dearest lord Thibaut [IV], by the grace of God, king of Navarre and count palatine of Champagne and Brie. They will hold that fief for two years from the Feast of Saint John the Baptist [June 24].

I asked the lord king to approve this mortgage to the monks because the fief moved from him. Since he approved, I promised him that unless I redeem the fief by the above term, he or his agent may seize my [other] property until that fief is redeemed. In testimony of which I have sealed this letter with my seal. Done in the year of our Lord 1238, in the month of December.

### 70. THE CUSTOM REGARDING FEUDAL MORTGAGES, CA. 1270
*In this undated decision the High Court of Troyes states the general custom governing the mortgage of fiefs in the late thirteenth century.*[31]

The custom in Champagne is that a nobleman who holds a fief may not sell or mortgage or alienate it to anyone for more than three years. After he has mortgaged it for three years, he must go to his lord and say: "Lord, I have sold the revenues of the fief that I hold from you, for three years." The lord must then consent, and may not object for any reason; nor may the overlord touch the mortgaged fief during those three years. But the feudal tenant must keep his domanial lands in his own hand so that he will be able to serve his lord, for he may not mortgage or sell the entire fief. This is the custom in Champagne.

### 71. A KNIGHT CREATES AN ANNUITY, 1202
*The knight Erlebaud of Vaubercey converted his feudal property into an annuity consisting of a grain rent payable by the Cistercian monastery of Larrivour. Here his wife and son appear before the bishop of Troyes to register a modification of the original agreement and to obtain a copy of it for the family's protection. A chirograph was a piece of parchment on which a text was written twice, either side-by-side or end-to-end, with the word* CHYROGRAPHUM *written in large letters between the texts. The parchment was then divided through that word so that each party received half.*[32]

Garnier, by the grace of God, bishop of Troyes, greeting in the name of the creator to all who receive this letter. Be it known that Erlebaud,

31. Text in Portejoie, *L'ancien coutumier,* 147–148, art. 4.
32. Text in "Cartulary of Larrivour," fol. 27r, no. 6.

knight of Vaubercey, and his wife Gila gave to the monks of Notre-Dame of Larrivour all their possessions in plain land and in woods between La Morge and Larrivour's forest. In return, the monks gave Erlebaud and Gila and their heirs six *modii* of grain, measure of Troyes, to be collected annually from their grange of Bonlieu.

After the death of her husband, Gila with the consent of her son John released the monks from one *modius* (one-half wheat, one-half oats) of that payment so that she would be buried at their abbey. Henceforth, the monks will pay her only son John and his heirs each year from their grange of Bonlieu: one-half of a *modius* of wheat, four *sextarii* of rye, and ten *sextarii* of oats on All Saints' Day [November 1], and the same amount at the Purification of Mary [February 2] and at Easter.

It is agreed that John and his heirs will not be able to sell, mortgage, or alienate this grain rent, nor even part of it, as long as the monks do not wish it. Also, John guarantees title [to the land] given by his father and mother against all claimants in all courts; if the title is in any way defective, the monks will not be held to pay the grain.

I have given each party a chirograph copy of this letter. Enacted in the year of our Lord 1201, in the month of February [1202].

[John died on the Albigensian Crusade in 1209 after selling the remaining grain rent to the abbey for 35*l.*]

## 72. A REAL ESTATE TRANSACTION, 1219–1220

*Property transfers became increasingly complex processes in the thirteenth century, as purchasers required sellers to provide clear titles. In this sale by a knight, six documents were required to complete the transaction: a deed of title (Doc. A), a promissory note (Doc. B), the approval of the feudal lord (Doc. C), the approval of the seller's wife (Doc. D), the formal transfer by investiture (Doc. E), and a receipt of payment (F).[33] Each document reveals a slightly different aspect of the transaction: one of the letters tells us that the seller's feudal lord was also his brother-in-law, while another states that the property sold was the wife's inheritance, which explains why the archbishop took care to obtain her divestiture before the new investiture (see Doc. 57). The receipt of payment reveals that the convent had made a 60l. (10 percent) downpayment at the time of the sale, and that the sale price was below full value, the difference being a gift to the abbey. That six related documents survive is quite exceptional; most often only the title deed survives, the other incidental documents having been destroyed.*

33. Texts in Paris, *Avenay*, 2 : 103–107, nos. 53–58.

(A) I, Giles, knight of Melun, make known to all, present and future, that I have sold all that I have in tithes and other rights at Mareuil-sur-Marne to the abbey of Saint-Pierre of Avenay, and that I guarantee the title against all claimants except the lady [Blanche] countess of Champagne and the lord Alan of Roucy. My wife Ermensend approved the sale and confirmed it by her oath. Also, Lord John, knight of Vallery, and his brother Hugh from whom I hold this fief, and their sister Lady Elizabeth, approved the sale.

The knights who witnessed this sale and who are my guarantors are: John of Vallery, Lord Guy of Cour-Guilleret, Lord James of Torcy, Lord Enguerran of Villers and his brother Lord John of Ablois-Saint-Martin, and Lord Peter the Younger of Moslins. I consummated this sale by a sworn oath. So that this remain valid, I sealed this charter with my seal. Done in the year of our Lord 1219, in the month of September.

(B) I, Eustachia, abbess, and the entire convent of Avenay, make known to all, present and future, that for the sale to us by Giles, knight of Melun, and his wife Ermensend, of the tithe and other rights that they have at Mareuil-sur-Marne, we owe them 600*l.*, money of Provins, payable in this manner at the monastery of Igny to its abbot, prior, or anyone else there: 200*l.* at the Feast of Saint Martin [November 11], 200*l.* within twenty days of the Feast of Saint-Remi [January 13, 1220], and 200*l.* at the Feast of Saint John the Baptist [June 24, 1220].

I, Eustachia, as abbess, and Isabel and Hodiard representing the nuns, swear to make the payments. These are our guarantors: the mayor Albric, John of La Forzy and his son Adin, Thibaut of Fonte, Heraud, Seuvin, the carpenter Garnier, the blacksmiths Guiot and Mainer, and our canons Pagan, Drogo, son of Dudo, Garnier of La Forzy, Dudet Coquin, and Fanquer—all these swore that if we do not pay, fifteen days after they are notified to that effect by Lord Giles of Melun, they will place themselves in his custody at Melun and remain there until the debt is paid off.

As greater warranty of payment, the following knights also are guarantors: Lord Guy of Sailly,[34] Lord Guy of Cour-Guilleret, Lord John of Ablois-Saint-Martin, Lord Clarembaud of Avenay and his brother William, Lord James of Torcy, Lord Enguerran of Villers and his brother Wacher, Lord Gaucher of Cormicy, Lord Pagan of Mareuil and his son

---

34. That is, Guy of Joinville; see Genealogical Table 2.

Philip—all of whom swore to place themselves in custody at Melun under the same conditions as stated above.

The guarantors also swore to pay Giles of Melun these sums of money if the nuns do not pay: 50*l.* each by Lord Renaud, canon of Avenay; Guiot of Mont, the falconer, and his brother, Erard of Rohais; and Thomas of Rohais. In testimony of which I have sealed this charter with the seal of the abbess, since the chapter of nuns lacks a seal. Done in the year of our Lord 1219, in the month of September.

(C) I, John, lord of Vallery, make known to all, present and future, that Lord Giles of Melun, knight, has sold to Saint-Pierre of Avenay all that he has in tithes and other revenue at Mareuil-sur-Marne which are held from me in fief, with the assent of his wife Ermensend—my sister—and I warrant the title. In addition, Giles made me his guarantor against all who might challenge the title except against the lady countess of Champagne and Lord Alan of Roucy. So that this remain valid, I have sealed this letter with my seal. Done in the year of our Lord 1219, in the month of September.

(D) H., priest of Saint-Jean of Le Jard, to his reverend father lord William, archbishop of Reims, greeting in the Lord. I notify your excellence that at your order I went to Ermensend, wife of Lord Giles, knight of Melun, and at my request she divested into my hand the tithe and revenue at Mareuil-sur-Marne which she possessed by hereditary right. And on her oath she conceded the sale of these things by her husband to Avenay abbey, and promised to warrant legitimate title. Done in the year of grace 1219, in the month of September.

(E) William [of Joinville],[35] by the grace of God, archbishop of Reims, greeting in the Lord to all who see this letter. Be it known that Giles, knight of Melun, acknowledged in my presence that he sold to the convent of Saint-Pierre of Avenay whatever he possessed in tithes and other things at Mareuil-sur-Marne, and he transferred possession into my hand, divesting himself of them. And he swore in my presence that he would guarantee legitimate title against all claimants except the lady countess of Champagne and the Lord Alan of Roucy.

35. See Genealogical Table 2.

I solemnly invested Avenay with these possessions.

Giles's wife Ermensend, to whom the tithe and other things belonged by inheritance, also conceded this sale on her oath and divested herself of them, promising to guarantee legitimate title. In testimony and confirmation of which, I have had my seal affixed to this letter. Done in the year of our Lord 1219, in the month of October.

(F) I, Giles, knight of Melun, to all, present and future, make known that Eustachia, the venerable abbess, and the convent of Saint-Pierre of Avenay paid me in full the 660*l*., money of Provins, which they owed me for my tithe at Mareuil-sur-Marne and other things there. And I, through divine piety and charity, give as a gift to the abbey whatever that tithe is worth above the sale price of 660*l*., money of Provins, with the assent of my wife Ermensend.

I release the guarantors of Eustachia and her convent from the oath of obligation they took for paying that sum. All this my wife concedes and confirms on oath. In testimony of which, so that no dispute arise later, I have sealed this letter with my seal. Done in the year of our Lord 1220, in the month of June.

### 73. A LADY HAS MISPLACED A LETTER OF DEBT, 1245

*The preservation of documents by laymen was always problematic, occasionally with serious consequences when documents were lost (see also Doc. 11B). In this letter Beatrice, widow of the seneschal Simon of Joinville and lady of Marnay,[36] explains that she lost a letter of debt. It is in French rather than Latin, as it was probably written directly from dictation.[37]*

I, Beatrice, lady of Marnay, make known to all, present and future, that the abbot and monastic community of Saint-Urbain contracted a debt of 200*l*., heavy money of Provins,[38] and gave me a letter sealed with the seals of the abbot and the chapter of Saint-Urbain. When they repaid me in full, the abbot asked me to return their letter of debt, but I was unable to find it. So I declare here that if that letter is found later, it will be null and void, not actionable by me or my heirs. In order to establish this firmly, I have affixed my seal to this letter at the request of the abbot and chapter of Saint-Urbain. Done in 1245, in the month of July.

36. See Genealogical Table 2.
37. Text in Gigot, *Chartes en langue française*, 13–14, no. 12.
38. See Doc. 68.

# Lordship

Lordship was a complex right whose exercise over nonfeudal tenants often depended on local circumstance.[39] While one lord could be prevented by a local monastery from exercising a legitimate right to establish a new village (Doc. 74), his nephew succeeded in taxing the tenants of another monastery who lived in his villages (Doc. 76). Even in stable communities, where all the residents came under a single lord's jurisdiction, the claims of lords over their tenants often were difficult to enforce, as outmigration of young men in search of better opportunities (see Docs. 3–4, 16–18) and of women through marriage to outsiders complicated the exercise of lordship (Doc. 75). Rights long exercised, however, were not easily circumscribed by the count or king (Doc. 77).

## 74. A NEW VILLAGE IS DISMANTLED, 1171

*The lords of Chacenay, like other barons, developed their lands by founding villages as new economic and population centers. In this case, the monks of Clairvaux feared that a new village would threaten the viability of their own grange, and they prevailed upon Thomas II of Chacenay to raze his new settlement.*[40]

I, Walter, by the grace of God, bishop of Langres, wish to notify all, present and future, that Thomas [lord] of Chacenay, penitent and acquiescing to the advice of his faithful [knights], dismantled the new village he had begun to construct near [Clairvaux's] grange of Fontarce and the village of Saint-Usage because it could jeopardize that grange. He promised on his oath that neither he nor his [younger] brother Erard, nor his heirs in perpetuity would ever build another village between the grange of Fontarce and the village of Vitry-le-Croisé [along the river Arce]. Within these bounds no village will be developed except those already long established there. Witnesses are: Drogo of Fontette and Michael of Chevrières, priests; and Guiard of Bricon, Hugh "Goriard" [of Magnant], and Erard of Chevrières, knights. Done in the year of our Lord 1171, during the rule of King Louis [VII] of the French, in the time of Abbot Girard and the cellarmasters of Clairvaux: Walter, Renaud, and John.

---

39. For a brief description of lordship, see Guy Fourquin, *Lordship and Feudalism in the Middle Ages*, trans. Iris and A. L. Lytton Sells (New York: Pica Press, 1976), esp. chap. 5.

40. Text in Waquet, *Recueil*, 2:148–149, no. 137.

75. A LORD'S RIGHTS OVER HIS VILLAGERS, 1203

*The component rights of lordship are described in community franchises and
pariages (see Docs. 16–18) but rarely for unfranchised communities. In this
unusual case, however, we can reconstruct the rights exercised by André (of
Brienne), lord of Ramerupt, who in 1188 mortgaged his village of Nogent-sur-
Aube to finance his journey on the Third Crusade. After his death overseas, the
holder of his mortgage—the count of Joigny—sold it to the abbey of Montiéramey, which already had the parish church and tithes there. But when André's
heir came of age and brought suit, the abbey agreed to relinquish half of the
village. In this variant of joint lordship, the two parties agreed to exercise lordship equally, neither having more rights than the other in this unfranchised
village.[41]*

I, Erard, lord of Ramerupt, make known to all, present and future,
that the abbot of Montiéramey and I reached a settlement in our dispute
over the justice and revenues of Nogent-sur-Aube in this manner:

[1] The abbot will retain his full right over his oven, mill, meadows,
and arable lands. Likewise his house and enclosure will be entirely his; and
if anyone of that household is accused of a misdeed, he will be answerable
only to the abbot. The abbot may have twenty oxen and ten cows attached
to that house with the right of pasture in the entire parish of Nogent. If
any of those animals causes damage, wise men will assess a fine according
to the local customs.

[2] As it is for the abbot, so it is for me: I will have my right over my
oven, mill, meadows, and arable lands. I will freely possess my house and
courtyard there. If any of my household servants living there commits a
misdeed, he will be answerable only to me. I may have twenty oxen and
ten cows there with the right of pasture in the entire parish; if any of those
animals causes damage, a fine will be assessed by wise men according to
the local customs.

[3] The residents of the village may grind their grain at either the
abbot's or my mill, and may bake at either oven, as they wish.

[4] The abbot and I each will have a mayor at Nogent who must
swear fidelity on their oath to me and to the abbot. The mayors will not
be more privileged than the other residents but will be liable to the same
justice, tallage, obligations, and taxes as the others. Neither mayor may

41. Text in Charles Lalore, ed., *Cartulaire de l'abbaye de Montiéramey* (Paris-Troyes:
E. Thorin-Lacroix, 1890), 212–216, no. 207. An analysis is in Evergates, *Feudal Society in the
Bailliage of Troyes*, 35–36.

unilaterally collect a tallage, levy a fine, hold pleas, or exercise any other right; the mayors must always act together.

[5] The abbot and I will share all revenues equally, that is, land rents, tithes, tallages, justice over residents, road taxes, and mortgages within the parish of Nogent, except for oblations in the church of Nogent and inheritance taxes on the abbot's own lands. In all these the abbot will not have more lordship (*dominium*) than I, nor I more than he.

[6] The Auzon river remains mine, except that whenever the abbot visits Rougevaux or Nogent, he may fish in the Auzon to feed his retinue.

[7] Neither the abbot nor I may acquire or sell property without the other; if either party does so, he must remit half of the price to the other.

[8] The abbot promised that neither he nor his successors will convert the abbey's lands there [from peasant tenures] to lands cultivated directly by the monks.[42]

[9] Whatever rights the abbey has over the men and women of Coclois on the day this document was drawn up, it will have in perpetuity. And if men and women of Nogent leave to settle on the abbey's other lands, or on my lands, or on the lands of another lord, they will continue to be under our joint lordship as they are at Nogent. If a man of the abbey marries a woman of Nogent and takes her away—and likewise for any of my men—the lord of the woman will be able to transfer a woman of equal value from Nogent.[43]

[10] Neither I nor the abbot may require any resident to appear at a court outside of Nogent: all cases of justice involving theft, murder, and duels will be conducted within the village. If the two mayors do not exercise that justice, the abbot and I will dispatch others to do it.

[11] If either mill deteriorates through age, it will be repaired as local wise men determine.

[12] When newcomers settle in Nogent, they will fall under the joint lordship of the abbot and me. The two mayors will collect the tallage so that neither party will have more lordship over it and each will receive the same amount.

I have sworn in good faith to observe this agreement with the abbey, and the abbot has promised on his sacred word to observe this agreement with me. So that this remain permanent, I have had this charter drawn up

---

42. That is, land now owing rent cannot be converted into the abbey's domain land worked by the monks themselves, free from rent.

43. This was required in order to retain parity between the lords at Nogent, and thus equal revenues. Omitted here is a clause regarding a specific woman at Nogent.

and sealed by my seal. Done in the year of our Lord 1203, in the month of May.

### 76. THE LORD OF CHACENAY EXACTS FOUR EXTRAORDINARY TAXES, 1218
*On the eve of his departure on crusade, Erard II, lord of Chacenay, restated the four occasions on which he collected an exceptional tax from his tenants. He claimed the same taxes from the tenants of Montiéramey abbey who resided in his villages.*[44]

I, Erard, lord of Chacenay, having decided to go to Jerusalem, reiterated [to the monks of Montiéramey] that I do not have the right to a tax (*rogatum*) from the men and women at [the nearby village of] Chervey belonging to the [abbey's] priory of Viviers. Also, I have only the right of justice in the woods of "Cochet," and I have returned the forest of "Wiler" to the priory and villagers of Viviers.

I have no right to collect a general tallage from the men and women of the abbey of Montiéramey who live in my castellany [of Chacenay], except on these occasions: for the knighting of myself and my sons; for the marriage of my daughter; for the ransom of my body if I am captured under arms; and for my journey to Jerusalem. On these occasions I may collect an aid (*auxilium*) from the villages of Viviers, Noé-les-Mallets, and Eguilly, but no more than 5s. [per person], in each of two years. Done in the year of our Lord 1218.

### 77. THE HIGH COURT UPHOLDS JEAN OF JOINVILLE'S RIGHTS, 1288
*In a session before the High Court of Champagne in September 1288, the former crusader and future biographer of Louis IX, Jean of Joinville, seneschal of Champagne, defended his ancient right of absolute jurisdiction within his fief. A court stenographer recorded the event.*[45]

[Jean], the lord of Joinville, seneschal of Champagne, brought suit against the bailiff of Chaumont, claiming that the bailiff unjustly seized the right of justice which he possessed over his village of Joinville: the bailiff so constrained him and his agents that Jean was unable to exercise his customary right of justice there, nor would he be able to do so in the

---

44. Abbreviated text in Lalore, *Montiéramey*, 290–291, no. 294. See Genealogical Table 3.

45. Text in Brussel, *Nouvel examen*, 2:865–866, note. See Genealogical Table 2.

future. Therefore Jean petitioned the court to have the situation rectified and to have his rights released to him.

The bailiff, in his defense, said that he took action because of a failure of justice (*defectum justitiae*) for this reason: after a man beat and viciously wounded another man in the village of Joinville, the two made peace in the presence of the provost of Wassy, who was acting in the name of the lord king [Philip IV]; but the attacker's accomplices remained at large within the jurisdiction of Joinville, and the lord of Joinville neither arrested those malefactors nor did anything to restrain them, all of which is well known. Because the wounded man was in danger of death, and also because of the violated oath [of the attacker], as well as the failure of the lord of Joinville to exercise his justice, the bailiff placed the village under the jurisdiction of the lord king.

The lord of Joinville responded that he allowed the truth of what the bailiff said and whatever else could be discovered about the facts, but the bailiff nevertheless had no right to confiscate his own right of justice nor even to impede his exercise thereof, since he was a noble castellan (*nobilis castellanus*) and had obtained his castellany and other rights in the highest nobility from the count of Champagne; nor did the bailiff have the right to summon him and his agents to answer in the bailiff's court for default of justice. Nor indeed did the bailiff have the right to prejudice a noble by seizing or impeding his justice without sufficient notification.

Having heard the case presented by the lord of Joinville and the bailiff's defense, the court decided that the bailiff retains jurisdiction over the broken sworn oath of peace, but that he must return the justice of the village of Joinville which he seized and may not molest that noble in his exercise thereof.

# 4 The Crusades

Pope Urban II (1088–1099), a native of the castle-town of Châtillon-sur-Marne, unleashed the crusading movement with his appeal to the French barons and knights at Clermont (1095). Although Count Stephen of Blois was among the leaders of the First Crusade,[1] his younger brother Hugh, count of Troyes (1093–1125), did not participate in that expedition. But Count Hugh later undertook several armed pilgrimages to the Holy Land and in 1125 joined the Templars, the new order of warrior-monks founded by a local lord, Hugh of Payns. The Second (1147–1149), Third (1190), and Fourth (1202–1204) Crusades attracted large contingents of barons and knights from Champagne, in part because the counts themselves were enthusiastic crusaders.

## The Templars

In 1118 Hugh of Payns, a baron from southern Champagne who was perhaps related to Count Hugh, founded a militia in Jerusalem to protect Western travelers visiting the holy sites. The early days of the Knights of the Temple of Jerusalem are described by William of Tyre, the foremost historian of the Latin East (Doc. 78). In 1127 Hugh returned home to recruit knights for his military confraternity and sought help from Bernard, the renowned abbot of Clairvaux. Reluctant at first to endorse a society organized for war, Bernard relented after Hugh appeared before the ecclesiastical Council of Troyes (January 14, 1128) and described the perilous conditions of pilgrims in the Holy Land. Bernard's *In Praise of the New Knighthood* presents the first justification of an order of warrior-monks (Doc. 79). Pope Innocent II accepted the constitution of the

1. See James A. Brundage, "An Errant Crusader: Stephen of Blois," *Traditio* 16 (1960): 380–395. Stephen's letter from Antioch to his wife Adele (daughter of William the Conqueror), is translated in Dana Carleton Munro, *Letters of the Crusaders* (Philadelphia: University of Pennsylvania, 1902), 5–8, no. 2.

Templars on March 29, 1139, when he placed the order under direct papal authority. During the next half-century Templar houses (called commanderies) became exceptionally wealthy as pilgrims donated lands and rents in gratitude for Templar assistance in the Holy Land (Doc. 80). The growing wealth of the Templars, however, prompted the counts first to restrict their acquisitions, then to prohibit them outright from acquiring feudal property in Champagne (see Doc. 12).

### 78. William of Tyre describes the Templars in 1118

*William of Tyre grew up in Jerusalem, where he was born ca. 1130. After studying in France and Italy for about twenty years (1145–1165), he returned home to become archbishop of Tyre and chancellor of the Latin kingdom of Jerusalem.[2] He wrote his* History of the Latin East *principally from 1175 to 1185. For the early years of the Templars, William relied on oral traditions among both eastern churchmen and the Templars themselves.[3]*

In that year [1118] certain pious and God-fearing nobles of the knighthood placed themselves in the hands of the patriarch [of Jerusalem], professing their wish to serve Christ and to live in poverty, chastity, and obedience, like regular canons. Foremost and most distinguished among them were the venerable Hugh of Payns and Geoffroy of Saint-Omer. Since they had neither a church nor a fixed domicile, the king [of Jerusalem] granted them a temporary dwelling place in his own palace on the south side of the Temple of the Lord. The canons of the Temple gave these men a nearby square for carrying out their duties.

The king and his barons, as well as the patriarch and his prelates, also donated properties, some for use during a limited period and some in perpetuity, whose revenues provided food and clothing for the new order. The main duty of this order—the one which the patriarch and the other bishops enjoined them to accept for the remission of their sins—was to keep the roads and highways safe from the menace of robbers and highwaymen, insofar as they could, and especially to protect pilgrims.

2. Peter W. Edbury and John Gordon Rowe, *William of Tyre: Historian of the Latin East* (Cambridge: Cambridge University Press, 1988), chaps. 2–3.

3. Translation (slightly modified here) by E. A. Babcock and A. C. Krey, *A History of Deeds Done beyond the Sea*, 2 vols. (New York: Columbia University Press, 1941), 1:524–526. Latin text in *Willelmi Tyrensis Archiepiscopi Chronicon*, ed. R. B. C. Huygens, 2 vols. (Turnhout: Brepols, 1986), 1:553–554 (bk. 12, ch. 7). For the early Templars, see Malcolm Barber, "The Origins of the Order of the Temple," *Studia Monastica* 12 (1970): 219–240, and Alain Demurger, *Vie et mort de l'Ordre du Temple* (Paris: Editions du Seuil, 1985).

Nine years after their founding, the brothers still wore secular clothing, that is, the garments that the people, for the salvation of their souls, had given them. . . . At the Council of Troyes [1128], by the order of Pope Honorius and of Stephen, patriarch of Jerusalem, the brothers were given a Rule[4] and were instructed to wear white [like the Cistercians]. . . . After this period they began to increase in numbers and their possessions multiplied.

At the time of Pope Eugenius III [1145–1153] the brothers began to sew red crosses on their mantles in order to distinguish themselves from everyone else. . . . [Today] they are said to have vast possessions, both on this side of the sea and beyond [in Europe]. There is not a province in the Christian world which does not bestow some of its possessions upon these brothers, and their wealth is said to equal the opulence of kings. Because they live in the royal palace next to the Temple [of Jerusalem], as I have said, these brothers are called Knights of the Temple.

### 79. Bernard of Clairvaux, *In Praise of the New Knighthood*, ca. 1130

*Bernard, a vociferous critic of knightly violence, endorsed a confraternity of knights organized to protect Westerners in the Holy Land after hearing Hugh of Payns describe the grim situation there. Bernard here justifies a "new" knighthood—a monastic military order—whose Christian purpose contrasted with the "old" or secular knighthood devoted to selfish, materialistic goals.[5] His writing is imbued with Scriptural references.*

To Hugh, knight of Christ and master of Christ's militia, Bernard, abbot in name only of Clairvaux, may you fight the good fight.

You have asked me, my dear Hugh, once, twice, and even a third time if I am not mistaken, to write a few words of exhortation for you and your knight comrades. Since I am not permitted to wield the lance against the tyrannical enemy, you wished me to help you at least by directing my pen in moral, rather than material, support for your cause. I have put you off

4. See *The Rule of the Templars: The French Text of the Rule of the Order of the Knights Templar*, trans. and intro. by J. M. Upton-Ward (Woodbridge: The Boydell Press, 1992).

5. Translation (slightly modified here) by M. Conrad Greenia, "In Praise of the New Knighthood," in *Bernard of Clairvaux: Treatises III* (Kalamazoo: Cistercian Publications, 1977), 127–128, 132–133, 138–142. Latin text in *Tractatus et Opuscula*, vol. 3 of *Sancti Bernardi Opera*, ed. J. Leclercq and H. M. Rochais (Rome: Editiones Cistercienses, 1963), 213–239. For Bernard's character, see Brian P. McGuire, *The Difficult Saint: Bernard of Clairvaux and His Tradition* (Kalamazoo: Cistercian Publications, 1991).

now for quite some time, not that I disdained your request but rather that I not be blamed for taking it lightly and hastily. I feared I might botch a task which remains difficult for me and which a more qualified hand could have done better. Having procrastinated to no purpose, I have now done what I could, lest my inability should be taken for unwillingness. May the reader judge the result. Some may find this proposal unsatisfactory or inadequate, but I shall be content nevertheless, as I have given you my best effort.

[After encouraging the "new " knighthood (chap. 1), Bernard depicts the evils of the "secular" knighthood (chap. 2):] What, then, is the purpose or the fruit of the secular knighthood (*secularis militiae*), or maliciousness (*malitiae*) as I should call it? What, if not the mortal sin of the victor [at tournaments] and the eternal death of the vanquished? To borrow a word from the apostle: he who plows or threshes does so with the expectation of a crop [1 Cor. 9:10]. What then, O knights, is this monstrous error and unbearable urge to devote such expense and labor in fighting, for no purpose except death and sin? You deck your horses with silk, and plume your armor with all manner of rags. You paint your saddles and shields [with emblems].[6] You adorn your bits and spurs with gold and silver and precious stones. And in all this glory you gallop in shameful frenzy and mindless stupidity to your own death! Are these the trappings of a warrior, or are they not rather the trinkets of a woman? Do you think your enemy's sword will bounce off your gold, spare your jewels, or fail to pierce your shields?

As you yourselves have certainly learned, a knight needs three things above all: he must have strength, energy, and shrewdness; he must be unencumbered in his movements; and he must be able to draw his sword quickly. Why then, on the contrary, do you blind yourselves with effeminate locks of hair, and trip yourselves up in long and flowing tunics with cumbersome sleeves in which you bury your tender, delicate hands? Beyond all this is a troubling question of conscience: that despite all your armor, you have presumed to undertake such a dangerous business with such levity and frivolity. For the root of your disputes and the cause of your wars is nothing more than irrational flashes of anger, a thirst for empty glory, and the lust for material possessions. To kill or to be killed for such reasons is senseless.

6. See Maurice Keen, *Chivalry* (New Haven and London: Yale University Press, 1984), chap. 7 ("Heraldry and Heralds").

[Bernard describes the life-style of the Templars (chap. 4):] In order to shame those knights who fight for the devil rather than for God, I will briefly describe the [ideal] life and virtues of the knights of Christ, how they conduct themselves on the battlefield and at home, how they appear in public, and how they differ from secular knights.

First, they are disciplined and obedient. As Scripture says, the undisciplined son shall perish, and rebellion is the sin of witchcraft; to refuse obedience is to commit idolatry [1 Sam. 15:23]. Therefore these knights come and go at the order of their superior. They wear what he gives them, and they do not presume to wear or eat anything from any other source. Thus they shun every excess in clothing and food, and are content with what is essential. They live as brothers in joyful and sober company, without wives or children. So that their spiritual perfection will lack nothing, they dwell in one family without any personal property, and carefully keep the unity of the Spirit in the bond of peace. You may say that they have but one heart and soul to the point that no one follows his own will but rather seeks to follow the commander.

They never sit idly nor wander aimlessly. On the rare occasion when they are not on duty, they earn their bread by repairing worn armor and torn clothing, or by simply putting things in order. For the rest, they are guided by the common needs and by the orders of the master.

There is no distinction [by rank] among them: deference is shown to merit rather than to noble birth. They rival one another in mutual consideration, and they carry one another's burdens, thus fulfilling the law of Christ [Gal. 6:2]. No inappropriate word, idle deed, unrestrained laughter, not even the slightest whisper or murmur is left uncorrected, once detected. They forswear dice and chess. They abhor hunting, and they take no delight in the ridiculous cruelty of falconry. As for jesters, magicians, bards, troubadours, and jousters, they despise and reject them as vanities and unhealthy distractions. They wear their hair short in accordance with the apostle's saying that it is shameful for a man to cultivate flowing locks [1 Cor. 11:14]. Indeed, seldom do they wash, and never do they set their hair, being content to appear tousled and dusty, bearing the marks of the sun and of their armor.

When the battle is at hand, they arm themselves inwardly with faith and outwardly with steel rather than with decorations of gold, since their business is to strike fear in the enemy rather than to incite cupidity. They seek out strong and fast horses rather than well-plumed ones, for they fight to win rather than to display pomp. They think not of glory but rather seek to be formidable. At the same time, they are not quarrelsome, rash, or unduly hasty, but draw themselves up into orderly ranks in a sober, prudent, and purposeful manner, as we read of the fathers: the true Israelite is a man of peace, even when he goes forth to battle.

In the thick of battle, this knight sets aside his previous gentleness, as if to say: "Do I not hate those who hate you, O Lord; am I not disgusted with your enemies?" [Psalms 139:21] They at once fall violently upon the enemy, regarding them as so many sheep. No matter how outnumbered, they never are awed by the fierce enemy hordes. Nor do they overestimate their own strength, but trust in the Lord to grant them victory. They remember the words of Maccabees: "It is simple enough for a multitude to be vanquished by a handful. It makes no difference to the God in heaven whether he grants deliverance by the hands of few or many, for victory in war depends not on a big army, and bravery is not a gift of heaven" [1 Macc. 3:18–20]. On many occasions they had seen one man pursue a thousand, and two put ten thousand to flight.

Thus, in a wondrous and unique way, these knights appear gentler than lambs, yet fiercer than lions. I do not know if it is more appropriate to call them monks or knights; perhaps it is better to recognize them as being both, for they lack neither monastic meekness nor military fortitude. What can I say except that God has empowered this [new order], and it is a marvelous sight to my eyes. God chose these men whom he recruited from the ends of the earth; they are valiant men of Israel chosen to guard the tomb of Solomon, each man, sword in hand, superbly trained to conduct war.

[The Temple of Jerusalem, chap. 5:] The quarters [of these knights] are in the very temple of Jerusalem, which is not as vast as the ancient masterpiece of Solomon but no less glorious. Truly all the magnificence of that first temple lay in perishable gold and silver, in polished stone and precious woods, whereas the beauty and gracious adornment of the present temple is in the religious fervor and well-disciplined behavior of its occupants. In the first temple one could contemplate all sorts of beautiful colors, while in the present temple one may venerate all sorts of virtues and good works. Indeed, holiness is the fitting ornament for God's house. Now one is able to delight in splendid merits rather than shining marble, and to be captivated by pure hearts rather than gilded paneling. Of course the facade of the temple is adorned, but with weapons rather than jewels, and its walls are decorated not by the ancient golden crowns but by shields. In place of candlesticks, censers, and ewers, this house is well appointed with saddles, bits, and lances.

### 80. A GIFT TO THE TEMPLARS, 1201

*Villain of Aulnay was the youngest brother of Erard, former marshal of Champagne,[7] and nephew of Geoffroy of Villehardouin, the current marshal, when he made this gift to the Templars. Villain had already made an oral donation while he was in Acre, probably in the late 1190s, in the presence of two Templar officials (who happened to be natives of Champagne, from villages not far from Aulnay). On his return home, Villain repeated his donation in the presence of his closest friends and had this charter drawn up to transfer title.[8] Such a generous gift suggests that Villain was repaying the Templars for their aid during his stay in the Holy Land.*

Be it known to all, present and future, that I, Villain of Aulnay, being of sound mind, have given in alms to the Knights Templar all that I possess in the village of Sancey with all its appurtenances, including mills, woods, meadows, arable land, and streams. This gift I made for the salvation of my soul and for the souls of my family and my lord Count Henry [II, d. 1197 in Acre], who gave me that village [in fief].

This gift I make freely and without any reservation. Witnesses [to the written act] are: Lord Oger of Saint-Chéron and his brother Lord William, Lord Guy of Chappes, Lord Clarembaud of Chappes, Lord Geoffroy of Villehardouin [marshal], and Lord Geoffroy "Putefin." This gift was made [originally in Acre] in the presence of Brother William of Arzillières, who was at that time marshal of the Knights Templar, and Brother Robert of Chamville, who was at that time preceptor of the Templar house in Acre. So that this gift remain firm and stable, I have confirmed this letter with my seal, and I have asked Lord Oger of Saint-Chéron to witness the donation and to seal this charter with his seal. Done in the year of grace 1201.

## Prince Henry and the Second Crusade

The future Count Henry the Liberal (1152–1181) was only nineteen years old when he took the cross on Easter Day, 1146, at Vézelay in the pres-

7. See Doc. 98.
8. Text in Petit, *Histoire* 3: 481–482, no. 1455 (erroneously dated 1205).

ence of King Louis VII and numerous barons. Having been exposed from an early age to public affairs by his father, Count Thibaut II ("the Great") of Champagne, Henry was acquainted with the leading political and religious figures of the day. Among them was the charismatic preacher at Vézelay, Bernard of Clairvaux, who was a special friend of the comital family and frequent recipient of its benefactions. Although Bernard had refused to use his influence to obtain an ecclesiastical placement for Henry's younger brother William (later archbishop of Reims, 1176–1202),[9] he did write a letter of introduction for Henry to the Byzantine emperor, Manuel Comnenus, asking the emperor to knight the young count (Doc. 81).

The royal expedition was a difficult one, marked by poor leadership, rough terrain, harsh weather, Byzantine fears, and effective Turkish archery, not to mention Queen Eleanor's disruptive presence. Young Henry's valorous deeds and loyalty to the king were much appreciated by the twenty-seven-year-old Louis, who wrote a letter of appreciation to Henry's father, Count Thibaut II (Doc. 82). As soon as Henry returned to France, however, he displayed his newly developed military prowess in a tournament challenging the king's own brother, Robert. Bernard of Clairvaux, who had long railed against the increasingly popular sport of tournaments because of their gratuitous violence, appealed to the regent, Abbot Suger of Saint-Denis, to prohibit the scheduled tournament (Doc. 83). The event must have taken place anyway because soon afterward Henry had to negotiate the release of a vassal who was captured at the tournament (Doc. 84). While deferent to Abbots Bernard and Suger, Henry must have treated his mother badly after he became count (January 1152), for she sought Bernard's intervention. Bernard consoled the countess with the hope that Henry would outgrow his youthful callousness (Doc. 85).

## 81. A LETTER OF INTRODUCTION TO THE BYZANTINE EMPEROR, 1147

*Bernard of Clairvaux writes a letter of introduction to Manuel Comnenus, emperor of Constantinople (1143–1180), on behalf of Count Henry requesting the emperor to gird the young man with the sword of knighthood.[10] If the emperor did comply, he probably did so in late October 1147 when the French barons,*

9. See *The Letters of Saint Bernard of Clairvaux*, trans. Bruno Scott James (London: Burns & Oates, 1953), 419–420, no. 341.

10. Text in *Recueil des historiens*, 15:607–608, no. 81. This letter, written by Bernard's secretary, Nicholas of Clairvaux, was not included in Bernard's official letter collections probably because it did not suit the anti-Byzantine feeling in France after the failure of the Second Crusade.

*promising to respect Byzantine imperial claims, did homage to Manuel before heading into Asia Minor.*[11]

To the exalted and glorious Manuel [Comnenus], emperor of Constantinople. Brother Bernard, called abbot of Clairvaux, sends greeting and prayers. If I have the audacity to write to your majesty, it is not because of insolence but rather my confidence in your charity. For who am I, and where is the house of my father in Israel, that I presume to address such a renowned emperor, pauper and unworthy person that I am, separated from you further by a vast expanse of land and an even larger body of water? What relation can there be between your high stature and my humble person if not in the humility of Christ, which is the glory of princes and judges, of kings as well as the common people? The magnificence and glory of your name have spread across the earth: "For this reason I bow my knees before the Father from whom every family in heaven and on earth is named" [Eph. 3:14–15], so that you may be promoted from your kingdom to that kingdom which is eternal.

Not deserving any favor on my own part, I have dared to send you the bearer of this letter, a young man of great nobility, so that you may receive his oath of knighthood and gird him with the sword against the enemies of Christ.[12] Many courts [for such a ceremony] are open to this young man, but I have thought it better for him to share your incomparable prestige so that he will remember for the rest of his life from whom he received the dignity of arms. Never would I have made this request if the cause of Christ were not at stake, the Christ for whom this young man has committed himself to a long and arduous journey. Whatever you do for him, you do for me.

For the rest, most exalted emperor, now is the time to show your generosity. The earth trembles because the King in heaven has lost the land he walked in. Soon the enemies of the Lord will attack his city [Jerusalem] and the tomb where the fruit of the Virgin Mary was embalmed in aromatic linen and where he was resurrected, the finest flower ever to appear on earth. So, at the command of the pope [Eugenius III] and after my own exhortations, the king of the French [Louis VII] and a multitude

11. It is not certain that Manuel did knight Henry, but given Bernard's sponsorship of the Second Crusade and Manuel's goodwill toward King Louis VII, it would seem highly likely that the ceremony did occur.

12. Jean Flori, *L'essor de la chevalerie, XIe-XIIe siècles* (Geneva: Droz, 1986), 211, notes that Bernard was not requesting a first, ordinary dubbing but rather the "giving of arms" to someone fighting on behalf of the church.

of princes, knights, and common people are preparing to cross your lands to reach the city of the living God. To you falls the honor of receiving them in accordance with your high dignity, power, and resources—for your own reputation and for the eternal salvation of your soul. Among these pilgrims I recommend to you above all others the son [Henry] of the illustrious prince Count Thibaut [II of Champagne]. He is young, noble, and of fine character, and he has devoted his first years under arms [as a knight] to the pursuit of justice rather than maliciousness.[13] He is the son of a man whose love of truth, kindness, and justice has made him honored among princes.

In gratitude for all these favors, I associate you with my house [Clairvaux] so that the bridegroom of the church, the son of Mary and our lord God, may grant you victory on earth and glory in heaven.

## 82. LOUIS VII PRAISES HENRY TO HIS FATHER, 1149

*On returning from the Holy Land in early 1149, Henry carried with him this laudatory letter to his father, Count Thibaut II, from King Louis VII, who remained in Antioch.[14] This was essentially a peace offering by Louis to heal the deep antagonism between him and Count Thibaut; moreover, while in the Holy Land Louis had betrothed his four-year-old daughter (the future Countess Marie) to Henry without the count's approval.[15]*

Louis, by the grace of God, king of the French, to his dearest Count Thibaut, greeting and deepest affection. The close friendship (*amor*) which I feel in my heart for your loyal son Henry has compelled me, in these remote parts, to write to you of his reputation. The devotion which he has shown me at all times and his loyal service have earned my ever increasing gratitude and have deepened my affection for him. For that, I thank you [for having sent him with me], and I point it out so that you may be even more proud of him yourself.

Know also that I wish to return to my kingdom with my barons but that the needs of the Eastern Church require my presence [in Antioch]

---

13. *Primitias suae militiae, non malitiae sed justiciae consecravit*: Bernard here evokes one of his favorite images in associating knighthood (*militia*) with evil deeds (*malitia*) (see Doc. 79). Henry was an exception.

14. Text in *Recueil des historiens*, 15:502, no. 53. Extreme dates are July 24, 1148, to April 3, 1149, but Arbois de Jubainville (*Histoire*, 2:391 n. 1) argues for late 1148 or early 1149 (before Easter, April 3).

15. See Theodore Evergates, "Louis VII and the Counts of Champagne," in *The Second Crusade and the Cistercians*, ed. Michael Gervers (New York: St. Martin's, 1992), 109–117.

until Easter [April 3, 1149]. Since the honor of my crown and the security of my kingdom rest especially on your fidelity [to me], I ask and pray that you diligently protect my kingdom and prevent any evil machinations against my crown.[16] Be assured that I will depart without fail immediately after Easter to return to my realm and resume its protection.

### 83.  BERNARD COMPLAINS TO ABBOT SUGER ABOUT A TOURNAMENT, 1149

*Bernard of Clairvaux asks Abbot Suger of Saint-Denis, regent of France, to prohibit a tournament planned by Henry of Champagne and the king's brother, Robert, on their return to France in the spring of 1149.[17] Robert was an aggressive young man known to have plotted against Louis during the crusade, and so the projected tournament seemed a deliberate provocation.[18] Bernard reminds Suger of the church's prohibition of tournaments.*

To his venerable father and lord Suger, by the grace of God abbot of Saint-Denis, Brother Bernard, called abbot of Clairvaux, greeting and prayers. Now is the time and the occasion to take up the sword of the Spirit, which is the Word of God, against an evil practice which has arisen again. The men who have returned [from the Second Crusade before King Louis VII himself] have arranged to hold an accursed tournament after Easter [April 3, 1149] at which Lord Henry, son of the count [Thibaut II of Champagne], and Lord Robert [of Dreux], the king's brother, plan to fight and kill one another. What can we think of their motives in setting out for Jerusalem if they returned with such an attitude? How rightly it can be said of those two: "We have healed Babylon but she is not healed" [Jer. 51:9], and "[Oh Lord] thou has smitten them but they felt no anguish, thou hast consumed them but they refused to take correction" [Jer. 5:3]. After such hardship and such dangers [of the crusade] in which we were worn down by evil and grief, and while the kingdom is at peace and the king abroad, these two return to trouble the land. I beg you, as

16. Thibaut was not, in fact, custodian of France (as he had been during Louis's early years) because of the ill will created by the king's invasion of Champagne in 1142–1143; Louis is attempting here to reestablish good terms with Thibaut, as he knew that his own brother Robert was planning a rebellion in France in the king's absence.

17. Translation (slightly modified here) by Bruno Scott James in *The Letters of Saint Bernard of Clairvaux*, 476–477, no. 405. Latin text in Bernard's *Epistolae*, vol. 8 of *Sancti Bernardi Opera*, ed. J. Leclercq, C. H. Talbot, and H. M. Rochais (Rome: Editiones Cistercienses, 1978), 339–340, *ep.* 376.

18. See Genealogical Table 3 and Andrew W. Lewis, "Fourteen Charters of Robert I of Dreux (1152–1188)," *Traditio* 41 (1985): 144–179.

the highest authority of the realm, to oppose them with all your might by either persuasion or force, and thus to bring credit to yourself and to the kingdom and benefit to the church. I appeal to you to restore the discipline of the church.[19] I have written likewise to the prelates of Reims, Sens, Soissons, and Auxerre, and to Counts Thibaut [II of Champagne] and Ralph [of Vermandois, royal seneschal]. You must prevent this event for the sake of the lord king and of the pope, who is guardian of the realm.[20]

## 84. Henry requests a meeting with Abbot Suger, 1149

*Henry seeks a meeting with Abbot Suger to arrange the release of Anseric [I], lord of Montréal, who was captured at the recent tournament (see Doc. 83).[21]*

To Suger, venerable abbot of Saint-Denis [and regent], Henry son of Count Thibaut [II of Champagne], greeting. No doubt it has come to your attention that your vassal (*homo*) Renaud of Pomponne captured Anseric [I] of Montréal in the recent tournament. In order to resolve this situation, I entreat you to meet me at Meaux a week from Sunday, if you are not overwhelmed by other responsibilities. Know that I am your most faithful friend and that I have inquired more deeply into this matter than any other, as much for the affection you have shown me as for the true discretion I value in you. With your wise counsel, I wish to resolve this issue in the presence of both Anseric and Lord Renaud.

## 85. Bernard consoles Countess Mathilda over her son's behavior, ca. 1152

*Bernard of Clairvaux was a close friend of the comital family and often involved in their personal affairs. Here he responds to Countess Mathilda's anguish over the bad behavior of her son Henry, who had just succeeded his father, Thibaut II, as count of Champagne.[22]*

19. Bernard refers to the Council of Clermont (1130), canon 9, which prohibited tournaments; it was repeated at Lateran II (1139) and the Council of Reims (1148); quoted in Richard Barber and Juliet Barker, *Tournaments: Jousts, Chivalry and Pageants in the Middle Ages* (New York: Weidenfeld & Nicolson, 1989), 16–17.

20. The bull of March 1, 1146, proclaiming the crusade provided papal protection for the families and properties of crusaders, as well as other privileges; that text is translated in Louise and Jonathan Riley-Smith, *The Crusades: Idea and Reality, 1095–1274*, Documents of Medieval History, 4 (London: Edward Arnold, 1981), 57–59.

21. Text in *Recueil des historiens*, 15:511, no. 72. For the lords of Montréal, see Bouchard, *Sword, Mitre, and Cloister*, 338–340.

22. Translation (slightly modified here) by Bruno Scott James in *The Letters of Saint Bernard of Clairvaux*, 436–437, no. 365. Latin text in Bernard's *Epistolae*, 216–217, *ep.* 300.

I am sorry that your son has behaved badly toward you. I deplore as much the excesses of a son as the wrongs of a mother, although the misdeeds of a young man are excusable insofar as youth itself is responsible for them. Are you not aware that a young man's disposition and thoughts are from an early age prone to evil ways? But be assured that the example of his father's good deeds and alms will influence him for the better. Even though he does not now show you proper filial respect, you must continue to pray to God for him, as a mother ought not and cannot lose her maternal affection for her children. "Can a mother ever forget the son she bore in her womb? And if she were to, I will not be forgetful of you" [Isaiah 49:15]. We must pray and beseech God that a such a fine young man should be led to emulate his father's goodness, and to encourage his good behavior, we must treat him gently rather than nag and scold him. I am confident that we will soon see a change in him for the better. I desire nothing else. I wish he would treat others as he has treated me, for he has always done whatever I have requested. May God reward him for that. Since you have frequently asked me, I have often reminded him about his conduct toward you, and I will continue to do so.

## Preparing for a Crusade

A journey to the Holy Land, whether on a pilgrimage or an official crusade, was an expensive proposition that entailed careful preparation. Although kings and princes occasionally supported their followers by collecting extraordinary taxes like the Saladin Tithe (Doc. 88), the barons and knights usually had to finance their own expeditions. It was prudent for crusaders to resolve outstanding conflicts (usually over property) with the church, to provide for their families in the event of death (Docs. 86, 87), and to obtain cash for the trip by mortgaging or selling property (Doc. 89; see also Doc. 76). Pope Eugenius III, in fact, had authorized knights to mortgage their fiefs to monasteries in order to finance the Second Crusade.[23] For some great nobles, preparing for a crusade was almost a ritual (Doc. 90).

23. Translated text in Riley-Smith, *The Crusades*, 57–59, no. 5. See also Giles Constable, "The Financing of the Crusades in the Twelfth Century," in *Outremer: Studies in the History of the Crusading Kingdom of Jerusalem*, ed. B. Z. Kedar, H. E. Mayer, and R. C. Smail (Jerusalem: Yad Izhak Ben-Zvi Institute, 1982), 64–88.

## 86. Josbert of La Ferté-sur-Aube settles his affairs, 1146

*Josbert of La Ferté-sur-Aube, viscount of Dijon and a relative of Bernard of Clairvaux, here gives property to Clairvaux in preparation for the Second Crusade.*[24]

I, Thibaut [II], count of Blois [-Champagne], make known to all men, present and future, that Josbert of La Ferté-sur-Aube, about to go to Jerusalem, has given to God and Notre-Dame of Clairvaux whatever he possesses in the village of Perrecin,[25] retaining nothing for himself or his heir. If, however, he returns from Jerusalem he may, if he chooses, enjoy for his lifetime the lordship (*dominatio*) and justice over the villagers there, a right that he shares with three other lords of that village; but after his death that right will revert to the abbey. All the rest of his possessions both in the village and within its district that he possesses alone he has given to Clairvaux in perpetuity, no matter whether he survives the crusade or dies on it.[26]

At La Ferté-sur-Aube Josbert invested Abbot Bernard of Clairvaux with the title to these possessions, with the approval of his wife Gertrude in the presence of Geoffroy, bishop of Langres, and myself [Count Thibaut]. I and my son Henry have approved this donation, since the property is held in fief from me, and I ordered this charter to be written. Witnesses to the donation were: Hilduin of Vendeuvre, Walter of Bernon, and Peter "the Purse," my knights, as well as Josbert's brother-in-law Hugh, lord of Beaumont, Roger of Orges, Guiard of Ville-sous-la-Ferté, and John, mayor of Perrecin.

This was done at La Ferté-sur-Aube, in the year of our Lord 1145,[27] during the reign of Louis [VII], son of Louis [VI], king of the French.

## 87. A townsman of Troyes finances his journey, 1147

*In the spring of 1147 Odo, a townsman of Troyes, sold his mills to the priory of Saint-Sépulchre for his crusade expenses. He also leased his oven to the priory for the duration of his journey, stipulating that it be restored to his family if he did not return.*[28]

24. Text in Waquet, *Recueil*, 1:16–17, no. 10.
25. A village near the abbey that has since disappeared.
26. In fact, Josbert's line ended with his death on the crusade; the only possession he did not alienate, the viscounty of Dijon, passed to his niece (see Petit, *Histoire*, 2:454).
27. In Champagne it was customary to begin the new year at Easter; since this document was probably drawn up after Christmas, 1145, and before the next Easter (March 31, 1146), it was dated "1145."
28. Text in Arbois de Jubainville, *Histoire*, 3:434–435, no. 103.

I, Thibaut [II], count of Blois [-Champagne], make known to all, present and future, that Odo [of Troyes], son of Goslen, setting out for Jerusalem, has given in perpetuity to God and the priory of Saint-Sépulchre[29] and to the monks serving God there: his [nearby] mills of Espincey for which he received 40*l.* in coin from the priory's generosity. When Odo returns from his journey, if God wills it, the monks will pay him [an additional] 20*l.* in coin. In his absence the monks may also hold his oven. Thus when he returns he will receive 20*l.* and the monks will return the oven to him in full possession. If however Odo dies en route, after certain knowledge of his death is received, the monks will return that oven and pay those 20*l.* to his wife and [eldest] son.

Odo's wife Ameline and his sons Hugh, Peter, and John, and his daughter Comitissa and her husband, Bauter of "Monteriniacus," approved of this arrangement. So that no dispute arise in the future, this agreement was reached in my presence and confirmed in my hand. And to preserve more certain memory of it, I have had this document drawn up and by my authority sealed with my seal. Witnesses were: Hugh "Bellus," Peter, son of David, Thibaut "Pullus," Bartholomew of "Wareis" and his nephew Peter, Arnulph, and Archer of Chappes. Done at Jouy-le-Châtel, in the year of our Lord 1147, in the year that Louis [VII], king of the French, and my son Henry [I] set out for Jerusalem with a large number of barons and commoners in order to conquer the defiant Turks.

## 88. COUNT HENRY II COLLECTS THE SALADIN TITHE, 1188

*In 1188 King Philip II of France decreed the Saladin Tithe within his kingdom to support the Third Crusade: a 10 percent tax on income to be collected from all those who did not take the cross, both laymen and ecclesiastics. The tax was widely resisted by the church, which feared that the payment of taxes to laymen would set a dangerous precedent.[30] Here Count Henry II delivers charters of non-prejudice to the canons of the cathedral church of Sens (Doc. A)[31] and to the residents of Chablis, an important wine-producing town under the count's protection (Doc. B).[32]*

(A) I, Henry, count palatine of Troyes, make known to all, present and future, that according to the decree of the lord king, Philip of France,

---

29. Located at Villacerf, near Payns.
30. See Elizabeth Siberry, *Criticism of Crusading, 1095–1274* (Oxford: Clarendon Press, 1985), 120–123.
31. Text in Quantin, *Cartulaire général*, 2:393, no. 385.
32. Text in ibid., 2:417, no. 412.

and the barons of the realm for support [of the expedition] to recapture Jerusalem, I should collect a 10 percent tax from the revenue of land that the canons of the cathedral of Sens possess in my county [of Champagne]. The canons, however, fearing that this instance might become a precedent, asked me to renounce all future claim to the tax. Wishing to repay their fidelity to me, I declare by this letter that I have collected the above-mentioned tax from their land in my county only for the above stated reason, and that henceforth I will not exact or accept any other tax or aid from those lands.

So that this renunciation will be valid in perpetuity, and so that my heirs will not presume to exact any kind of tax or aid, I have validated this letter with my seal. Done at Provins, in the year of our Lord 1188. Written by William [chancery scribe].

(B) I, Henry, count palatine of Troyes, make known to all, present and future, that when I decided to go to Jerusalem, I took 300*l.* from the residents of Chablis. Since I do not have any other right or authority to tax them except for Christ's business and as an aid for my journey, that money was collected for me with the consent and permission of Saint-Martin of Tours [the monastery to which the town belonged]. So that this notice retain its validity in the future, I have confirmed this letter with my seal. Done at Troyes, in the year of our Lord 1190. [This document was] given [to the residents of Chablis] by the hand of Haice [of Plancy], chancellor [of Champagne]. Written by John [chancery scribe].[33]

### 89. A knight finances his sons' trip to Constantinople, 1212

*In 1212 the knight Hagan of Ervy, who had survived the Third Crusade (see Doc. 51), sold an 8l. rent to the chapter of Saint-Etienne of Troyes so that his two sons could travel to Constantinople.[34] By this act Hagan completed the alienation of a 10l. fief that Count Henry I had granted him fifty years earlier.[35]*

To all who see this letter, greeting from Hagan of Ervy. Be it known to all that I used to collect an annual revenue of 10*l.* assigned on the sales tax paid by the merchants of Ypres at Troyes [during the Fairs of Champagne], which Count Henry [I] the father gave me. With the consent of

---

33. In 1239 Count Thibaut IV seems to have used this letter as a precedent to collect 300*l.* for his own crusade.

34. Text in "Cartulary of Saint-Etienne of Troyes," fol. 79v.

35. See Evergates, *Feudal Society in the Bailliage of Troyes,* 180.

my sons Henry and Guy, I gave 2*l*. of that annual revenue to the church of Saint-Etienne of Troyes [in 1205 and 1207] for the celebration of an annual commemorative Mass for me in perpetuity.

Later, since my sons wished to go to Constantinople but lacked the means to outfit themselves for that journey, I sold the remaining 8*l*. of that revenue, with my sons' approval, to Saint-Etienne for 70*l*., in coin of Provins, so that they would be able to pay their way.

I have affirmed and sworn that neither I nor anyone at my instigation will reclaim this revenue, and I will guarantee valid title to Saint-Etienne. In testimony of which I have sealed this letter with my seal. Done in the year of our Lord 1212.

90. THE SENESCHAL DESCRIBES HIS PREPARATIONS, 1248
*In his "Life of Saint Louis" written in the early fourteenth century, Jean of Joinville, seneschal of Champagne, recalls his preparations for the first crusade of Louis IX.*[36]

At Easter, in the year of our Lord 1248, I summoned my men and my feudal tenants to Joinville. On Easter eve, when all the people I had summoned had arrived, my son John, [later] lord of Ancerville, was born to my first wife [Alice], who was the sister of the count of Grandpré.[37] All that week we feasted and danced, and my brother [Geoffroy], the lord of Vaucouleurs, and other wealthy men sponsored banquets, one after another, on Easter Monday, Tuesday, Wednesday, and Thursday.

On Friday I said to them: "My lords, I am going overseas and I do not know whether I will return, so if I have injured anyone, come forward and I will make amends, as I have always done for anyone who has a claim against me or my agents." And I dealt with each claim in the way the men on my lands considered right; so as not to influence the decisions, I withdrew from the discussion, and later I agreed without reservation to their recommendations.

Since I did not wish to take with me even a penny unjustly,[38] I went to Metz in Lorraine and mortgaged the greater part of my land. I can

36. Translation (slightly modified here) by M. R. B. Shaw from "The Life of Saint Louis," in *Joinville and Villehardouin: Chronicles of the Crusades* (London: Penguin Books, 1963), 192. French text in *Jean, sire de Joinville: Histoire de Saint Louis*, ed. Natalis de Wailly, 2d ed. (Paris: Firmin Didot, 1874), 63–64.

37. See Genealogical Table 2.

38. That is, to impose a crusade tax on his tenants, as most lords must have (see Doc. 76).

assure you that on the day I left my lands to go to the Holy Land, I did not have more than 1,000*l.* annual income, for my mother [Beatrice] was still alive.[39] Nevertheless, I took with me nine knights and two knights banneret. I bring these things to your [the reader's] attention so that you may understand that if God, who has never failed me, had not come to my help [while overseas], I would not have been able to have stayed the six years that I remained in the Holy Land.

## Consequences of the Crusades

Crusades were lengthy, perilous expeditions which often had serious repercussions at home. Prolonged absences raised a host of problems, some of which required judicial resolution (Doc. 91). Although well-born crusaders expected to be ransomed if they were captured (Doc. 92), the fall of Jerusalem to Saladin (1187) and the subsequent failure of the Third Crusade resulted in the death and capture of a staggering number of Westerners. John of Matha was so touched by the plight of the hostages that he founded a religious order called the Trinitarians whose mission was to redeem Christian captives (Doc. 93). The Fourth Crusade exacted its own toll; some unfortunates of that expedition would languish in captivity for many years (Docs. 94, 95).

91. THE HIGH COURT CONSIDERS A PILGRIM'S PROLONGED ABSENCE, 1166

*In the early 1160s Guy III, lord of Possesse, mortgaged his castle to Count Henry I and left the county, presumably for the Holy Land. His younger brother John succeeded to the lordship of Possesse (excluding its castle), but in 1165 decided to become a monk at Clairvaux. In that same year, the youngest brother Hugh placed his share of the inheritance under Count Henry's protection and left for the Holy Land. But Hugh only reached Calabria, Italy, where he married and settled, leaving the status of Possesse and its castle in abeyance. At this point the husband of Hugh's deceased sister, Guy of Garlande, brought suit claiming the castle on behalf of her eldest son, Hugh's nephew. Here the High Court allows the transfer of the castle if Hugh does not return within one year.[40]*

---

39. She retained her dower lands comprising at least one-third of Jean's inheritance.

40. Text in Henri d'Arbois de Jubainville, "Document sur l'obligation de la résidence imposée aux barons par le droit féodal champenois au douzième siècle," *Revue historique de droit français et étranger* 7 (1861): 69–70.

I, Henry, count palatine of Troyes, wish to announce by this letter that Guy of Garlande and his son Anselm petitioned me at a session of my court at Troyes for possession of the barony (*honore*) of Possesse because Hugh of Possesse, having married in Calabria, remains there. To decide this case, I convened a session of my court at Troyes on the Thursday following Christmas [December 29, 1166]. At that session the petitioners requested the barony by hereditary right, and I recognized the legitimacy of their claim. But Hugh, when he left for Jerusalem, placed his lands in my hand and later notified me by appropriate and well-known messengers that he wanted me to be guardian of his lands.

So my barons (*barones*) who were present at this hearing, namely Count Thibaut [V of Blois], my brother; Anselm of Traînel [butler of Champagne] and his brother Garnier; Simon of Broyes; William of Dampierre; Hugh of Plancy; Odo [of Pougy], constable [of Champagne]; Girard of Châlons-sur-Marne; Drogo of Provins and his brother Peter; Peter "the Purse" [chamberlain]; William [of Provins], marshal; and others decided that, to be fair, I should allow Hugh one year to return and reclaim his land. If Hugh does not return within the year, I will invest Guy and Anselm with their inheritance, saving however Hugh's right—if he should return later—and saving the [mortgage] redemption owed me for that fief.

It was also decided that in the interim I may, at my discretion, give possession of that fief to Guy and Anselm as custodians. Done at Troyes, in the year of our Lord 1166, in the presence of the above named witnesses. [Document] presented [to Guy and Anselm] by William the chancellor.

[Hugh did not return to Champagne. Guy redeemed the mortgage and gave Possesse to his son Anselm, whose descendants continued as lords of Possesse through the next century.]

## 92. COUNT HENRY'S VOW WHILE A HOSTAGE, 1182

*In May 1179 Count Henry I set out to revisit the Holy Land that he had seen as a young man on the Second Crusade. Captured while traveling from Jerusalem to Constantinople, he was eventually ransomed by the Byzantine emperor, Manuel Comnenus, the very person who may have dubbed him in 1147 (see Doc. 81). Henry was still in Constantinople when Manuel died and was succeeded by Alexis II; the new empress was Henry's niece Agnes, daughter of his sister, Queen Adele of France. Shortly after returning home, Henry died (March 1181). Here his brother William, the archbishop of Reims (1176–1202), recounts Henry's vow.*[41]

---

41. Text in Martène and Durand, *Thesaurus novus anecdotorum*, 1:619.

I, William, by the grace of God, archbishop of Reims and cardinal of S. Sabina, to all, present and future, who see this letter, greeting in the Lord. Be it known that my dearest brother Henry, while he was being held captive by the Muslims, made a vow to give 30*l*. annual revenue from the fairs of Bar-sur-Aube to the cathedral chapter of Saint-Mammès of Langres, as I have heard from his friends who were with him there. Since the lord God returned him safely to his own land, Henry repeated his vow publicly in front of his great men [his barons] and invested Manasses, bishop of Langres, with that 30*l*. revenue for the chapter. The count then ordered his chancellor, Haice [of Plancy], to draw up a charter attesting to that donation and to validate it with the count's seal. But in the commotion and grief following the count's death, the chancellor, occupied by more serious matters, forgot to draw up the document.

The said bishop of Langres requested the assignment of that revenue from me and my dearest sister-in-law Marie [of France], countess of Troyes. After conducting an inquiry into the truth of the matter with me and my brother Stephen [count of Sancerre] and other barons who were present [at her court], she granted that 30*l*. revenue to the chapter of Langres: it is to be collected each year from the payment made by the men of Bar-sur-Aube on the Feast of Saint-Remi [January 13]. If by chance that payment does not yield 30*l*., the revenue will be collected instead from the fair revenues of Bar-sur-Aube between the first Sunday before Easter and Easter Day.

That 30*l*. revenue is to be distributed to the canons who are present at Matins. Each week in that church a Mass will be celebrated for the soul of the count, and his name is to be inscribed in the missal book so that his anniversary may be solemnly observed.

In testimony of which I have had this charter written at the request of both parties [the bishop and the countess], and I have confirmed it with my seal. Done in the year of our Lord 1182. Given [to the bishop] by Lambinus, my chancellor.

### 93. The Rule of the Order of Trinitarians, 1198

*Saladin's rapid conquest of crusader settlements in the 1180s, culminating in the capture of Jerusalem itself in late 1187, resulted in enormous numbers of killed and captured Westerners. The plight of the prisoners led John of Matha in the early 1190s to found a religious order, called the Trinitarians, dedicated to securing the release of Christian captives.[42] The center of the Trinitarians and the*

42. For a comparison with Spain, see James W. Brodman, *Ransoming Captives in Crusader Spain: The Order of Merced on the Christian-Islamic Frontier* (Philadelphia: University of Pennsylvania Press, 1986).

*site of their general chapter meetings was Cerfroid in Champagne. Pope Inno-*
*cent III recognized the new order and recorded its Rule in his bull of De-*
*cember 17, 1198.*[43]

[1] The brothers of the house of the Holy Trinity shall live in chastity, without personal possessions, and in obedience to the prelate of their house who shall be called "minister."

[2] The brothers will divide all things lawfully acquired into three equal parts. Two parts will support works of mercy and provide modest support for the brothers and their household staff. The third part is to be reserved for the ransom of captives who are imprisoned for the faith of Christ by pagans [Muslims]: that sum may be used to purchase their ransom or the ransom of pagan captives who can be exchanged for Christian ones, according to their personal merits and status. When money or any other gift is received by the brothers, one-third will be reserved for this purpose, always with the donor's consent; otherwise, it is not to be accepted. However, gifts of land, meadows, vineyards, woods, buildings, livestock, and the like, are not to be divided; rather their produce will be divided into three equal parts after deducting expenses (which are calculated at one-half of the produce). Produce which requires little expense is to be entirely divided into three equal parts. But clothing, shoes, and other small items for the brothers' use and which do not yield much profit if sold, are exempted from the equal division unless the minister of the house and the brothers decide otherwise. These matters are to be discussed every Sunday, if possible, in chapter meeting. If any of these things—such as clothing, land, livestock or small items—is sold, the sum is to be divided into three equal parts.

[3] All the churches of this order are to be named Holy Trinity, and are to be of simple construction.

[4–5] In each residence there may be three cleric-brothers, three lay-brothers, and one procurator who will be called "minister." He will be addressed "Brother X, minister of the house of the Holy Trinity." The brothers are bound to promise and to give him obedience, and he is to administer faithfully to them.

43. Translation of the Rule (slightly abridged and modified here) by Joseph J. Gross, based on his edition, *The Trinitarians' Rule of Life: Texts of the Six Principle Editions* (Rome: The Trinitarian Historical Institute, 1983), 9–15. The growth of the order is traced in Joseph J. Gross, "The Trinitarian Order's Apostolate of the Ransom of Christian Captives and Works of Mercy during the First Centuries of its History: A Special Consideration of the Communities Located in the Interior of the European Continent and in Great Britain," in *Captivis Libertas: Congresso dell'Apostolato Redentivo-Misericordioso dell'Ordine Trinitario*, vol. 1 (Rome: Centro Trinitario, 1982), 51–82.

[6–7] The brothers are to wear white, woolen garments. They may have a fur-lined overgarment and breeches, which they may not remove while reposing. They are to sleep in their woolen garments without featherbeds or mattresses except during illness. They may, however, have a pillow to support their heads.

[8] The brothers will wear the emblem [the cross of the Order] on their capes.

[9] The brothers may not mount or possess horses. They may ride only asses.

[10] The brothers will drink wine so watered down that it can be consumed in sobriety.

[11] The brothers will fast on Monday, Wednesday, Friday, and Saturday from September 13 until Easter, except on solemn feast days. From Advent to Christmas, and from the Sunday before Lent until Easter, they are to fast on Lenten foods except on Sundays. They will also observe other customary fasts. But at certain times the minister may, at his discretion, relax the fast on account of a brother's age, travel, or other good reason, or he may even prolong the fast.

[12] The brothers may eat meat given as gifts or from their own livestock only on Sundays from Easter to Advent, and from Christmas to the third Sunday before Lent, and on Christmas, Epiphany, Ascension, Assumption, Purification, and All Saints' Day.

[13] The brothers may not buy anything to consume except bread and food taken with bread, namely beans and peas and like vegetables, greens, oil, eggs, milk, cheese, and fruit. They may not buy meat, fish, or wine except for the needs of the infirm, weak, or poor, or for use at great feasts. The brothers may, however, purchase and raise livestock. While traveling the brothers may buy—but sparingly—wine and fish during Lent; if they receive gifts, they are to consume whatever is necessary and to divide the remainder in three parts. But if they are on the way to ransom captives, they must retain the totality of all gifts—less expenses—for the ransom of captives.

[14] In cities, villages, and fortified places where the brothers have houses, they may not eat or drink outside the house, even if invited to do so, except to take water in a religious house or in a respectable dwelling. They may not remain outside their house at night, nor are they to dwell, eat or drink in taverns or disreputable places. If a brother does so, his minister will punish him.

[15] Cleric-brothers and lay-brothers shall eat the same food and use the same clothing, dormitory, refectory, and table.

[16] The infirm are to eat and sleep apart under the care of a lay- or cleric-brother. The infirm are warned not to ask for rich or sumptuous foods but should be content with suitable and healthful moderation.

[17] One of the more discreet and kinder brothers is to care for guests, the poor, and travelers. He is to attend them and give them the comfort of charity, but he is to ask before admitting them whether they will be content with what is served to the brothers, for it is not proper for anyone to be served rich and sumptuous foods. Whatever is offered them will be presented cheerfully; to no one will evil be returned in kind. If anyone, and especially a religious, comes to receive hospitality, he is to be received kindly with charity, to the extent possible.

[18] No brother, lay or cleric, is to be without a duty, if possible. Anyone able but unwilling to work will be expelled, for the Apostle says "he who does not work should not eat."

[19] The brothers will observe silence always in their church, always in the refectory, and always in the dormitory. In other places they may speak about necessary matters, but at the proper time and in subdued voice, humbly and respectfully. Elsewhere, they must speak honestly and without scandal. And they must be above reproach in their comportment, gestures, life, and behavior.

[20] The minister will hold a chapter meeting with his brothers every Sunday if possible. They are to be honest with him, and he with them, about the business of the house and about the gifts, so that one-third may be set aside for the ransom of captives.

[21] Every Sunday the brothers and members of the household are to be exhorted about their religious beliefs and moral responsibilities.

[22] The brothers are to be judged in chapter meeting regarding all matters and complaints.

[23] No brother is to accuse another in public unless he can prove the accusation. Whoever makes an unfounded charge is to suffer the punishment the accused might have incurred if he were found guilty, unless the minister pardons the accuser. If anyone causes a scandal or, God forbid, strikes another, he is to be punished according to the judgment of the minister. If anyone should suffer an offense from a brother, the injured one should suffer patiently; when emotions have calmed down, the injured brother will admonish and correct the offender in a kind and fraternal manner between themselves up to three times, both to do penance for the offense and to refrain from repeating it. If the offender does not listen, he is to be reported to the minister for correction. If a brother who has

caused scandal wishes to make amends, he is to prostrate himself fully at the feet of the minister begging forgiveness.

[24] The general chapter meeting is to be held annually during the week following Pentecost.

[25] If a house must contract a debt for some necessity, the brothers must give their advice and consent in chapter meeting to prevent suspicions and rumors [of corruption].

[26] If anyone damages a house's property, he is first to be warned charitably by the brothers and then by other neighbors before the matter is taken to court.

[27] The minister is elected by general agreement of the brothers. He is not to be chosen on the basis of his family's standing but rather for his own meritorious life, wisdom, and learning. He must be a priest or cleric suitable for orders. The minister, whether major or minor, must be a priest. [Items 28–30 deal with confessions by the brothers, the responsibilities of the minister, and procedures for deposing the minister.]

[31] Anyone who wishes to be a brother of this order must first serve in the order for God's sake for one year at his own expense, except for food, retaining his own clothing and all his belongings. After one year he is to be received in the order, if the minister and brothers deem him suitable and if there is an opening. Nothing [that is, no gift] may be required for his admission. If he does give something to the order, it may be received provided that it does not involve the church in litigation. If there is any doubt about a person's suitability in the order, the probation may be extended. If anyone becomes impatient with the discipline or cannot adjust to the life of the house, he may leave with all his possessions. No one is to be received into the order before completing his twentieth year.

[32] The brothers may not accept mortgaged property from laymen except for tithes, and then only with the bishop's permission.

[33] The brothers may not take oaths, except under dire necessity and with the minister's permission, or when ordered to do so by their bishop or apostolic legate.

[34] Anything sold [by a house] with a defect is to be indicated as such.

[35] The brothers may not accept for deposit any gold or silver or coins [as did the Templars].

[36] When a brother becomes ill, he must on that day confess his sins and receive communion. [Item 37 deals with the absolution of the deceased.]

[38] Every night—at least in the hospice in the presence of the poor—common prayer is to be held for the security and peace of the holy Roman Church and of all Christendom, for its benefactors, and for those for whom the church customarily prays.

### 94. A MOTHER SEEKS TO RANSOM HER SON, 1215

*Rosceline of La Ferté-sur-Aube contracted with the Hospitallers to secure the release of her captured son Guiard in Acre. Here Countess Blanche of Champagne approves of Rosceline's alienation from her fief to pay the Hospitallers.*[44]

I, Blanche, countess palatine of Troyes, make known to all, present and future, that my loyal and faithful Rosceline of La Ferté-sur-Aube has affirmed in my presence that she made this contract with the Hospitallers: that if they secure the unrestricted release in Acre of her son Guiard, who is held captive by the Muslims, she will give the Hospitallers 10*l.* rent collectible from the fief that she holds from me at Bar-sur-Aube. And I, for the love of God and at Rosceline's request, have approved that grant [that is, alienation] from my fief; my dearest son Count Thibaut [aged fourteen years] also has approved. In testimony of which I have had this letter drawn up and validated with my seal. Done in the year of grace 1214, in the month of February [1215].

### 95. A THIRTY-YEAR CAPTIVITY, 1233

*In 1202 Renaud II, lord of Dampierre-le-Château, led a large contingent of knights from eastern France on the Fourth Crusade. He and his party, however, did not join the main body of crusaders at Venice, but rather headed south from Piacenza to Apulia. From there they sailed directly to Syria and entered the service of Bohemond IV, prince of Antioch. Ambushed and captured on May 16, 1203, near Laodicia in Syria, Renaud would spend the next thirty years in captivity in Aleppo. He was ransomed by the Hospitallers in 1231 and returned home by 1233.*

*Renaud's return after such a long absence was not easy: his sons had alienated some of his property and, more seriously, the monks of Montiers-en-Argonne had usurped much of the rest. In 1233 the marshal of Champagne, Geoffroy of Louppy, arbitrated Renaud's dispute with the monks and awarded him an indemnity. Renaud also took the monks to the court of the bishop of Châlons-sur-Marne, claiming 1,500l. lost revenue (50l. annually for thirty years) but later*

---

44. Text in Delaville le Roulx, *Cartulaire général*, 2:171, no. 1434.

*dropped that case. Here Renaud explains his claim and the resolution of his two lawsuits.*[45]

I, Renaud, lord of Dampierre, wish all present and future to know that when I returned from overseas, I became involved in many disputes with the abbot and monks of Montiers-en-Argonne over property which I claimed that they took from me while I was detained overseas, namely: part of a wood called the Allod of Sommevesle which I claimed that the monks had enclosed within the dike of Tilloy; the land rents of that village; the major and minor tithes of Le Châtellier and Remicourt, except for two parts of the minor tithe of Le Châtellier which the chaplain of Gomicourt has; two parts of the major and minor tithes of La Neuville-aux-Bois; the sale of the woods of Tilloy and other woods, half of whose revenues I used to give to Saint-Martin of Paris; the woods which Renarth "Chainoi" held from me; the acquisitions which the monks made beyond the bridge of the mill at Vière, which I claimed they were not allowed to make; two carucates of land which I claimed in the parish of Freginville and two carucates in the parish of Epensival; the new grange which I claimed was built within my territory and justice; the old woods of the abbey and the tile works built in those woods; the field next to Epense overgrown by neglect; the pool and the mill of Vière; the damages committed by the monks in my woods, and the trees felled by the monks of which I claim half.

A settlement to these claims was arranged through the mediation of the discreet Geoffroy, lord of Louppy and marshal of Champagne, who first conducted an inquest to determine the truth of the charges in order better to arrange a settlement. Having diligently studied the matter, and with the unanimous consent of a council of wise men and with my approval, the marshal decided: that I would receive 600*l.*, heavy coin of Champagne, and ten cows and one hundred sheep from the monks, to whom I quitclaim all quarrels and disputed possessions now and in the future, for me and my heirs. So that this settlement be firmly observed, I bound myself by oath in the church of Saint-Medard in the presence of many worth men. My dear and only son Anselm,[46] who gave his consent and approval to the settlement, swore to what I have sworn in the same church.

45. Document in AD, Marne, 20 H 11 (Montiers-en-Argonne), no. 7.
46. Renaud's eldest son, Renaud, had died before his father's return.

Be it noted in this letter that whatever the monks acquired after my departure overseas up to the time of my return, in any place under my lordship and power, from either my own lands or my fiefs, whether they acquired it from my sons Renaud and Anselm or from my brother Henry or my sister Marie, I, Renaud, lord of Dampierre, approve and confirm; that is, I approve and confirm whatever is contained in the [abbey's] charters of acquisition.

I also brought suit against the monks in the court of the venerable Philip, bishop of Châlons-sur-Marne, seeking 1,500*l.* which I claimed they took from the produce of my land [during the past thirty years]. I abandoned that claim in the hand of the abbot, in return for which the monks released me from the suit they brought against me before the papal legates John, Garin, and Ralph, archdeacons of Châlons-sur-Marne, over damages they said I committed in the woods of Tilloy.

So that neither I nor my heirs will ever trouble the monks again, and so that this settlement remain in perpetuity, I and my heirs have agreed to all that is contained in this charter. I have corroborated this charter by my seal. Done in the year of grace 1233.

[Renaud died within months of this settlement.]

# 5 Acts of Violence, Liberality, and Charity

Although the documents drawn up primarily for legal and administrative purposes furnish a large dossier for reconstructing medieval practices, they lack the compelling narrative of human events described by Orderic Vitalis,[1] Galbert of Bruges,[2] and crusade historians like William of Tyre, Geoffroy of Villehardouin, and Jean of Joinville.[3] Occasionally, however, the scribe of a routine document was able to capture the fear, anger, generosity, or anguish of those whose affairs he was reporting, as the documents in this section illustrate.

## Violence

The cases of violence presented here range from a personal assault, which nearly cost the young Count Hugh his life (Doc. 96), to the dramatic execution of religious dissidents (Doc. 100). Conflicts between lay lords and the church were a common source of violence, as the former resorted to arms while the latter brandished ecclesiastical sanctions, occasionally with tragic results (Docs. 97, 98). But physical violence was not unknown among ecclesiastics, even among the nuns of an aristocratic convent whose brazen attempt to demolish a new church in Troyes brought them all under excommunication (Doc. 101). A constant source of environmental violence, of course, was fire, which frequently struck the wooden-frame houses that predominated in most medieval towns (Doc. 99).

1. Orderic Vitalis, *The Ecclesiastical History of Orderic Vitalis*, ed. and trans. Marjorie Chibnall, 6 vols. (Oxford: Clarendon Press, 1969–1980).
2. Galbert of Bruges, *The Murder of Charles the Good, Count of Flanders*, trans. James Bruce Ross (New York: Harper & Row, 1967).
3. William of Tyre, *A History of the Deeds Done beyond the Sea*; Villehardouin and Joinville in *Joinville and Villehardouin: Chronicles of the Crusades*.

96. An assassination attempt on Count Hugh, 1104

*Gravely wounded by a household servant in late 1103, Count Hugh was taken to the convent of Avenay for recuperation. A scribe recounted the event when Hugh, after a difficult recovery, made a donation to the abbey in the presence of his eleven-year-old nephew Thibaut [IV of Blois, II of Champagne], his closest relative who would have succeeded to his lands if Hugh had died (Doc. A).[4] Later, in a donation to the monastery of Saint-Loup of Troyes, the count himself recalled his ordeal (Doc. B).[5]*

(A) At the time when the most noble Count Hugh was governing his lands in a most excellent way, it happened that the devil, the giver of death who hated good deeds and who was obsessed by envy, tried to kill the count through the hands of a traitor. For Hugh, who was greatly devoted to God by his prayers and his generosity to the poor, used to ransom captives and aid the destitute. Among those was a certain Alexander, an impoverished man from overseas whom the count took into his own household. The most noble count and his family treated this man so well that he even ate and often slept in the count's personal quarters.

One night while the count was staying in the village of Dontrien, Alexander, judging the time and place appropriate, tried to slit the throat of the sleeping count. But through divine intervention, the count escaped only half-dead. Usually, when such a great personage is afflicted, a crowd of physicians gathers around him to treat him, but in this case, they were unable to heal the deep wounds. Thus the count was taken to Avenay abbey so that his open wounds might be healed by the intercession of that abbey's saints. The good Count Hugh remained there three months during which he suffered intensely. Realizing that his recovery was due less to his physicians than to the intercession of the saints and God's mercy, he showed his appreciation for that, and for the souls of his parents and ancestors, by donating to the abbey two-and-one-half manses of land in Avenay village, with the consent of his nephew Thibaut [count of Blois]. Hugh also donated a tenant woman, the wife of Gilboud, with her family who live in the village of Loges, as well as the wife of Constantius with her family in Plévy.

The venerable count, inspired by God, gave another favor: permission to anyone who holds a fief from him to donate it to Avenay for the follow-

4. Text in Paris, *Avenay*, 2:72–73, no. 4.
5. Extract from the text in Charles Lalore, ed., *Cartulaire de l'abbaye de Saint-Loup de Troyes* (Paris: E. Thorin, 1875), 14–16, no. 4.

ing reasons: for burial in the abbey, for the endowment of a daughter as nun there, and for any other good cause.

Hugh's nephew Thibaut approved, as did the count's entire household. This charter was redacted in 1103, in the ninth indiction, on the kalends of March [March 1, 1104], in the reign of Philip I, king of France, and of Manasses, archbishop of Reims, and of Abbess Fredeburge [of Avenay]. Witnesses were: Thibaut, the count's nephew; André, count [of Ramerupt]; Geoffroy, seneschal [of Champagne]; Guinebert, butler [of Champagne]; Odo, baker; Pagan, provost of Mareuil; Hernaud, mayor. Clerics: Gilbert, Albert, Berengar, Guy. Nuns: Emeline, dean; Agnes, chantress; Martha, cellarmaster. Gilbert, the estate steward of Avenay, and Hugh, dean. Whoever seeks to contradict this act, may he be anathema and, like Judas, thrown into hell.

(B) [April 2, 1104] I, Hugh, by the grace of God, count of Troyes, having with great difficulty recovered from my wounds, for which God was the physician who saved me, and having realized that many of my acts may have offended God and that my wounds were just punishment for my sins, render thanks to God by conferring gifts to certain churches. . . .

## 97. COUNT HENRY RESISTS THE ARCHBISHOP OF REIMS, 1171–1172

*King Louis VII's brother Henry, archbishop of Reims (1162–1175), was a difficult man whose prelateship was marked by poor relations not only with the townsmen of Reims and the barons in the countryside, but even with Pope Alexander III. In 1170, while attempting to clear the road between Reims and Châlons-sur-Marne of the brigands who harassed travelers and merchants, the archbishop's forces demolished a troublesome castle and constructed a powerful new one under his direct control. Henry's brother-in-law, Count Henry of Champagne, objected to such a fortification at the very edge of his lands. Armed clashes erupted along the border and the archbishop, in a fit of anger, excommunicated the count. As the archbishop explained to his suffragans, he withheld a public excommunication while the two parties appealed to the pope (A).[6] During this interval, however, the archbishop pronounced the excommunication, but his reason for doing so was not clear to Pope Alexander III, who delegated a commission of inquiry (B).[7] At the same time, the pope asked Louis VII to decide whether the archbishop had the right to construct the new castle (C).[8]*

6. Text in *Recueil des historiens* 16 : 194–195, no. 174.
7. Text in *Patrologia Latina*, ed. J. P. Migne et al., 221 vols. (Paris, 1844–1864), 200 : 798–800, no. 896.
8. Text (slightly condensed here) in ibid., 200 : 803–804, no. 899.

(A)  Henry, called archbishop of Reims, to his venerable brothers and suffragan bishops, greeting and apostolic benediction.[9] According to wise words, "A brother helped is like a strong city" [Prov. 18:19], and in the execution of justice, let there be no dispute in the pursuit of eternal justice. Wherefore I must explain to you, brothers, how Count Henry perpetrated a certain malice against both my person and my church and fails to desist in it. For while he was my liegeman, save fidelity to the lord king—and he has not disavowed me—he trapped and captured some of my knights who were waging war [against brigands] in my feudal lands, taking booty from me and my churches. I warned him and sent formal representation that he release the captives, but he did not, nor did he expel the brigands from my fiefs. Rather, as it became apparent, he sought a subterfuge by asking me to submit the case to the lord pope. I did not consent, for a plunderer does not have the right of appeal. Soon in fact he dropped his pretense and displayed his anger openly, for his knights and hired hands invaded my lands, attacked the churches under my protection, and committed horrible cruelties against my men, killing some and taking others away in chains to prison. In one church thirty-six people died when it was burned down; no one of either sex was spared. Plunder and destruction pervade the entire region.

I sent representatives to the count, requesting the return of my property and that of the churches, but I was unable to speak with him.[10] Then, in the presence of my clerics, I hurled the sentence of excommunication against him, although I did not publish the sentence in my church at the time.

Later, however, the count sought a truce between us, and I accepted on the understanding that the status quo be maintained: that the excommunication would not be proclaimed in church but that my property would be returned. The truce continued, but neither my property nor the churches were returned. So I published the sentence of excommunication, extinguishing candles, against him. After the sentence was published, he again appealed for an audience with the lord pope.

Because of this injury against me and my churches, I order you, my brothers, to have the sentence of excommunication proclaimed in all the

---

9. This is a papal greeting whose use here reflects the archbishop's arrogant nature. The pope's letters to him were remarkably cool in tone, even terse.

10. It sounds as if the archbishop went to the count's quarters seeking a personal meeting, was rebuffed, and then reacted with anger in the quarters where he was awaiting a reply.

churches of your dioceses every Sunday against him and all who offer him aid against me and my church.

(B) Alexander [III], bishop and servant of the servants of God, to his venerable brothers the archbishop of Tours and the bishop of Rouen, greeting and apostolic benediction. My dear sons Masters Stephen and Milo of Châlons-sur-Marne, nuncios of my venerable brother Henry, archbishop of Reims, came to me with his letter asking me to confirm by apostolic authority the sentence of excommunication that he pronounced against Count Henry for the latter's excesses. But my dear sons John "Sound as a Wolf" and Master Melior, who came to me about the same matter on behalf of the count, argued that the excommunication should not be confirmed because it was pronounced after the dispute had been appealed to the Holy See. The archbishop's nuncios countered that although the excommunication was published after the two parties had agreed to take the case to the pope, it was published in response to the invasion of the church of Reims's lands by the count's provosts and military forces, and after churches under the archbishop's jurisdiction were torched at will and residents of those lands were killed or led away captive and held unjustly for ransom, despite the archbishop's request for their release.

The count's ambassadors replied that if the count's provosts and armed men did those things after the appeal to the Holy See, they did so without the count's order and without his knowledge. When the ambassadors were asked about the captives, they responded that the incident itself was provoked, and the count's men did not in fact invade the archbishop's lands; rather the archbishop's own provosts had invaded the count's land with armed men and killed some of his men, and when fortune turned against the invaders, several of them were killed and others captured [that is, on the count's land].

Since there is disagreement over this affair, and since I wish to remain neutral—as both parties appealed to me—and since the archbishop's excommunication occurred after the appeal was lodged, I cannot and should not confirm that sentence of excommunication until I am certain about the case. In order to dispel my doubts, I order you [the archbishop of Tours and the bishop of Rouen] by my apostolic authority to inquire diligently into the truth of this matter within eleven days of receipt of this letter to determine:

• Whether the count's provosts and armed men acted on his authority or knowledge, after the appeal but before the excommunication, and as aggressors on the archbishop's land

• Whether the count refused to release his captives which he holds in chains, despite the archbishop's request for their release

If all this is true, you are to confirm the sentence of excommunication, unless an amicable settlement can be reached between the parties, which I would much prefer. You are to excommunicate those who outrageously set fire to churches [and not lift it] until they render satisfaction. Otherwise, the sentence of excommunication should not be confirmed because it was proclaimed after an appeal.

Moreover, I order you to represent the church in seeking a compromise regarding the construction of castles [by the archbishop], if you are summoned by our dearest son in Christ, Louis [VII], king of the French. Failing a compromise, I order you to resolve that issue through legal proceedings. But, just as with the above excommunication, I order you to enforce the interdict. Given at Tusculum, the eleventh kalends of April [March 22, 1172].

(C) [Alexander III to King Louis VII.] Nuncios of the venerable Henry, archbishop of Reims and your own brother, as well as representatives of the noble Count Henry [his brother-in-law], appealed to me to resolve their dispute. But I have not done so because I wish to preserve the peace of your realm, especially in this serious case between two such noble and powerful personages. Wishing to end the dispute regarding the excommunication [of Count Henry], which does fall under my authority, I have ordered the archbishop of Tours and the bishop of Rouen, both discreet and prudent men, to terminate that dispute after an inquiry [Doc. B above].

Since Count Henry maintained that the newly built castles of the archbishop caused him great harm, and since this is at the root of a serious dispute between the parties, I ask you to decide the case and either find an amicable compromise or render a judgment, whichever you think best, for it is better and healthier to treat a disease at the start than after it has become entrenched.

If you yourself do not wish to enter this case of castle-building (which I doubt), assign it to discreet men for investigation and the arrangement of an amicable settlement or an imposed judicial decision. May peace and harmony between those two great and powerful persons be quickly restored for the benefit of you and your realm. Given at Tusculum, the eleventh kalends of April [March 22, 1172].

## 98. THE DEATH OF AN EXCOMMUNICATED MARSHAL, 1185

*This matter-of-fact document relates a dramatic moment for the family of Erard of Aulnay, marshal of Champagne, who died while under excommunication.*[11] *It is not known what specific deed led the chapter of Châlons-sur-Marne to impose the sentence that deprived him of a Christian burial. Erard's widow collected the entire family to beseech the archbishop of Reims to intercede with the chapter of Châlons to ensure her husband's burial; she offered, as another document put it, "restitution for Erard's damages and for the salvation of his soul."*[12] *Erard finally was buried in the cemetery of the Cistercian abbey of Trois-Fontaines. This text is also significant in that it marks the first documented appearance of Geoffroy of Villehardouin, the chronicler of the Fourth Crusade, just before he was named to succeed Erard as marshal of Champagne.*

William, by the grace of God, archbishop of Reims, cardinal of S. Sabina, and legate of the Apostolic See [and brother of the recently deceased Count Henry I], greeting in the Lord to all who receive this letter. Be it known that after Erard of Aulnay [marshal of Champagne] died while under excommunication by the church of Châlons-sur-Marne for damage that he inflicted on [the village of] Saint-Amand, his widow Helvide, his brothers, and several of his friends came before me to make peace with the dean and chapter of Châlons. Helvide gave the chapter all the rents, jurisdiction, and whatever else she and Erard used to have at Saint-Amand, with the consent of Marie, the illustrious countess of Troyes and of her dearest son—my nephew—Henry [Count Henry II, still a minor], as well as with the consent of Erard's brothers Oudard and Villain,[13] and of Erard's sister Mathilda and her son Erard. Also present were Helvide's sister's son, Guy [II] of Dampierre; her brother John [I] of Arcis-sur-Aube; Erard's uncle [and successor as marshal] Geoffroy of Villehardouin; Erard's brothers already mentioned; Milo [II, lord] of Nogent-sur-Seine; and Oger of Saint-Chéron. Geoffroy of Mousson and his uncle Erard also promised to uphold this agreement.

The canons of Châlons promised that they would celebrate every year

---

11. Text in Jean Longnon, *Recherches sur la vie de Geoffroy de Villehardouin* (Paris: Honoré Champion, 1939), 152–153, no. 8.
12. Ibid., 153, no. 9
13. See Doc. 80.

an anniversary Mass for Erard appropriate for a knight (*iuxta morem militum*). Done in the year of our Lord 1185. Presented [to the chapter of Châlons, as a title deed] by my chancellor Lambin.

### 99. THE GREAT FIRE AT TROYES, 1188

*The city of Troyes underwent explosive growth from the middle decades of the twelfth century, in part because the fairs of Champagne increasingly drew merchants from the Mediterranean as well as northern Europe. The inner city was a maze of small streets and alleys between blocks of two- and three-story wooden-frame buildings that served as living quarters, shops, and warehouses. Until the construction of stone structures became more common, medieval cities were tinderboxes (see Doc. 20). Here the chronicler Robert of Auxerre describes the devastating fire at Troyes in 1188.[14]*

On the eve of July 23 [1188], the heavily built up and densely populated city of Troyes, crammed with goods [for sale at the international fair] burned down almost to the ground. It was the time of the fair [of Saint John] at which merchants from many diverse parts brought their wares to sell. Suddenly that night, a swell of fire rose out of control, fanned every which way by turbulent winds. Some people were overtaken by flames as they tried to save their possessions and those of their neighbors, while others who stayed put also were consumed by fire. There was an incalculable loss of goods, and many people perished in the flames.

The cathedral church [of Saint-Pierre], covered with fine leaden roof tiles, was destroyed by the fire. And the church of Saint-Etienne, which Count Henry [I] had founded [in 1157], endowed with rents, and equipped with gold and silver ornaments and furnishings, also perished with its entire accumulation of remarkable objects.

On those very days the populous and wealthy cities of Provins, Beauvais, and Poitiers, as well as large parts of Chartres, were ravaged by fire and calamity. By the judgment of God, a vast destruction befell those places.

### 100. A HOLOCAUST OF HERETICS, 1239

*In May 1235 Pope Gregory IX authorized a general inquisition in France, with special attention to the heretic-infested sees of Reims and Sens (which included the diocese of Troyes). He appointed as chief inquisitor Robert le Bougre, a for-*

---

14. Text in Robert of Auxerre, *Chronicon*, ed. O. Holder-Egger, in *Monumenta Germaniae Historica: Scriptores*, 31 vols. (Hannover, 1826–1933), 26:253.

*mer heretic who had spent twenty years in Milan mastering heretical doctrines before rejecting them.*[15] *A ferocious, even maniacal, pursuer of heretics, Robert unleashed a reign of persecution and heretic burnings in northern France that culminated in the great burning in Champagne on May 13, 1239. Suspects— called Bulgars because their ideas were thought to have been brought westward by Bulgarians—were gathered for examination in the courtyard of the large comital castle of Mont-Aimé. The event must have been billed as a spectacular affair, perhaps as a send-off for Count Thibaut's crusade, for it attracted an exceptionally large crowd. Aubri, the Cistercian monk and chronicler at Trois-Fontaines who recorded this event, seems to have collected details from an eye witness.*[16]

On the Friday before Pentecost [May 13, 1239], there was a great burnt-offering (*holocaustum*) pleasing to God in which 183 Bulgars were burned in the presence of the king of Navarre [Count Thibaut IV] and the barons of Champagne at Mont-Aimé, the ancient "Mons Wedoma-rus." Also present were: Henry, archbishop of Reims; James, bishop of Soissons; Master Gautier, bishop of Tournai; Master of theology Guiard, bishop of Cambrai; Master Alzo, bishop of Arras; Peter, bishop of Thé-rouanne; Nicolas, bishop of Noyon; Master Garnier, bishop of Laon; Master Adam, bishop of Senlis; Robert, bishop-elect of Beauvais; Geof-froy, bishop-elect of Châlons-sur-Marne and paternal uncle of the count of Grandpré; Master William, bishop of Orléans; Master Nicolas, bishop of Troyes; Peter, bishop of Meaux; Ralph of Thourotte, bishop of Verdun, and his brother Robert, bishop of Langres; and many other prelates, in-cluding abbots, priors, and deans.

Not all [of the suspects] were burned, for during that week some recanted after being examined [by the inquisitor Robert]. There was such a large crowd there of both sexes and of various social classes that it was estimated to number about 700,000.[!] Just as in antiquity, it is said, dogs coming together to fight and tear one another apart in this very place had a premonition of their future, so it is with the Bulgars, worse than dogs, who were exterminated in one day to the triumph of the holy church.

Their leader, who was called "archbishop," spoke to them [before

15. See Charles Homer Haskins, "Robert le Bougre and the Beginnings of the Inqui-sition in Northern France," chap. 10 of his *Studies in Medieval Culture* (Oxford: Clarendon Press, 1929).

16. Text in Aubri of Trois-Fontaines, *Chronicon*, ed. P. Scheffer-Boichorst, in *Monu-menta Germaniae Historica: Scriptores*, 31 vols. (Hannover, 1826–1933), 23:944–945 (year 1239). Translated texts of similar events in R. I. Moore, *The Birth of Popular Heresy* (New York: St. Martin's, 1975).

their death] in a loud voice: "You will all be saved, absolved by my hand. I alone am damned because I do not have a superior to absolve me." They also esteemed certain old women who took deceptive names, such as the one called "Holy Mary," and another called "Holy Church" or "Roman Law," and another called "Holy Baptism" or "Holy Marriage" or "Holy Communion." And they would say, while being examined, "I believe whatever Holy Church or Roman Law believes," referring, of course, to those old women!

One very highly regarded old woman from Provins by the name of Gisele, who was called "Abbess," had her death delayed when she promised Brother Robert that she would reveal the names of a great number of heretics. Another woman acknowledged under Robert's examination that on Good Friday she was transported [from Champagne] to Milan to waitress Bulgar tables, and that in her absence a demon transformed himself into her image next to her sleeping husband.

Those heretics are said to have originated with the detestable Manes. At least what they do in secret need not be made public, for they are horrible and smelly; they stink so much that they are [easily] detected by wise men.

Brother Robert and popular opinion held that Fortunatus, the Manichean whom Saint Augustine expelled from Africa, came to Champagne and encountered Widoma, prince of thieves, at Mont-Aimé and converted him and his companions to that belief; since that time the seed of that belief has remained in the vicinity of Mont-Aimé.

101. THE WRATH OF NUNS, 1266

*Pope Urban IV (1261–1264), son of a shoemaker of Troyes, decided to commemorate his family and native city by constructing a large church in the latest gothic style on the very site of his childhood home. In 1262 he ordered the owner of the house, the convent of Notre-Dame of Troyes, to sell it at a reasonable price to papal procurators, who at the time were buying up all the adjacent properties on which the new church would be built. The nuns were not pleased, as Urban had just reversed a very close election of their abbess and imposed the minority candidate.[17] After the dedication of Saint-Urbain in 1265, the nuns' resentment turned to violence, as explained in the letters of Urban's successor, Pope Clement IV. First the nuns willfully damaged the new altar (Doc. A) and perhaps were*

17. A summary of these events is in Penelope D. Johnson, *Equal in Monastic Profession: Religious Women in Medieval France* (Chicago and London: The University of Chicago Press, 1991), 87–89, 171–172.

*responsible for the fire which seriously damaged the roof;*[18] *then they attacked a papal envoy in order to prevent the dedication of Saint-Urbain's cemetery (Doc. B).*[19]

(A)  Clement [IV] to his dear sons the archdeacon of Luxeuil and the dean of Saint-Etienne of Troyes, my chaplains, greeting and apostolic benediction. Through unheard of insolence and arrogance against God and religious propriety, the abbess and nuns of the convent of Notre-Dame of Troyes vilely wished to demolish the new church of Saint-Urbain of Troyes which was built through privileges and subsidies from the Holy See. They and their accomplices destroyed the altar which by papal mandate the dean and chapter [of Saint-Urbain] erected to celebrate the divine mysteries: they sawed through the church doors, cut up the marble altar stone, and destroyed the stone-moving machines, ropes, timbers, carpenters' tools, tiles, and other things which they violently carried off. Not content with that, they later compounded the damage by destroying the doors which the canons installed as replacements [for the damaged ones] and carried them off to their convent.

Such acts, produced not by gentleness or devotion but rather by a pitiless and insolent attitude, deeply offend the Holy See, which cannot overlook grave excesses in contempt of the divine majesty. Since the nuns' accomplices, both clerics and laymen—whose names are not known to the dean and chapter of Saint-Urbain—encouraged and aided the nuns in perpetrating their malice, I am unwilling to let such a heinous crime pass under silence, nor to let them off with impunity; nor will I permit such an example to stand.

I therefore order you [his chaplains] to summon those clerics and laymen [accomplices] publicly in churches to give full satisfaction to the dean and chapter of Saint-Urbain within fifteen days (unless you set another deadline) under pain of general excommunication, which you may have published as you see fit, notwithstanding anyone's papal indulgence of exemption from excommunication or interdict.

Given at Viterbo, the kalends of October [October 1], in the second year of my pontificate [1266].

18. For the damage caused by the nuns, see Michael T. Davis, "On the Threshold of the Flamboyant: The Second Campaign of Construction of Saint-Urbain, Troyes," *Speculum* 59 (1984): 847–884,

19. Texts in Charles Lalore, ed., "Documents sur l'abbaye de Notre-Dame-aux-Nonnains de Troyes," *Mémoires de la Société académique d'agriculture, des sciences, arts et belles-lettres du département de l'Aube* 38 (1874): 120–121, no. 194; 123–124, no. 199.

(B) Clement [IV], bishop and servant of God, to his sons the arch-deacon of Luxeuil and the dean of Saint-Etienne of Troyes, my chaplains, greeting and apostolic benediction.

Wishing to bestow appropriate honor on the church of Saint-Urbain of Troyes, which was founded by subsidies from the Roman Church, I ordered the former bishop of Auxerre, now the archbishop of Tyre, who was consulting in that region of France, to dedicate the cemetery of Saint-Urbain that is reserved for its canons, clerics, and their servants. However, the abbess and some nuns of the Benedictine convent of Notre-Dame of Troyes along with armed men—as the dean and chapter of Saint-Urbain related to me—surrounded the archbishop and prevented him from enter-ing the church by closing the church doors, even though he was carrying out a papal mandate. Although he threatened them with excommuni-cation if they did not open the doors and let him through, they forcefully placed hands on him and pushed him back.

Later, as the archbishop was returning to Saint-Urbain to carry out his mandate, the nuns intercepted him in the street and threatened to pre-vent him again from entering the church. They explained why they had impeded him earlier: primarily because the abbess and the convent were compelled by the Holy See [by Pope Urban IV] to sell their houses, reve-nues, rents, legal rights, jurisdiction, and other things for which they were not fully compensated, and the arbitrator appointed to work out a com-promise in this dispute had not yet announced a decision.

Although the dean and chapter of Saint-Urbain said they were pre-pared to carry out all terms of the arbitration, they humbly petitioned me to intervene in the case. Therefore I order you [his chaplains] by this ap-ostolic letter that in the presence of the people in churches you publicly, by my papal authority, warn those clerics and laymen accomplices of the abbess and nuns—whose names are not known by the dean and chapter of Saint-Urbain—to render satisfaction within fifteen days (or any other term you fix). If they do not, you are to promulgate a general sentence of excommunication that will be solemnly declared on every Sunday and feast day, with church bells ringing and candles lit, in all places you deem appropriate.

Given at Viterbo, the ides of July [July 15], in the fourth year of my pontificate [1268].

[The nuns and their accomplices were excommunicated on March 15, 1269, and finally released from that sentence on March 23, 1274.]

# Liberality

The twelfth-century counts were widely known for their largess to the church. Their generosity included both traditional Benedictine houses, which received an assortment of gifts, privileges, and even revenues from the fairs (see Docs. 21, 22), and newly founded collegiate chapters of canons, such as Saint-Etienne of Troyes (see Doc. 99). But it was the Cistercians who were most privileged in Champagne. Bernard of Clairvaux drew enthusiastic support not only from Counts Hugh and Thibaut II but also from the noble families whose sons were captivated by the Cistercian message of an alternate life-style. Unlike the Benedictines, the Cistercians did not accept child oblates, only adults who had made considered commitments to monastic life (see Docs. 47, 48).[20] Bernard's personal charisma attracted talented men whose leadership as Cistercian abbots assured the material success of the order (Doc. 102), while Count Henry and other great lords exempted the Cistercians from tolls and sales taxes (Doc. 103). The countesses, for their part, supported female convents (see Doc. 44), their most notable benefaction being the foundation of Argensolles by Countess Blanche (Doc. 104).

102. THE CISTERCIAN MONASTERY OF VAULUISANT, 1127
*Bernard, abbot of Clairvaux (1115–1153), was the prime mover of the extraordinary expansion of Cistercian monasteries in the first half of the twelfth century. Within a few years of Clairvaux's foundation (1115) at the southern edge of the county, Bernard sent monks to found daughter houses in Champagne and Burgundy. Abbot Artaud, who founded Preuilly (1118), was so successful in attracting new monks that nine years later, in 1127, he founded another house, Vauluisant. This notice recalls Abbot Artaud's effort to secure the support of powerful local nobles in order to assure the new community's success.[21]*

In the year of our Lord 1127, Lord Artaud, the first abbot of Preuilly, having attracted by divine inspiration many monks [to join that community], decided to found a new monastery in a place called Vauluisant[22] to

20. See Jean Leclercq, *Monks and Love in Twelfth-Century France: Psycho-Historical Essays* (Oxford: Clarendon Press, 1979).
21. Text in Albert Catel and Maurice Lecomte, eds., *Chartes et documents de l'abbaye cistercienne de Preuilly* (Montereau: Imprimerie Claverie, 1927), 8–9, no. 5
22. *Vallis Lucens*, that is, valley of light.

alleviate the overcrowding at his monastery. In order to secure approval, he traveled to a place called "Monstuz" where the nobles Anselm [I, lord] of Traînel and Odo [lord] of Villemaur were meeting for their own business. Artaud asked them, for the salvation of their souls, to allow the monks to acquire whatever rights they had in that place [Vauluisant]. The two nobles accordingly distinguished themselves before God by conceding that in perpetuity. These [vassals of Anselm and Odo] witnessed the grant: Hugh "the Red," Bovo [of Villemaur, uncle of Odo], Arnulf of Isle, Ayric, Milo "the Saint," Hugh of Rhèges, Havinus of Traînel, and too many others to name.

Be it known that the illustrious Milo [I, lord] of Nogent-sur-Seine, for the salvation of his soul and of his parents' souls, conceded to the monks of Vauluisant that they may acquire lands under his jurisdiction as gifts to the Lord. He did this at the request of Artaud, first lord abbot of Preuilly and founder of Vauluisant. These witnessed the grant: Anselm of Traînel and his brother Garin, Fulk of Jouarre, and Milo "the Saint."

103. CLAIRVAUX IS EXEMPTED FROM TOLLS AND TAXES, 1154
*Count Henry I was called "the Liberal" by contemporaries in recognition of his many benefactions to the church. Shortly after his accession, and not long after Bernard's death, Henry conferred this substantial privilege on Clairvaux and its daughter houses, whose monks apparently were frequenting the fairs of Bar-sur-Aube.*[23]

I, Henry, count palatine of Troyes, have granted to the servants of God at Clairvaux and its related abbeys, for the salvation of my soul and that of my father, that the monks be exempt from all tolls, duties, and taxes [on goods in transit] in all my lands; that they may freely buy and sell goods at my fairs without paying sales tax on the items necessary for their own use; that they will be free from molestation and harassment by my agents and officials; and that my own men everywhere will leave the monks in peace.

So that this benefaction may remain in force and not be forgotten, I have had this charter written for the monks and sealed with my seal. I have confirmed this grant as immutable, not to be circumscribed later by my successors and heirs, nor by anyone else for any reason. Witnesses to this grant are: Hilduin of Vendeuvre, Walter of Bernon, and Drogo of Provins

23. Text in Waquet, *Recueil,* 1:50–51, no. 26.

[knights formerly in service to Henry's father]. Done in the year of our Lord 1154, in the reign of the most Christian king, Louis [VII] the younger, and of Geoffroy, bishop of Langres. Given [to the monks] at Bar-sur-Aube by William, my notary.

## 104. THE CISTERCIAN CONVENT OF ARGENSOLLES, 1224

*The late twelfth century witnessed a surge in female spirituality, as many young women chose celibate life over marriage and married women left their husbands for the convent.[24] Since the older convents were overwhelmed by applicants (see Docs. 44, 46), new convents and other unofficial communities were created. The monastic orders resisted the pressure to accept women, and in 1220 the Cistercians even prohibited new convents altogether.[25] In 1222, however, when Countess Blanche retired from public life, she founded a convent at Argensolles, and over the next two years she used her substantial dower income to purchase a variety of economic resources needed to sustain the community (Doc. A).[26] Her high standing with the church overcame any opposition to the convent, which was accepted into the Cistercian order and allowed to grow to ninety nuns, making it one of the largest convents of the time (Doc. B).[27]*

(A)  I, Blanche, countess palatine of Troyes [retired], make known to all, present and future, that when I purchased [in 1222] the place called Argensolles with all its annexes, both in woodland and in plain land, from the monastery of Hautvillers, with the assent of the venerable William [of Joinville], archbishop of Reims, and of James, bishop of Soissons in whose diocese it is located, I gave it as a perpetual gift to Lady Ida, abbess, and the nuns serving God there in the Cistercian order. I did this both for the salvation of my soul and the soul of my dearest son Thibaut [IV], count palatine of Champagne and Brie, as well as for the good memory of my husband Thibaut [III, d. 1201] and all our ancestors. Later I added these items to that original gift, with the consent of the bishop:

• About one thousand *arpents* of woods beyond the woods already belonging to Argensolles, consisting of: two hundred *arpents* which I pur-

24. See Brenda M. Bolton, "Mulieres Sanctae," in *Studies in Church History* 10 (1973): 77–85, reprinted in *Women in Medieval Society*, ed. Susan Mosher Stuard (Philadelphia: University of Pennsylvania Press, 1976), 141–158.

25. See Sally Thompson, "The Problem of the Cistercian Nuns in the Twelfth and Early Thirteenth Centuries," in *Medieval Women*, ed. Derek Baker (Oxford: Basil Blackwell, 1978), 227–252.

26. Text in *Gallia Christiana in provincias ecclesiasticas distributa*, 13 vols. (Paris, 1715–1785), 9:*instrumenta*, 132–133, no. 53.

27. Text in ibid., 133, no. 54.

chased from William "Peuchet"; what I purchased from Guy of Couroy
and his wife and heirs in the woods of Loye; what I purchased from
Nicholas and his brothers in the woods of "Kifelard"; and what I purchased from the lord of Mancy in the woods of "Taveon" in the community of Mancy.

   • Part of the tithe of Ferreux which the monastery holds as security
for 120*l*. [owed by] Peter, knight of Montfelix, with the consent of the
lord of Pleurs from whom that tithe moved in fief; the tithe of Le Belocier
of Germinon and one-third of the tithe of Trécon—by which the nuns
collect the entire tithe every third year—which I purchased from Baldwin
of Fismes and his heirs; one-sixth of the tithe of Servolles which I purchased from Henry of Loisy-en-Brie and his brothers, with their mother's
consent.

   • Forty *sextarii* of rye annually from the land rent and mill of Germinon which the miller, my Jew, purchased from my faithful [vassal] Milo of
Germinon and which I, in turn, purchased from that Jew; twenty-four
*sextarii* of rye annually from the mill of Sourdun which belonged to
Goyod.

   • Eleven measures of meadowland at Chouilly which I bought from
Guyot of Epernay; the meadow of Brancon near Grauves which I bought
from Simon of Tréloup, who bought it from Henry of Mancy; the
meadow of Braux which Adam, dean of Vertus, gave to the nuns; two
measures of meadowland at Chouilly, 20*s*. *census*, two *modii* of wine, and
one *sextarius* of oats which I bought from Odo of Brie and his wife.

   • The vineyard of twenty-four *arpents* called "the count's vineyard" at
Montferré; two *arpents* of a newly planted vineyard at Barre, which I
bought from the sisters of the hospital of Barre;[28] a newly planted vineyard of one *arpent* that I bought from Boschet; a vineyard of three *arpents*
at "Chef d'ail" bequeathed by Milo, cleric of Vertus; two *arpents* at Oger
which I bought from Remi, mayor of Oger, and one-half an *arpent* there
and 5*s*. rent and one *arpent* of a vineyard at Gravour which came to the
monks [of Hautvillers]; four *arpents* of a new vineyard at Moslins which I
bought from Peter, lord of Moslins; four *arpents* at Mantes as a gift from
the lady Contessa after her death—Simon of Tréloup and John the Bache-
lor exempted it from all rents and taxes.

   • An annual revenue of 10*l*. at Provins which I purchased from the
marshal of Chartres; 60*s*. rent from the wine tax and carriage tax of Oger

28. See Doc. 105.

which Marie, lady of Conflans, gave to the nuns for celebrating an annual anniversary Mass for Girard of Saint-Obert; 10*l.* annual revenue which Baldwin of Reims gave to nuns for the salvation of his soul; seven *modii* of grain (half oats and half rye) which I purchased from the sisters of the wife of Philip "Putus."

• The stone mill on the road of Dandon at Sézanne which I bought from Lord Peter [of Moslins].

• And also my grange of Sercy with all the lands I bought from Pagan of Oger; the vacant land of Ado, dean of Vertus, going up to the dean's ditch; the land I bought from William "Peuchet" adjacent to the woods I bought from him; and likewise the land of Guy of Couroy next to the woods I bought from him.

So that this remain secure, I have confirmed this letter with my seal. Done in the year of our lord 1224.

(B) Brother Conrad, abbot of Cîteaux, Brother Odo, abbot of La Ferté, Brother Peter, abbot of Pontigny, Brother Robert, abbot of Clairvaux, and Brother Guy, abbot of Morimond, send greeting in the Lord to all abbots, priors, subpriors, and others of the Cistercian order. We wish all to know that by the authority of the chapter general and of the entire Cistercian order, we have allowed the abbess and convent of Argensolles to expand up to ninety nuns, ten lay converts, and twenty clerics and laymen, God willing.

That convent is fully part of our order with the right to wear the prescribed habit, that is, cloaks and monastic cowls without hoods. Lay converts may wear the same habit so that when they are sent to other abbeys and granges of our order, they will be received just as we are in the chapels and refectories of lay converts. Clerics who serve as novitiates in the order of monks may be received behind the choir in our churches; they will conduct services within the holy space that is closed to laymen. Those clerics and lay converts will promise the abbess and chapter of nuns that they will abide by this regulation, and they will profess their faith to the abbess.

We declare that the nuns will wear the prescribed habit, a single coat without fur mantle, and that the abbot of Clairvaux will be the father of the house, as he is of monasteries of monks. Done in the year of our Lord 1224, during the meeting of the chapter general. [Sealed with the seals of the above named abbots.]

## Charity

Two particular forms of charity (as opposed to largess) were notable in the High Middle Ages: the foundation of hospitals and hospices to care for the ill and travelers; and benefactions to the poor, whose presence was increasingly felt in the burgeoning towns.[29] The counts had long supported hospitals in their towns, and occasionally—usually at their deaths—sponsored lavish feedings of the poor (see Doc. 53). The texts here represent quite different individual responses to social needs: a chaplain commits his entire inheritance to endow a new hospital for the poor and ill (Doc. 105); the seneschal helps feed the Cistercian abbots at their annual chapter general meeting (Doc. 106); Count Thibaut IV, in one of his first actions as count, tries to improve conditions within Clairvaux monastery (Doc. 107); and a noblewoman donates a large sum of money for establishing an endowment to feed the poor (Doc. 108).

105. FOUNDATION OF THE HOSPITAL OF LA BARRE, 1211
*When Guy of Barre, chaplain in the castle of Château-Thierry, decided to use his inheritance to found a new hospital just outside the castle walls not far from the leper colony there, he asked Countess Blanche to exempt it from her jurisdiction (Doc. A).[30] He also needed permission from the abbot whose parish rights would be reduced by the planned construction of a chapel and cemetery at the hospital (Doc. B).[31] Within a year Countess Blanche took over the new community, built the chapel with her own funds, and introduced women to minister to the ill and poor. So many people flocked to the place that by the summer of 1214 they had overwhelmed its resources (Doc. C).[32]*

(A) I, Blanche, countess palatine of Troyes, make known to all, present and future, that Lord Guy, chaplain of Saint-Thibaut of Château-Thierry, has given as a perpetual gift, for the salvation of his soul, his

---

29. See Edward J. Kealey, "Hospitals and Poor Relief," in *Dictionary of the Middle Ages*, ed. Joseph R. Strayer, 13 vols. (New York: Charles Scribner's Sons, 1982–1989), 6 : 292–297, and Timothy S. Miller, "The Knights of Saint John and the Hospitals of the Latin West," *Speculum* 53 (1978): 709–733. On the poor in general, see Michel Mollat, *The Poor in the Middle Ages. An Essay in Social History*, trans. Arthur Goldhammer (New Haven and London: Yale University Press, 1986).

30. Text in C. Nusse, ed., "Charte de fondation d'un Hôtel-Dieu à la Barre," *Annales de la Société historique et archéologique de Château-Thierry* (1874): 191–192.

31. Text in A. E. Poquet, "L'abbaye de Barre et son recueil de chartes," *Annales de la Société historique et archéologique de Château-Thierry* (1884): 133–134, no. 2.

32. Text in ibid., 136–137, no. 6.

houses, grange, and their attached enclosure located between the castle [wall] and the leper colony in order to establish a hospital to serve the poor. And I, for my soul and for the soul of my dearest husband Count Thibaut [III], have exempted that property from my taxes and jurisdiction.

Gautier, chaplain of Saint-Crépin, Baldwin of Verneuil, knight, Anselm, squire of Essômes, and Marie of Sancy, widow of the knight Hugh of Sancy, quit to the hospital the eleven *sextarii* of wine and 12*d.* in rent that they collect from Guy's land, for which I gave them in exchange ten *sextarii* of wine and 20*d.* annual rent elsewhere in the following manner: the chaplain Gautier will collect four *sextarii* of wine and 12*d.* in rent from the house of Hugh the Carpenter and from the tenement of Roland of Navarre; Baldwin, André, and Marie will collect six *sextarii* of wine and 8*d.* in rent from the land of Oudard, son of Tafornel, and his brother in the parish of Saint-Martin in Château-Thierry.

In order to preserve perpetual memory of this act, I have had this charter drawn up and sealed with my seal. Done at Château-Thierry in the year of our Lord 1211, in the month of March. Given by Remi, my chancellor.[33]

(B) I, Haymard, bishop of Soissons, make known that Guy of Barre, through divine inspiration, exchanged his temporal inheritance for an eternal one and, as the Scripture says, sold all his possessions for his salvation. He has given his house with all its appurtenances in the parish of Saint-Martin for use by the poor.

Odo, abbot of Essômes, and his monastic community, at the request of the illustrious Blanche, countess palatine of Champagne, have freed that house with its appurtenances consisting of six *arpents* of land from all parish obligations [to Essômes] and allow the brothers [of the hospital] to erect a chapel with bells and to have a cemetery for the burial of the brothers and the poor. The monastery of Essômes allows those brothers to carry on their work without interference by Essômes.

It is stipulated, however, that the chaplain [in charge of the hospital] will turn over to the prior of Saint-Martin [the parish church operated by Essômes] the oblations received there on the five annual feast days which by custom belong to that prior. But the brothers of the hospital may keep the daily oblations.

33. Remi of Navarre was Blanche's illegitimate half-brother who served as her chancellor (1211–1220) before becoming bishop of Pamplona.

The chaplain of the hospital chapel is prohibited from giving the sacraments to the parishioners of Saint-Martin, for those belong to the prior of Saint-Martin: that is, the Mass, baptism, marriage, the blessing of a new mother, and burial. Exception is made for ill parishioners who on their deathbeds have not yet chosen a burial place. The chaplain may, however, give the sacraments to the brothers of the hospital and to the poor there. In compensation for these concessions [by Essômes], the hospital of Barre will pay the canons of Essômes 10*s.* annually. [The bishop approved on December 11, 1211, and appended his seal.]

(C) I, Blanche, countess palatine of Troyes, to all her provosts, bailiffs, and all her faithful men. Be it known that the bearer of this letter represents the hospital of La Barre, which I founded.[34] Since the resources of the hospital are inadequate to support the poor who have sought refuge there, the charity of other people is necessary. Help and protect the bearer of this letter, and assist him in anyway to do what must be done. [Done in July 1214.]

### 106. Fish for the Cistercian Chapter General meeting, 1216

*This act might have served political as well as charitable ends, for in 1216 Simon of Joinville was at loggerheads with the regent Countess Blanche over whether the office of seneschal was his by inheritance. By this one act Simon obtained the goodwill of all the Cistercian abbots of the region. The document seems to have been written directly from his dictation.[35]*

I, Simon, lord of Joinville, seneschal of Champagne, make known to all, present and future, that I have granted in perpetual gift to God, to holy Mary, and to the brothers of Clairvaux the right to fish in all my streams for three days and three nights before their chapter general meeting in order to supply food for the abbots coming to that meeting.

The brothers may fish freely, in whatever way they wish, each year in all my streams, as I have said, for three days and nights, but not in my fish ponds.

My wife Ermengard, my son Geoffroy, and my daughters Isabel and Beatrice approved this gift.[36] Done in the year of grace 1216.

34. The countess took over the hospital in 1212, built the chapel with her own funds, and thereafter considered the hospital as her foundation. In 1234 Barre became a female convent.

35. Text in M. Champollion-Figeac, *Documents historiques inédits tirés des collections manuscrits de la Bibliothèque Royale*, 4 vols. (Paris: Imprimerie Nationale, 1841–1848), 1: 618.

36. See Genealogical Table 2.

### 107. Light for Clairvaux and its Charnel House, 1223

*The twenty-one year old Count Thibaut IV must have heard about conditions at Clairvaux shortly after his accession in May 1222. He seems to have been genuinely concerned about the monks' personal safety.*[37]

[I] Thibaut, count palatine of Champagne and Brie, [make known] to all in perpetuity. I was amazed to hear that the monks of Clairvaux do not burn wax [that is, candles] for light when celebrating their private Masses but rather use torches, which often create dangerous situations. Wishing therefore to remove that danger, I have given to the monks as a perpetual gift 18*l.*, money of Provins, in annual rent to be collected from my fair revenues at the fair of Bar-sur-Aube, in order to purchase wax for this purpose.[38] The monks promised me that henceforth they would not celebrate Mass without lit wax candles.

In addition I have given the monks 2*l.* annual rent from the same fair revenues at Bar-sur-Aube for keeping a torch burning continuously in their charnel house where the bones of the deceased faithful remain at the abbey.

So that this may endure, I have had my seal affixed to this letter. Done in the year of our Lord 1223, in the month of March.

### 108. Clothing and shoes for the poor, 1228

*Elizabeth, widow of Lord Hugh III of Broyes-Commercy,*[39] *was troubled by the number of paupers in the countryside. In presenting Clairvaux with an exceedingly generous gift to help the rural poor, she acted like some modern benefactors in requiring the recipient to maintain her bequest as she intended it.*[40]

I, Brother Ralph, called abbot of Clairvaux, and the entire chapter of Clairvaux make known to all, present and future, who see this letter that the noble and our dearest lady Elizabeth of Châteauvillain gave to us in Christ 620*l.*, money of Provins, in pure and perpetual free gift [which she assigned] to our gate at Clairvaux. With that sum we purchased the great tithe of Meurville—except for a part of it held by the priest there—and at her request, for the salvation of her soul, we assigned that tithe to our gate

---

37. Text in "Cartulary of Clairvaux," pp. 137–138, no. 13. The scribe who copied this grant into Clairvaux's title book abbreviated the address and the closing.

38. In 1231 the count increased that rent to 35*l.*

39. She was widowed in 1199; see Genealogical Table 3.

40. Text in "Cartulary of Clairvaux," pp. 53–54, no. 48.

at Clairvaux in perpetuity for the purchase of clothing for the poor, in this manner: the gatekeeper of Clairvaux must distribute garments and shoes every year to eighty paupers from that tithe-revenue of Meurville. Each pauper will have five ells [about twenty feet] of new coarse wool and new shoes.

If that tithe ever produces additional revenue, the gatekeeper must expend it entirely on the purchase of shoes for the paupers. He must distribute the cloth and shoes in good faith between the Nativity of Our Lady [September 8] and the Nativity of the Lord [December 25].

We have approved the above gift and wish it to be observed in perpetuity. The said lady conceded it to us and our successors on the understanding that the tithe never be used for any other purpose. To acknowledge this gift, we give her this sealed letter to ensure it in perpetuity. We have also given her letters from Lord Hugh, bishop of Langres, and Lord G[eoffroy], abbot of Cîteaux, which confirm the above stated restriction. Done in the year of our Lord 1228, in the month of March.

# Bibliography

## Sources

### ABBREVIATIONS

AD: Archives Départementales (Aube, Marne, Haute-Marne)
AN: Archives Nationales (Paris)
BN: Bibliothèque Nationale (Paris)

### DOCUMENTS

AD, Marne, 20 H 11, no. 7.
AD, Haute-Marne, 1 H 37, 5 H 10.
AN, J 193, nos. 2, 28.

### CARTULARIES

Cartulary of Clairvaux: AD, Aube, 3 H 9.
Cartulary of Larrivour: AD, Aube, 4 H 1.
Cartulary of Saint-Etienne of Troyes: BN, Latin 17098.
Cartulary-Registers of the counts of Champagne:
      no. 3: BN, Latin 5993.
      no. 4: AN, KK 1064, fols. 1–207.
      no. 5: AN, KK 1064, fols. 267–371.
      no. 7: BN, Cinq Cents de Colbert, vols. 56–58
        [ = vols. 1–3], copy of the lost *Liber Principum*.
Collection Moreau: BN, Collection Moreau, vol. 185.
Recueil historique by A. Caulart: BN, Français 11559.

### PRINTED WORKS

Arbois de Jubainville, Henri d'. "Document sur l'obligation de la résidence impo-
    sée aux barons par le droit féodal champenois au douzième siècle." *Revue
    historique de droit français et étranger* 7 (1861): 69–70.

————. *Histoire des ducs et des comtes de Champagne.* 7 vols. Paris-Troyes: Aug. Aubry, Dufey-Robert, et al., 1859–1869.

Aubri of Trois-Fontaines. *Chronicon.* Edited by P. Scheffer-Boichorst. Vol. 23: 674–950, in *Monumenta Germaniae Historica: Scriptores.* 31 vols. Hannover, 1826–1933.

Barthélemy, Edouard, ed. *Recueil des chartes de l'abbaye de Notre-Dame de Cheminon.* Paris: Champion, 1883.

Benton, John F. "Philip the Fair and the *Jours* of Troyes." In *Studies in Medieval and Renaissance History* 6 (1969): 281–344. Reprinted in his *Culture, Power and Personality,* 191–254.

Bernard of Clairvaux. "In Praise of the New Knighthood." In *Bernard of Clairvaux: Treatises III*, translated by M. Conrad Greenia, 125–167. Kalamazoo: Cistercian Publications, 1977. Latin text in *Sancti Bernardi Opera.* Vol. 3, *Tractatus et Opuscula*, edited by J. Leclercq and H. M. Rochais. Rome: Editiones Cistercienses, 1963.

————. *The Letters of Saint Bernard of Clairvaux.* Translated by Bruno Scott James. London: Burns & Oates, 1953. Latin texts in *Sancti Bernardi Opera.* Vol. 8, *Epistolae*, edited by J. Leclercq, C. H. Talbot, and H. M. Rochais. Rome: Editiones Cistercienses, 1978.

Brussel, Nicolas. *Nouvel examen de l'usage général des fiefs en France.* 2d ed. 2 vols. Paris: C. Prud'homme-C. Robustel, 1750.

Catel, Albert, and Maurice Lecomte, eds. *Chartes et documents de l'abbaye cistercienne de Preuilly.* Montereau: Imprimerie Claverie, 1927.

Champollion-Figeac, M. *Documents historiques inédits tirés des collections manuscrits de la Bibliothèque Royale.* 4 vols. Paris: Imprimerie Nationale, 1841–1848.

Chantereau-Lefebvre, Louis. *Traité des fiefs et de leur origine.* Paris: L. Billaine, 1662. Part 2 is an edition of selected acts from the Champagne chancery cartularies.

Chapin, Elizabeth. *Les villes de foires de Champagne.* Paris: Honoré Champion, 1937.

"Chronique et mélanges." *Bibliothèque de l'Ecole des Chartes* 39 (1878): 561.

Coq, Dominique, ed. *Chartes en langue française antérieures à 1271 conservées dans les départements de l'Aube, de la Seine-et-Marne, et de l'Yonne.* Documents linguistiques de la France, série française, 3. Paris: Editions du CNRS, 1988.

Cossé-Durlin, Jeannine, ed. *Cartulaire de Saint-Nicaise de Reims (XIIIe siècle).* Paris: Editions du CNRS, 1991.

Delaville le Roulx, J., ed. *Cartulaire général de l'Ordre des Hospitaliers de S. Jean de Jérusalem.* 4 vols. Paris: E. Leroux, 1894–1906.

Didot, Ambroise Firmin. *Etudes sur la vie et les travaux de Jean, sire de Joinville.* Paris: Typographie de Ambroise Firmin Didot, 1870.

*Gallia Christiana in provincias ecclesiasticas distributa.* 13 vols. Paris, 1715–1785.

Gigot, Jean-Gabriel, ed. *Chartes en langue française antérieures à 1271 conservées dans le département de la Haute-Marne.* Documents linguistiques de la France, série française, 1. Paris: Editions du CNRS, 1974.

Grayzel, Solomon. *The Church and the Jews in the XIIIth Century.* 2d ed. New York: Hermon Press, 1966.

Gross, Joseph J., ed. *The Trinitarians' Rule of Life: Texts of the Six Principle Editions.* Rome: The Trinitarian Historical Institute, 1983.

Joinville. "The Life of Saint Louis." In *Joinville and Villehardouin: Chronicles of the Crusades*, translated by M. R. B. Shaw. London: Penguin Books, 1963. French text in *Jean, sire de Joinville: Histoire de Saint Louis*, edited by Natalis de Wailly. 2d ed. Paris: Firmin Didot, 1874.

Lalore, Charles, ed. *Cartulaire de l'abbaye de Montiéramey*. Paris-Troyes: E. Thorin-Lacroix, 1890.

———. *Cartulaire de l'abbaye de Saint-Loup de Troyes*. Paris: E. Thorin, 1875.

———. *Cartulaire de l'abbaye du Paraclete*. Paris: E. Thorin, 1878.

———. "Documents sur l'abbaye de Notre-Dame-aux-Nonnains de Troyes." *Mémoires de la Société académique d'agriculture, des sciences, arts et belles-lettres du département de l'Aube* 38 (1874): 5–148.

Laurière, Eusèbe de, et al., eds. *Ordonnances des rois de France de la troisième race*. 22 vols. Paris: Imprimerie Royale, 1723–1849.

Longnon, Auguste, ed. *Documents relatifs au comté de Champagne et de Brie (1172–1361)*. 3 vols. Paris: Imprimerie Nationale, 1901–1914.

———. *Rôles des fiefs du comté de Champagne sous le règne de Thibaud le Chansonnier (1249–1252)*. Paris: Henri Menu, 1877.

Longnon, Jean. *Recherches sur la vie de Geoffroy de Villehardouin*. Paris: Honoré Champion, 1939.

Martène, Edmond, and Ursin Durand, eds. *Thesaurus novus anecdotorum*. 5 vols. Paris: F. Delaulne et al., 1717.

Nusse, C., ed. "Charte de fondation d'un Hôtel-Dieu à la Barre." *Annales de la Société historique et archéologique de Château-Thierry* (1874): 191–192.

Paris, Louis. *Histoire de l'abbaye d'Avenay*. 2 vols. Paris: Picard, 1879.

*Patrologia Latina*. Edited by J. P. Migne et al. 221 vols. Paris, 1844–1864.

Pérard, Estienne, ed. *Recueil de plusieurs pièces curieuses servant à l'histoire de Bourgogne*. Paris: C. Cramoisy, 1664.

Petit, Ernest. *Histoire des ducs de Bourgogne de la race capétienne*. 9 vols. Paris: Picard, 1885–1905.

Poquet, A. E. "L'abbaye de Barre et son recueil de chartes." *Annales de la Société historique et archéologique de Château-Thierry* (1884): 117–177.

Portejoie, Paulette, ed. *L'ancien coutumier de Champagne (XIIIe siècle)*. Poitiers: P. Oudin, 1956.

Quantin, Maximilien, ed. *Cartulaire général de l'Yonne*. 2 vols. Auxerre: Perriquet, 1854, 1860.

———. *Recueil de pièces pour faire suite au Cartulaire général de l'Yonne*. Auxerre-Paris: Durand, Pédrone-Lauriel, 1873.

*Recueil des historiens des Gaules et de la France*. Edited by Dom Bouquet et al. 24 vols. Paris, 1737–1904.

Robert of Auxerre. *Chronicon*. Edited by O. Holder-Egger. Vol. 26:219–276, in *Monumenta Germaniae Historica*: *Scriptores*. 31 vols. Hannover, 1826–1933.

Roger, Jean-Marc. "Les Morhier champenois." *Bulletin philologique et historique* (1978): 77–130.

Saige, Gustave, Henri Lacaille, and L. H. Labande, eds. *Trésor des chartes du comté de Rethel*. 5 vols. Monaco: Imprimerie de Monaco, 1902–1916.

Teulet, A., et al, eds. *Layettes du Trésor des chartes*. 5 vols. Paris: Henri Plon, 1863–1909.

Viollet, Paul, ed. *Les Etablissements de Saint Louis*. 4 vols. Paris: Renouard, 1881–1886.

Waquet, Jean, et al., eds. *Recueil des chartes de l'abbaye de Clairvaux*. Fascicules 1–2. Troyes: Archives Départementales de l'Aube, 1950, 1982.

William of Tyre. *A History of Deeds Done beyond the Sea*. Translated by E. A. Babcock and A. C. Krey. 2 vols. New York: Columbia University Press, 1941. Latin text in *Willelmi Tyrensis Archiepiscopi Chronicon*, edited by R. B. C. Huygens. 2 vols. Turnhout: Brepols, 1986.

## Other Works

Barber, Malcolm. "The Origins of the Order of the Temple." *Studia Monastica* 12 (1970): 219–240.

Barber, Richard, and Juliet Barker. *Tournaments: Jousts, Chivalry and Pageants in the Middle Ages*. New York: Weidenfeld & Nicolson, 1989.

Benton, John F. "The Accounts of Cepperello da Prato for the Tax on *nouveaux acquêts* in the Bailliage of Troyes." In *Order and Innovation in the Middle Ages: Essays in Honor of Joseph R. Strayer*, edited by William C. Jordan, Bruce McNab, and Teofilo R. Ruiz, 111–135, 453–457. Princeton: Princeton University Press, 1976. Reprinted in Benton's *Culture, Power and Personality*, 255–274.

———. *Culture, Power and Personality in Medieval France* [collected articles]. Edited by Thomas N. Bisson. London: The Hambledon Press, 1991.

———. "Written Records and the Development of Systematic Feudal Relations." In Benton's *Culture, Power and Personality*, 275–290.

Berlow, Rosalind Kent. "The Development of Business Techniques Used at the Fairs of Champagne from the End of the Twelfth Century to the Middle of the Thirteenth Century." In *Studies in Medieval and Renaissance History* 8 (1971): 3–31.

Bloch, Marc. *Feudal Society*. Translated by L. A. Manyon. Chicago: The University of Chicago Press, 1961.

Bolton, Brenda M. "Mulieres Sanctae." In *Studies in Church History* 10 (1973): 77–85. Reprinted in *Women in Medieval Society*, edited by Susan Mosher Stuard, 141–158. Philadelphia: University of Pennsylvania Press, 1976.

Boswell, John. *The Kindness of Strangers: The Abandonment of Children in Western Europe from Late Antiquity to the Renaissance*. New York: Pantheon, 1988.

Bouchard, Constance Brittain. *Sword, Mitre, and Cloister: Nobility and the Church in Burgundy, 980–1198*. Ithaca: Cornell University Press, 1987.

Brodman, James W. *Ransoming Captives in Crusader Spain: The Order of Merced on the Christian-Islamic Frontier*. Philadelphia: University of Pennsylvania Press, 1986.

Brooke, Christopher N. L. *The Medieval Idea of Marriage*. Oxford: Oxford University Press, 1989.

Brown, Elizabeth A. R. "Reform and Resistance to Royal Authority in Fourteenth-Century France: The League of 1314–1315." In *Parliaments, Estates and*

*Representation*. Vol. 1:109–137. London, 1981. Reprinted in Brown's *Politics and Institutions in Capetian France*. Great Yarmouth: Variorum, 1991.

———. "The Tyranny of a Construct: Feudalism and Historians of Medieval Europe." *American Historical Review* 79 (1974): 1063–1088.

Brundage, James A. "An Errant Crusader: Stephen of Blois." *Traditio* 16 (1960): 380–395.

———. *Law, Sex, and Christian Society in Medieval Europe*. Chicago and London: The University of Chicago Press, 1987.

Bur, Michel. *La formation du comté de Champagne, v.950–v.1150*. Mémoires des Annales de l'Est, no. 54. Nancy: Université de Nancy-II, 1977.

Chazan, Robert. *Medieval Jewry in Northern France: A Political and Social History*. Baltimore and London: The Johns Hopkins University Press, 1973.

Clanchy, M. T. *From Memory to Written Record: England, 1066–1307*. Cambridge, Mass.: Harvard University Press, 1979.

Constable, Giles. "The Financing of the Crusades in the Twelfth Century." In *Outremer: Studies in the History of the Crusading Kingdom of Jerusalem*, edited by B. Z. Kedar, H. E. Mayer, and R. C. Smail, 64–88. Jerusalem: Yad Izhak Ben-Zvi Institute, 1982.

Davis, Michael T. "On the Threshold of the Flamboyant: The Second Campaign of Construction of Saint-Urbain, Troyes." *Speculum* 59 (1984): 847–884.

Delaborde, Henri-François. *Jean de Joinville et les seigneurs de Joinville*. Paris: Imprimerie Nationale, 1894.

Demurger, Alain. *Vie et mort de l'Ordre du Temple*. Paris: Editions du Seuil, 1985.

Donahue, Charles, Jr. "The Canon Law on the Formation of Marriage and Social Practice in the Later Middle Ages." *Journal of Family History* 8 (1983): 144–158.

Duby, Georges. *The Knight, the Lady and the Priest: The Making of Modern Marriage in Medieval France*. Translated by Barbara Bray. New York: Pantheon, 1983.

———. *The Three Orders: Feudal Society Imagined*. Translated by Arthur Goldhammer. Chicago and London: The University of Chicago Press, 1980.

Edbury, Peter W., and John Gordon Rowe. *William of Tyre: Historian of the Latin East*. Cambridge: Cambridge University Press, 1988.

Evergates, Theodore. "Champagne." In *Dictionary of the Middle Ages*, edited by Joseph R. Strayer, 3:243–250. 13 vols. New York: Charles Scribner's Sons, 1982–1989.

———. "The Chancery Archives of the Counts of Champagne: Codicology and Historiography of the Cartulary-Registers." *Viator* 16 (1985): 159–179.

———. *Feudal Society in the Bailliage of Troyes under the Counts of Champagne, 1152–1284*. Baltimore and London: The Johns Hopkins University Press, 1975.

———. "Louis VII and the Counts of Champagne." In *The Second Crusade and the Cistercians*, edited by Michael Gervers, 109–117. New York: St. Martin's, 1992.

Flori, Jean. *L'essor de la chevalerie, XIe–XIIe siècles*. Geneva: Droz, 1986.

Fourquin, Guy. *Lordship and Feudalism in the Middle Ages*. Translated by Iris and A. L. Lytton Sells. New York: Pica Press, 1976.

Galbert of Bruges. *The Murder of Charles the Good, Count of Flanders*. Translated by James Bruce Ross. New York: Harper & Row, 1967.

Gross, Joseph J. "The Trinitarian Order's Apostolate of the Ransom of Christian Captives and Works of Mercy during the First Centuries of its History: A Special Consideration of the Communities Located in the Interior of the European Continent and in Great Britain." In *Captivis Libertas: Congresso dell'Apostolato Redentivo-Misericordioso dell'Ordine Trinitario*, vol. 1:51–82. Rome: Centro Trinitario, 1982.

Haskins, Charles Homer. "Robert le Bougre and the Beginnings of the Inquisition in Northern France." Chap. 10 of Homer's *Studies in Medieval Culture*. Oxford: Clarendon Press, 1929.

Herlihy, David. *Medieval Households*. Cambridge, Mass.: Harvard University Press, 1985.

Johnson, Penelope D. *Equal in Monastic Profession: Religious Women in Medieval France*. Chicago and London: The University of Chicago Press, 1991.

Jordan, William Chester. *The French Monarchy and the Jews: From Philip Augustus to the Last Capetians*. Philadelphia: University of Pennsylvania Press, 1989.

Kealey, Edward J. "Hospitals and Poor Relief." In *Dictionary of the Middle Ages*, edited by Joseph R. Strayer, 6:292–297. 13 vols. New York: Charles Scribner's Sons, 1982–1989.

Keen, Maurice. *Chivalry*. New Haven and London: Yale University Press, 1984.

Kelley, Donald R. *Foundations of Modern Historical Scholarship: Language, Law, and History in the French Renaissance*. New York: Columbia University Press, 1970.

Leclercq, Jean. *Monks and Love in Twelfth-Century France: Psycho-Historical Essays*. Oxford: Clarendon Press, 1979.

Lewis, Andrew W. "Fourteen Charters of Robert I of Dreux (1152–1188)." *Traditio* 41 (1985): 144–179.

McGuire, Brian P. *The Difficult Saint: Bernard of Clairvaux and His Tradition*. Kalamazoo: Cistercian Publications, 1991.

Miller, Timothy S. "The Knights of Saint John and the Hospitals of the Latin West." *Speculum* 53 (1978): 709–733.

Mollat, Michel. *The Poor in the Middle Ages: An Essay in Social History*. Translated by Arthur Goldhammer. New Haven and London: Yale University Press, 1986.

Moore, R. I. *The Birth of Popular Heresy*. New York: St. Martin's, 1975.

Munro, Dana Carleton. *Letters of the Crusaders*. Philadelphia: University of Pennsylvania, 1902.

Newman, William Mendel. *Les seigneurs de Nesle en Picardie (XIIe-XIIIe siècle)*. 2 vols. Philadelphia: The American Philosophical Society, 1971.

Orderic Vitalis. *The Ecclesiastical History of Orderic Vitalis*. Edited and translated by Marjorie Chibnall. 6 vols. Oxford: Clarendon Press, 1969–1980.

Philippe of Beaumanoir. *The Coutumes de Beauvaisis of Philippe de Beaumanoir*. Translated by F. R. P. Akehurst. Philadelphia: University of Pennsylvania Press, 1992.

Poly, Jean-Pierre, and Eric Bournazel. *The Feudal Transformation, 900-1200*. Translated by Caroline Higgitt. New York and London: Holmes & Meier, 1991.

Riley-Smith, Louise, and Jonathan Riley-Smith. *The Crusades: Idea and Reality, 1095–1274*. Documents of Medieval History, 4. London: Edward Arnold, 1981.

Reuter, Timothy, ed. *The Medieval Nobility: Studies on the Ruling Classes of France and Germany from the Sixth to the Twelfth Century.* Amsterdam-New York-Oxford: North Holland, 1979.

*The Rule of the Templars: The French Text of the Rule of the Order of the Knights Templar.* Translated and introduced by J. M. Upton-Ward. Woodbridge: The Boydell Press, 1992

Siberry, Elizabeth. *Criticism of Crusading, 1095–1274.* Oxford: Clarendon Press, 1985.

Thompson, Sally. "The Problem of the Cistercian Nuns in the Twelfth and Early Thirteenth Centuries." In *Medieval Women*, edited by Derek Baker, 227–252. Oxford: Basil Blackwell, 1978.

Turner, Ralph V. "The *Miles Literatus* in Twelfth- and Thirteenth-Century England: How Rare a Phenomenon?" *American Historical Review* 83 (1978): 928–945.

Verlinden, O. "Markets and Fairs." In *The Cambridge Economic History of Europe*, 3:119–153. Cambridge: Cambridge University Press, 1963.

White, Stephen D. *Custom, Kinship, and Gifts to Saints: The* Laudatio Parentum *in Western France, 1050–1150.* Chapel Hill: The University of North Carolina Press, 1988.

# Index

Reference is to the document number. Placenames within the county of Champagne are identified by *département* and *arrondissement* (ar.); those located on the map are marked by an asterisk.

University of Pennsylvania Press
MIDDLE AGES SERIES
Edward Peters, General Editor

F. R. P. Akehurst, trans. *The* Coutumes de Beauvaisis *of Philippe de Beaumanoir.* 1992

Peter L. Allen. *The Art of Love: Amatory Fiction from Ovid to the* Romance of the Rose. 1992

David Anderson. *Before the Knight's Tale: Imitation of Classical Epic in Boccaccio's* Teseida. 1988

Benjamin Arnold. *Count and Bishop in Medieval Germany: A Study of Regional Power, 1100–1350.* 1991

Mark C. Bartusis. *The Late Byzantine Army: Arms and Society, 1204–1453.* 1992

J. M. W. Bean. *From Lord to Patron: Lordship in Late Medieval England.* 1990

Uta-Renate Blumenthal. *The Investiture Controversy: Church and Monarchy from the Ninth to the Twelfth Century.* 1988

Daniel Bornstein, trans. *Dino Compagni's* Chronicle *of Florence.* 1986

Maureen Boulton. *The Song in the Story: Lyric Insertions in French Narrative Fiction, 1200–1400.* 1993.

Betsy Bowden. *Chaucer Aloud: The Varieties of Textual Interpretation.* 1987

James William Brodman. *Ransoming Captives in Crusader Spain: The Order of Merced on the Christian-Islamic Frontier.* 1986

Kevin Brownlee and Sylvia Huot, eds. *Rethinking the* Romance of the Rose: *Text, Image, Reception.* 1992

Otto Brunner (Howard Kaminsky and James Van Horn Melton, eds. and trans.). Land *and Lordship: Structures of Governance in Medieval Austria.* 1992

Robert I. Burns, S.J., ed. *Emperor of Culture: Alfonso X the Learned of Castile and His Thirteenth-Century Renaissance.* 1990

David Burr. *Olivi and Franciscan Poverty: The Origins of the* Usus Pauper *Controversy.* 1989

David Burr. *Olivi's Peaceable Kingdom: A Reading of the Apocalypse Commentary.* 1993

Thomas Cable. *The English Alliterative Tradition.* 1991

Anthony K. Cassell and Victoria Kirkham, eds. and trans. *Diana's Hunt/Caccia di Diana: Boccaccio's First Fiction.* 1991

John C. Cavadini. *The Last Christology of the West: Adoptionism in Spain and Gaul, 785–820.* 1993

Brigitte Cazelles. *The Lady as Saint: A Collection of French Hagiographic Romances of the Thirteenth Century.* 1991

Karen Cherewatuk and Ulrike Wiethaus, eds. *Dear Sister: Medieval Women and the Epistolary Genre.* 1993

Anne L. Clark. *Elisabeth of Schönau: A Twelfth-Century Visionary.* 1992

Willene B. Clark and Meradith T. McMunn, eds. *Beasts and Birds of the Middle Ages: The Bestiary and Its Legacy.* 1989

Richard C. Dales. *The Scientific Achievement of the Middle Ages.* 1973

Charles T. Davis. *Dante's Italy and Other Essays.* 1984

Katherine Fischer Drew, trans. *The Burgundian Code.* 1972

Katherine Fischer Drew, trans. *The Laws of the Salian Franks.* 1991

Katherine Fisher Drew, trans. *The Lombard Laws.* 1973

Nancy Edwards. *The Archaeology of Early Medieval Ireland.* 1990

Margaret J. Ehrhart. *The Judgment of the Trojan Prince Paris in Medieval Literature.* 1987

Richard K. Emmerson and Ronald B. Herzman. *The Apocalyptic Imagination in Medieval Literature.* 1992

Theodore Evergates. *Feudal Society in Medieval France: Documents from the County of Champagne.* 1993

Felipe Fernández-Armesto. *Before Columbus: Exploration and Colonization from the Mediterranean to the Atlantic, 1229–1492.* 1987

R. D. Fulk. *A History of Old English Meter.* 1992

Patrick J. Geary. *Aristocracy in Provence: The Rhône Basin at the Dawn of the Carolingian Age.* 1985

Peter Heath. *Allegory and Philosophy in Avicenna (Ibn Sînâ), with a Translation of the Book of the Prophet Muḥammad's Ascent to Heaven.* 1992

J. N. Hillgarth, ed. *Christianity and Paganism, 350–750: The Conversion of Western Europe.* 1986

Richard C. Hoffmann. *Land, Liberties, and Lordship in a Late Medieval Countryside: Agrarian Structures and Change in the Duchy of Wrocław.* 1990

Robert Hollander. *Boccaccio's Last Fiction: Il Corbaccio.* 1988

Edward B. Irving, Jr. *Rereading* Beowulf. 1989

C. Stephen Jaeger. *The Origins of Courtliness: Civilizing Trends and the Formation of Courtly Ideals, 939–1210.* 1985

William Chester Jordan. *The French Monarchy and the Jews: From Philip Augustus to the Last Capetians.* 1989

William Chester Jordan. *From Servitude to Freedom: Manumission in the Sénonais in the Thirteenth Century.* 1986

Ellen E. Kittell. *From* Ad Hoc *to Routine: A Case Study in Medieval Bureaucracy.* 1991

Alan C. Kors and Edward Peters, eds. *Witchcraft in Europe, 1100–1700: A Documentary History.* 1972

Barbara M. Kreutz. *Before the Normans: Southern Italy in the Ninth and Tenth Centuries.* 1992

E. Ann Matter. *The Voice of My Beloved: The Song of Songs in Western Medieval Christianity.* 1990

María Rosa Menocal. *The Arabic Role in Medieval Literary History.* 1987

A. J. Minnis. *Medieval Theory of Authorship.* 1988

Lawrence Nees. *A Tainted Mantle: Hercules and the Classical Tradition at the Carolingian Court.* 1991

Lynn H. Nelson, trans. *The Chronicle of San Juan de la Peña: A Fourteenth-Century Official History of the Crown of Aragon.* 1991

Charlotte A. Newman. *The Anglo-Norman Nobility in the Reign of Henry I: The Second Generation.* 1988

Joseph F. O'Callaghan. *The Cortes of Castile-León, 1188–1350.* 1989

Joseph F. O'Callaghan. *The Learned King: The Reign of Alfonso X of Castile.* 1993

William D. Paden, ed. *The Voice of the Trobairitz: Perspectives on the Women Troubadours.* 1989

Edward Peters. *The Magician, the Witch, and the Law.* 1982

Edward Peters, ed. *Christian Society and the Crusades, 1198–1229: Sources in Translation, including* The Capture of Damietta *by Oliver of Paderborn.* 1971

Edward Peters, ed. *The First Crusade: The* Chronicle of Fulcher of Chartres *and Other Source Materials.* 1971

Edward Peters, ed. *Heresy and Authority in Medieval Europe.* 1980

James M. Powell. *Albertanus of Brescia: The Pursuit of Happiness in the Early Thirteenth Century.* 1992

James M. Powell. *Anatomy of a Crusade, 1213–1221.* 1986

Michael Resler, trans. Erec *by Hartmann von Aue.* 1987

Pierre Riché (Michael Idomir Allen, trans.). *The Carolingians: A Family Who Forged Europe.* 1993

Pierre Riché (Jo Ann McNamara, trans.). *Daily Life in the World of Charlemagne.* 1978

Jonathan Riley-Smith. *The First Crusade and the Idea of Crusading.* 1986

Joel T. Rosenthal. *Patriarchy and Families of Privilege in Fifteenth-Century England.* 1991

Teofilo F. Ruiz. *Crisis and Continuity: Land and Town in Late Medieval Castile.* 1993

Steven D. Sargent, ed. and trans. *On the Threshold of Exact Science: Selected Writings of Anneliese Maier on Late Medieval Natural Philosophy.* 1982

Sarah Stanbury. *Seeing the* Gawain-Poet: *Description and the Act of Perception.* 1992

Thomas C. Stillinger. *The Song of Troilus: Lyric Authority in the Medieval Book.* 1992

Susan Mosher Stuard. *A State of Deference: Ragusa/Dubrovnik in the Medieval Centuries.* 1992

Susan Mosher Stuard, ed. *Women in Medieval History and Historiography.* 1987

Susan Mosher Stuard, ed. *Women in Medieval Society.* 1976

Jonathan Sumption. *The Hundred Years War: Trial by Battle.* 1992

Ronald E. Surtz. *The Guitar of God: Gender, Power, and Authority in the Visionary World of Mother Juana de la Cruz (1481–1534).* 1990

Patricia Terry, trans. *Poems of the Elder Edda.* 1990

Hugh M. Thomas. *Vassals, Heiresses, Crusaders, and Thugs: The Gentry of Angevin Yorkshire, 1154–1216.* 1993

Frank Tobin. *Meister Eckhart: Thought and Language.* 1986

Ralph V. Turner. *Men Raised from the Dust: Administrative Service and Upward Mobility in Angevin England.* 1988

Harry Turtledove, trans. *The Chronicle of Theophanes: An English Translation of Anni Mundi 6095–6305 (A.D. 602–813).* 1982

Mary F. Wack. *Lovesickness in the Middle Ages: The* Viaticum *and Its Commentaries.* 1990

Benedicta Ward. *Miracles and the Medieval Mind: Theory, Record, and Event, 1000–1215.* 1982

Suzanne Fonay Wemple. *Women in Frankish Society: Marriage and the Cloister, 500–900.* 1981

Jan M. Ziolkowski. *Talking Animals: Medieval Latin Beast Poetry, 750–1150.* 1993

This book has been set in Linotron Galliard. Galliard was designed for Mergenthaler in 1978 by Matthew Carter. Galliard retains many of the features of a sixteenth-century typeface cut by Robert Granjon but has some modifications that give it a more contemporary look.

Printed on acid-free paper.